The Travels of Pietro della Valle in India

From the Old English Translation of 1664

VOLUME 1

EDITED BY EDWARD GREY

CAMBRIDGE
UNIVERSITY PRESS

CAMBRIDGE UNIVERSITY PRESS

Cambridge, New York, Melbourne, Madrid, Cape Town, Singapore,
São Paolo, Delhi, Dubai, Tokyo

Published in the United States of America by Cambridge University Press, New York

www.cambridge.org
Information on this title: www.cambridge.org/9781108014939

© in this compilation Cambridge University Press 2010

This edition first published 1892
This digitally printed version 2010

ISBN 978-1-108-01493-9 Paperback

CAMBRIDGE LIBRARY COLLECTION

Books of enduring scholarly value

Travel and Exploration

The history of travel writing dates back to the Bible, Caesar, the Vikings and the Crusaders, and its many themes include war, trade, science and recreation. Explorers from Columbus to Cook charted lands not previously visited by Western travellers, and were followed by merchants, missionaries, and colonists, who wrote accounts of their experiences. The development of steam power in the nineteenth century provided opportunities for increasing numbers of 'ordinary' people to travel further, more economically, and more safely, and resulted in great enthusiasm for travel writing among the reading public. Works included in this series range from first-hand descriptions of previously unrecorded places, to literary accounts of the strange habits of foreigners, to examples of the burgeoning numbers of guidebooks produced to satisfy the needs of a new kind of traveller - the tourist.

The Travels of Pietro della Valle in India

The publications of the Hakluyt Society (founded in 1846) made available edited (and sometimes translated) early accounts of exploration. The first series, which ran from 1847 to 1899, consists of 100 books containing published or previously unpublished works by authors from Christopher Columbus to Sir Francis Drake, and covering voyages to the New World, to China and Japan, to Russia and to Africa and India. A member of a noble Roman family, Pietro della Valle began travelling in 1614 at the suggestion of a doctor, as an alternative to suicide after a failed love affair. The letters describing his travels in Turkey, Persia and India were addressed to this advisor. This 1664 English translation of della Valle's letters from India, republished by the Hakluyt Society in 1892, contains fascinating ethnographic details, particularly on religious beliefs, and is an important source for the history of the Keladi region of South India.

Cambridge University Press has long been a pioneer in the reissuing of out-of-print titles from its own backlist, producing digital reprints of books that are still sought after by scholars and students but could not be reprinted economically using traditional technology. The Cambridge Library Collection extends this activity to a wider range of books which are still of importance to researchers and professionals, either for the source material they contain, or as landmarks in the history of their academic discipline.

Drawing from the world-renowned collections in the Cambridge University Library, and guided by the advice of experts in each subject area, Cambridge University Press is using state-of-the-art scanning machines in its own Printing House to capture the content of each book selected for inclusion. The files are processed to give a consistently clear, crisp image, and the books finished to the high quality standard for which the Press is recognised around the world. The latest print-on-demand technology ensures that the books will remain available indefinitely, and that orders for single or multiple copies can quickly be supplied.

The Cambridge Library Collection will bring back to life books of enduring scholarly value (including out-of-copyright works originally issued by other publishers) across a wide range of disciplines in the humanities and social sciences and in science and technology.

WORKS ISSUED BY

The Ibakluyt Society.

———o———

THE TRAVELS

OF

PIETRO DELLA VALLE IN INDIA.

No, LXXXIV,

THE TRAVELS

OF

PIETRO DELLA VALLE

IN

INDIA.

FROM THE OLD ENGLISH TRANSLATION OF 1664,
BY G. HAVERS.

IN TWO VOLUMES.

Edited, with a Life of the Author, an Introduction and Notes,

BY

EDWARD GREY

(LATE BENGAL CIVIL SERVICE).

LONDON:

PRINTED FOR THE HAKLUYT SOCIETY,

4, LINCOLN'S INN FIELDS, W.C.

M.DCCC.XCII.

COUNCIL

OF

THE HAKLUYT SOCIETY.

PIETRO DELLA VALLE
IL PELLEGRINO
Hic peragro peregrinus adhuc: tellüs tamen ulla
Hic peregrina mihi, Sed domus, et patria est.

CONTENTS OF VOL. I.

PREFACE.

 FEW words may not be out of place regarding the circumstances under which the preparation of this edition of the " Letters from India" of P. della Valle was entrusted to the present Editor.

Some years ago a translation of these letters was made by Professor E. Rehatsek, of Bombay University (who died there in January of this present year), apparently in ignorance of the fact that an English translation of the letters (which forms the text of the present edition) was already in existence. The Professor, being unwilling to undertake the task of annotating the translation made by him, sent it to the Hakluyt Society, in the hope that the work might be published by that Society. The letters were included in the list of works "suggested to the Council for publication", and one of the members of the Council proposed to the present Editor that he should undertake the work of revising and annotating the translation referred to.

The present Editor, though he had not had any previous experience of editorial work, ventured to undertake the task. A residence of twenty-one years in India, in the Civil Service, and some acquaintance with previous publications of the Hakluyt Society, several of which had come into his possession through his relationship with a former member of the Council, Mr. Ralph William Grey, formed a slight foundation, on which he felt bold enough to rest the attempt of which the result is now brought before the public.

On examination of the translation already referred to it became evident that a considerable amount of revision and correction would be required, and it was therefore decided, with the concurrence of the Secretary of the Society, to adopt the old translation of 1664, by G. Havers, instead of that made by Professor Rehatsek.

An additional reason for adopting the old translation was that the somewhat archaic form of the language used in it seems to be in keeping with that of the original letters, and to give them a character and flavour which would be wanting in a modern translation.

A few alterations in the text have been made where such appeared to be necessary, and a few short passages, omitted by the translator, have been added. But the translation now reprinted is substantially the same as that published in 1664.

The Editor has added notes wherever such appeared to be called for. Though they must necessarily be of a more or less imperfect character, he trusts that they may be found useful in some respects, and such as will be found to add in some slight degree to the interest of the letters. His object has been to avoid as far as possible the repetition of information easily obtainable from ordinary works of reference, and to assist the reader without fatiguing him with irrelevant matter.

In conclusion, the Editor wishes to express his thanks to Mr. E. Delmar Morgan, the Honorary Secretary of the Hakluyt Society, for the "Bibliographical Notice" included in this volume, and also for many valuable suggestions, and for information on various points, supplied by him during the preparation of this edition, and also for the trouble taken by him in superintending the press-work, and engraving of the frontispiece, etc.

Also to Mr. Coutts Trotter, a member of the Council of the Hakluyt Society, for his kind help in the acquisition of information on several subjects ; and to two ladies who have kindly supplied the Editor with the translation of the Italian Dedication. The Editor's thanks are due also to the late Professor Rehatsek for some of the facts stated in the " Life of P. della Valle", as recorded in a memorandum prepared by him.

It is right to mention also that some of the latter part of the "Historical Sketch of the Portuguese Power in India" is supplied from an unpublished manuscript written by the Editor's father, the late Rt. Hon. Sir C. E. Grey, formerly Chief Justice of Bengal, and afterwards Governor of Jamaica.

LIFE

OF

PIETRO DELLA VALLE.

IETRO DELLA VALLE, the son of Pompeo della Valle and his wife Giovanna Alberini, was born at Rome, April $\frac{1st}{11th}$, 1586. His family was one of the most ancient and illustrious in Rome, and numbered among its members two Cardinals, viz., Rustico under Pope Honorius II, and Andrea under Leo X. From the latter the street and church in Rome of " St. Andrea della Valle" took their name. Little is known of his early life except that he received a good education, travelled over Italy, and was admitted into the Academy of *Umoristi,* a scientific and literary society of those days which had been instituted at Rome.

On differences arising between the Pope and the Venetians, and when also the troubles which ensued on the death of Henry IV of France led to expectations of war, he entered the military service ; but it does not appear that he actually took part in any campaign.

Later on, in the year 1611, he joined a Spanish fleet in an expedition to Barbary, and took part in

the capture of the Karkenssa Islands (the ancient
Cercina and Cercinitis) in the Gulf of Cabes, off the
coast of Africa, which were then the stronghold of
pirates, and in other engagements, which, he says
however, that he regarded "rather as skirmishes
than fights".

Subsequently, owing to a disappointment in a love
affair, he went to Naples, and assumed the habit of
a pilgrim and the title of "Pellegrino", which he
ever afterwards added to his signature.

In consequence of this disappointment, and by the
advice of his friend, Signor Mario Schipano, a professor of medicine, he determined on travelling in
the East, and embarked at Venice for Constantinople
on board the *Gran Delfino* on June 8th, 1614. He
remained at Constantinople until September 1615,
and proceeded thence to Asia Minor and Egypt, and
from there to Mount Sinai, the monastery of St.
Catherine, and to Palestine. He visited Jerusalem,
Damascus, Aleppo and Baghdad, besides Anah on
the Euphrates and Hillah, the site of Babylon. On
his return thence to Baghdad he married Maani
Gioerida, a young Assyrian Christian, eighteen years
old. Her father was an Assyrian, her mother an
Armenian. Maani (which signifies "intelligence" in
Arabic) was born at Mardin, a principal town of
Mesopotamia, whence she came, at the age of
four, with her father and mother to Baghdad, when
her native town was ravaged by the Kurds. She
appears to have been well educated and was acquainted with the Turkish language in addition to

her own, which was Arabic. In one of his letters, written from Baghdad, Pietro describes at great length the history of his marriage with this lady, after repeated efforts to overcome the reluctance, whether real or assumed, on the part of her mother to the proposed union, and he enters into considerable details on the subject of the personal charms of his bride. This marriage took place in the year 1616, and he proceeded in company with his wife to Persia. He visited Hamadan and Ispahan, and, hearing that the King, Shah Abbas, was at that time in the vicinity of the Caspian Sea, proceeded to seek an interview with him in his camp. He was hospitably received by the King, and remained for some time at his Court. He had at this time two objects in view—viz., a desire to serve in a military expedition against the Turks, which was then talked of, and also to obtain certain advantages for the Christians who were the subjects of persecution in the Ottoman Empire. He accompanied the King to Ardebil, where the army was assembled, and took part in a sanguinary battle with the Turks. His wife accompanied him, and he speaks of her (in Letter No. III from Persia) as "a warrior who fears neither to see blood, nor to hear the sound of firing". He then returned to Ispahan, and, quitting it on October 1st, 1621, visited the ruins of Persepolis and city of Shiraz. Thence he travelled towards the coast of the Persian Gulf. At Mina, near the Gulf of Ormuz, his wife died on December 30th, 1622, of fever brought on by hardship and an unhealthy climate. In one of his letters (No. xvi from Persia) he describes her illness and death in very affecting terms. He caused his wife's body to be embalmed and placed in a coffin, and taking it with him, and also a Georgian girl, Maria Tinatin di Ziba, whom his wife had taken under her protection, endeavoured to embark for India at Bender Ser. Owing, however, to the fact that the Persians, aided by the English, were at that time besieging Ormuz, then occupied by the Portuguese, his intention was frustrated for a time, and he returned to Lar. Afterwards, on January 19th, 1623, he embarked at Gombroon (Bandar Abbas) for India. He arrived at Súrat on February 10th, 1623, and thence visited Cambay (Khambáyat), Ahmadábád, Cháwal, Goa, Ikkeri, Barcelor, Mangalúr, and Calicut (Kálíkót), which last place was the limit of his travels in India. Thence he returned along the coast to Goa, and, embarking there on November 16th, 1624, sailed to Mascat. Thence he travelled by Bassora to Aleppo, and from that port sailed by Cyprus, Malta and Sicily, to Naples, where he arrived on February 5th, 1626, and finally reached Rome on March 28th of that year. Here he buried the remains of his wife, which he had conveyed with him throughout his travels, in the Church of Ara Cœli in the vault of the Della Valle family. He was well received by the Pope Urban VIII, and by his friends at Rome. He soon afterwards became honorary Chamberlain to the Pope, and married the young Georgian, already mentioned as having been taken under protection by his wife in Persia, who had been the companion of his travels ever since his wife's death. She was the daughter of an officer in the Georgian army, who had been killed in the course of an attempt to resist the invasion of his country by the army of the King of Persia, and had been carried with other captives to Ispahan, where Sitti Maani saw her and took her under her protection. By her marriage with P. della Valle she became the mother of fourteen sons. It does not appear that any of these sons attained to any distinction in after life. It is stated that on account of their turbulent conduct at Rome, after their father's death, they, with their mother, were compelled to leave Rome and to take up their residence at Urbino.

Subsequently to his marriage Pietro della Valle continued to reside at Rome until an event happened in consequence of which he was compelled to seek for a time another place of residence. On the occasion of a procession taking place in the streets of Rome a quarrel arose between an Indian servant in the employment of Della Valle and one of the Pope's servants, in the course of which the latter deprived the Indian of his sword, which he was about to break in two, when P. della Valle, drawing his own sword, ran it through the man's body, killing him on the spot in the presence of the Pope. He left Rome and retired to the Fort of Paliano and thence to Naples, but after a short time he was allowed by the Pope, through the intercession of Cardinal Francesco Barberini, to return to Rome, where he con-

tinued to reside until his death in the month of April
1652. He was buried in the Chapel of San Ber-
nardino di Siena in the Church of Ara Cœli, where
a tomb may still be seen with the following inscription on it :

> " Hic requiescit Petrus de Valle
> Ci (cujus) Aia (anima)
> Requiescat in pace. Amen ;"

though there is reason to doubt whether this inscription refers to the great traveller, or to some one less
well known of his ancestors. His widow was still
living in 1662, but the date of her death is uncertain.

From the time of his return to Rome until his
death he appears to have led a retired life, receiving
the visits of friends who came to hear the history of
his travels and to inspect the museum of curiosities
which he had collected in the course of his wanderings. The society of the *Umoristi*, of which he
was a member, conferred upon him the title of *Il
Fantastico*. He had always been a great admirer
of music, and, besides composing several melodies,
became the inventor of two new musical instruments,
to which he gave the names of *cimbalo esarmo-
nico* and *violino panormonico*.

But his claims to posthumous fame must, no doubt,
be based on his merits as a bold and observant
traveller. We cannot forget that he was the first
traveller to penetrate into the second Pyramid, and
to send to Europe two mummies, now preserved in
the collection of antiquities at Dresden. He was
the first who directed attention to the rock inscrip-

tions and cuneiform writings in Assyria, of which he brought back some copies, and, though he was incapable of deciphering them, he was clever enough to discover that the inscriptions must be read from left to right, contrary to the direction prevailing in more modern inscriptions written in Oriental languages. He came to this conclusion by noticing that in the formation of the arrow-headed characters the thicker ends of those in a horizontal position were invariably towards the left hand of the inscription.

His travels were described in a narrative divided into three parts, comprising his wanderings in Turkey, Persia and India respectively. The first part only was published in his lifetime. The second and third parts appeared several years after his death, being published under the care of four of his sons, Valerio, Erasmo, Francesco and Paolo. They are all composed in the form of letters addressed to his friend, Signor Mario Schipano, who resided at Naples, and are evidently written by an acute observer, who knew how to make use of his uncommon learning, and who had an advantage over many other previous travellers in his knowledge of Eastern languages, of which we know that he wrote and spoke Turkish, Persian and Arabic, besides having some acquaintance with Coptic and Chaldæan. As to his merits as a traveller, Gibbon —a man not given to praise anyone unduly—has recorded his opinion that "no traveller knew and described Persia so well as P. della Valle". Southey

speaks of him as "that excellent traveller"; and the
late Sir Henry Yule, than whom few persons could
form a better ópinion of the merits of an Eastern
traveller, says—speaking "of travellers whose steps
have led them to India by no inducements of trade
or service, but who came for their own pleasure or
convenience"—"The prince of all such who have
related their experiences is Pietro della Valle, the
most insatiate in curiosity, the most intelligent in
apprehension, the fullest and most accurate in
description." (See *Diary of Sir W. Hedges*, published by the Hakluyt Society, vol. ii, p. 343.)

The present volume comprises only the eight
letters which contain an account of P. della Valle's
travels in India. His wanderings in that country were
confined to a comparatively limited area, extending,
as has been already stated, only to Ahmadábád
towards the north, and to Calicut (Kálíkót) on
the south, and comprising (with the exception of
expeditions to Cambay, Ahmadábád and Ikkeri,
towns in the interior) visits only to settlements
on the western coast of the peninsula. It is to be
regretted that he did not extend his travels further ;
but these letters, describing as they do only a very
limited extent of country, are nevertheless full of
graphic descriptions, and bring before the mind's
eye a vivid and life-like representation of men and
manners as they existed in the early part of the
seventeenth century in the Portuguese settlements
on the coast and in the native territories adjacent to
them. Nor is there wanting in some of them a deeper

vein of thought, which crops up every now and then in the attempt to penetrate into and to explain the mystery underlying the outward semblance of religion among the Hindus, as represented by their idols their temples, and their pagan ceremonies of religious worship. And, although the interest of the reader is more likely to be attracted towards the descriptions of native life, the account of Portuguese towns and of the mode of life adopted by their European inhabitants will be found little less interesting. To us, who in the present day see nothing in these settlements but the relics of departed greatness, the pictures here laid before us of the commercial activity and political enterprise which were exhibited in those days must have a fascination which is all the greater because they owe their attractions to the "touch of a vanish'd hand" and the charm of "a voice that is still".

HISTORICAL SKETCH
OF THE
RISE AND FALL OF THE PORTUGUESE
POWER IN INDIA.

S an introduction to the following letters of P. della Valle, it may be useful to the reader to have a short account of the rise, progress and decline of the Portuguese power in India, extending over a period of about 270 years, from the arrival of Vasco da Gama at Kálíkót, in the year 1498, to the capture of Bassín by the Maráthas in 1765; a period which may be roughly divided into two halves, of which the first half comprises the rise, and the last half the decline, of Portuguese dominion in India. It was not long after the arrival of Vasco da Gama at Kálíkót—viz., in the year 1499—that the Portuguese obtained permission to build their first fort at Kúchi (Cochin), which was completed in 1503, and in the same year they commenced to build another at Kananúr, which was finished in 1505. In 1509 they built a third fort near Kálíkót, and in 1513 a fort was erected at that port.

The year 1508 had been marked by the arrival in

India of the second Portuguese Viceroy (Don Francisco Dalmeida being the first), the renowned Don Afonso Dalboquerque (better known, perhaps, as Albuquerque), who arrived at Kananúr in the month of December 1508, though it was not until November 1509 that he actually obtained possession of the Viceroyalty from Don Francisco Dalmeida, who objected to be superseded by the Admiral. The next great event was the expedition on December 31st, 1509, against Kálíkót, under the command of Dalboquerque, when the Portuguese destroyed and sacked the city and the King's palace, though they were ultimately compelled to retreat with severe loss.

The year 1510 was signalised by an event of greater importance—viz., the expedition against Goa, which resulted in the storming and capture of the fort of Panjim at the entrance of the port, followed by the occupation of the island of Goa and the adjacent territory by the Portuguese. This event may be regarded as the actual foundation of their dominion in India ; for, although they were forced to abandon Goa in the month of May, they succeeded in November of the same year in regaining possession of the place and have held it ever since.

The subsequent chief events may be briefly stated. In 1515 permission was obtained to build a factory at Kálíkót. About this time the greater part of the island of Ceylon submitted to the Portuguese. In 1521 a fort was built near Cháwal, and in 1526 Mangalúr and the town of Mahim were taken. In 1531 another fort was built at Shália, near Kálíkót,

and in 1534 the port of Swálya (Swally) was captured, and the town of Damán and the island of Diu,
where a fort was built ; in the same year the towns
of Bassín, Cháwal and Bombay were ceded to the
Portuguese by Bahádur Sháh, King of Guzarát, and
by the defeat of the King of Bíjápúr they obtained
the two peninsulas of Bardes and Salsette, which
adjoin the island of Goa.   In 1554 their territory
was further increased by the cession to them by
Malú 'Adil Shah of the whole of the Konkan—*i.e.*,
the territory lying between the Gháts and the sea
from about lat. 17° to lat. 19° N.   In the year 1569
the town of Honáwar was taken.   The year 1570
was marked by the unsuccessful siege of Goa by 'Alí
'Adil Shah, and the year 1592 by the siege of
Cháwal.

In the year 1595 the first Dutch ships arrived on
the coast of India, and from that time there commenced a struggle for mercantile supremacy between
the Dutch and Portuguese, which resulted in the
gradual extinction of the Portuguese power in India.
In the year 1603 the Dutch blockaded Goa, and,
though they were then compelled to withdraw, they
again besieged it in the year 1643, and soon afterwards succeeded in driving the Portuguese out of
Ceylon, Malacca and the Moluccas, and in excluding
them by their intrigues and influence from the trade
of Japan.   So that it came to pass that by the year
1640 nearly all their ports and forts had been wrested
from them.   As an instance of the ruin which now
fell upon the nation Tavernier mentions that, when

he visited Goa in 1648, many of the inhabitants
who at the time of his first visit in 1642 enjoyed
incomes of 2,000 crowns, were now reduced to beg
alms secretly ; and P. della Valle, in one of his letters
(Letter III, p. 157) mentions a similar state of things
even as early as 1623. Bombay was given up to the
English (as part of the marriage dower of the
Infanta Katherina) in 1662, and Kúchi (Cochin) was
taken from them in 1663. Further losses took
place from time to time. Finally, Bassín was taken
by the Maráthas in 1765, together with the island
of Salsette. Only Goa, Diu and Damán were left
to them, and these ports they still retain.

The first blow which fell upon the Portuguese
power was, no doubt, inflicted by the competition of
the Dutch merchants, who were better fitted for the
struggle by their national training and natural temperament, and also by the fact that their settlement
at the Cape of Good Hope, half-way from Europe,
gave them an advantage which was wanting to the
Portuguese. To these advantages must be added a
greater tact and facility on the part of the Dutch
merchants in providing for the wants of the markets
in Europe, as compared with the Portuguese traders.
But other causes also contributed to the rapid decline
of their power. The union of Portugal with Spain in
1579 had an injurious effect in this respect, not only by
its direct result in involving Portugal in the war with
the Dutch Republic, but also by indirectly weakening
the attention and support which the Portuguese
dominion in India received from the home Govern-

ment, so long as Portugal remained an independent kingdom. The discovery and conquest of Brazil, and consequent attention directed towards South America, contributed in some degree also to weaken the control of Indian affairs, and a want of proper discrimination in the selection of men appointed as Viceroys at Goa was another cause of the gradual decay of Portuguese power. These men showed an indifference to their duties as governors which not only of necessity produced disastrous results in the weakening of control over public affairs, but they also by their example brought about an extravagant and luxurious mode of life among the Portuguese residents, which gradually sapped their energy and gave an opportunity to their rivals of which they were not slow to take advantage ; while, by depriving the Government of men willing to serve as soldiers and seamen, it also seriously crippled its military power.[1] Intermarriage with people of the country had also an injurious effect in the diminution of energy and moral qualifications of the Portuguese. To these causes must be added a natural tendency

---

[1] " Society was almost rotten to the core. The morals of the community were extremely lax. Profligacy had become the predominant and fashionable vice, and men gave themselves up to the sensual pleasures peculiar to Oriental life. Nor was the public administration less tainted. The civic virtues of Albuquerque and Castro were supplanted by corruption and venality ; justice was bought, public offices were put up for sale, and the martial spirit of the nation degenerated into effeminacy, sloth and indolence, as in the last days of the Roman Empire." (*Soldado Pratico*, pp. 34 *et seq.*, quoted by Fonseca in *Historical Sketch of Goa*, p. 168.)

on their part to despise other nations as inferior to themselves, and a consequent disinclination to make the necessary efforts to retain the position which they had formerly held, but which they were now rapidly losing. Another cause of decay is to be found in the too great increase in numbers and wealth of the numerous religious orders which had established themselves at Goa and other settlements. These constituted a dead weight on the resources of the Portuguese settlements which could not but tend to produce a disastrous effect on the inhabitants, who required all their wealth and energy to enable them to contend against such formidable rivals as they had to meet with in their competitors for mercantile supremacy. Lastly, the epidemic fever which broke out for the second time in 1635 with unprecedented violence tended in no slight degree to complete the ruin which was being brought about by the causes already mentioned. Owing to the poverty of the Government treasury at that time no proper measures could be taken to arrest the ravages of the disease, and the Government officials contented themselves with merely joining with the clergy in imploring the Divine mercy. (See Fonseca's *Sketch of Goa*, p. 169.) Nor must it be forgotten that from their very first landing in India the Portuguese had been far too impetuous and venturesome in their attempts to establish themselves as a power in India. Instead of concentrating themselves in one or two settlements and thence gradually extending their power, they established isolated ports at various points on the coast, from which, when the time of adversity arrived, they were gradually driven by their enemies.

To sum up in a few words the history of the decline and fall of Portuguese power in India, it may be said that it was a tree planted with the sword and watered with blood, which, "because it had no root, withered away."

For the use of those who wish to inquire further into the subject, thus briefly referred to, it is only necessary to state that an ample list of authorities is quoted in the Introduction to the *Commentaries of Afonso Dalboquerque* (published by the Hakluyt Society in 1875), vol. ii, p. cvii *et seq*, and in a paper by T. W. H. Tolbort, Esq., B.C.S., on "Authorities for the History of the Portuguese in India", in the *Journal of the Asiatic Society of Bengal*, vol. xlii, Part I, 1873, pp. 193-208.

In *The Times* of August 15th and 21st, 1891, will be found letters making mention of valuable records at Lisbon and in the Library of Lincoln's Inn in London on this subject, to which the attention of the British Indian Government has lately been directed. An announcement has lately been made also of two works on the *History of the Portuguese in India*, and. on *The Causes which led to the Decline of Portuguese Power in India*, about to be published by Senor J. da Pinheiro of Goa.

As frequent reference is made in the following letters to the English and Dutch merchants, and as these two nations were the rivals of the Portuguese power in India, and constantly in collision with its representatives both in war and in matters of trade, a brief sketch of the origin and growth of the British and Dutch East India Companies up to the period when the Portuguese power ceased to hold sway on the continent of India may be useful to the reader of these letters, and may tend to a better understanding of affairs as they existed at the time referred to therein.

The spirit of enterprise and the spread of commerce which had ensued upon the discovery of America and of the passage to India by the Cape of Good Hope, the successes of the Spaniards and the Portuguese and the commercial efforts of the Dutch, disposed the English Government in the latter part of the sixteenth century to encourage plans for securing to the people a share of the increasing benefits of trade ; and, in consequence, several mercantile companies were established by letters patent. In 1589 a memorial was presented by divers merchants to the Lords of the Council, setting forth the public advantages which would result from trade in the East Indies ; and, at length, a charter of incorporation was granted, which is dated the 31st of December in the forty-third year of the reign of Elizabeth, A.D. 1600, the last day of the sixteenth century.

In this charter it is recited that two hundred and nineteen individuals, who are named, have petitioned for licence that they, "for the increase of navigation and the advancement of trade of mer-

chandise within the realms and dominions of the
Queen", might make trading voyages to the East
Indies.   It is then declared that the Queen has
granted to the individuals before named to be "a
body corporate and politic", by the name of "The
Governor and Company of Merchants of London
trading into the East Indies"; and then it is
granted to the Company and their servants that
"they may, by the space of fifteen years, freely traffick and use the trade of merchandise anywhere
beyond the Cape of Good Hope to the streights
of Magellan; so always that the same be not addressed to any place in the lawful and actual possession of any such Christian prince, or state, as
shall be in league, or amity, with the English Crown,
and who shall publicly declare that they will not
accept of such trade; and that neither the East
Indies, nor any of the places aforesaid, shall be
visited by the subjects of the Crown during the
fifteen years."

The commanders of the first ships which were
dispatched by the Company carried with them
letters of recommendation from the Queen, to be
presented to the kings of the countries at which
they might arrive in the Indian seas.   These
letters were each addressed "to the great and
mighty King of ——, our loving brother"; and,
after setting forth the advantages of commerce, held
out the prospect of a better supply of merchandise
and commodities than the Spaniards, or Portuguese,
had before furnished, and informed the King of

———, that "the Portugales pretended to be the sovereign Lords and princes of all his territories, and gave it out that they held his nation and people as subjects". The letter then proceeded to state that, if the King should accept that introduction to a continuance of friendship and of commerce and intercourse between the Queen's subjects and his own, the Queen had given orders to the bearer of her letter, if his Majesty should be pleased therewith, "to leave in the country some persons to reside under the King's protection, to learn the language and fashions of the people, and establish an amicable intercourse"; and if for this purpose his Majesty should require promises and capitulations, which the Queen could not in her letter take knowledge of, he was prayed to give credit to the bearer in whatsoever he should promise, or undertake, concerning the Queen's amity and intercourse, which, on the word of a prince, the Queen promised to see performed.

At Achín,[1] in the island of Sumatra, this letter was first used; and one Captain Lancaster made a treaty of commerce with "the mighty King of Dachein[2] and Sumatra", and obtained permission to settle a factory,[3] and that the factor and his servants,

---

[1] More correctly Atcheh. (See Yule's *"Cathay and the Way Thither*, vol. i, p. 120.)

[2] Balbi mentions the "Rey del Dagin", which he afterwards lets us see is meant for Achín. (See Sir H. Yule's *Cathay and the Way Thither*, vol. i, p. 101.)

[3] This factory was closed in 1785.

c 2

in their own private concerns, might conform to the laws of England, but in their transactions with nations to the laws and usages of the country ; and that they should have the right to dispose of their private property by will. Similar arrangements were made with the King of Bantam in the Island of Java in the year 1603.[1]

It is worthy of remark that it was within less than a year after the grant of this important charter to the East India Company that a successful attempt was made in the English House of Commons, for the first time, to restrain the prerogative of granting monopolies. On the 20th and 21st of November in the year 1601 this matter was debated with an earnestness not too great for the occasion, but which excites a smile when we look back upon it from a point of time nearly three hundred years in advance.

On the 25th of November, however, the Speaker delivered to the House a most gracious message from the Queen, in which it was expressed that she herself "would take present order of reformation ; and that some of the patents for monopolies should be repealed ; some suspended ; and none put in execution but such as should first have a trial according to the law for the good of the people". Mr. Secretary Cecil announced the glad tidings in a still more cheering strain, saying, "And because you

---

[1] This factory was withdrawn to Surat in India in 1682 or 1683.

may eat your meat more savoury than you have
done every man shall have salt as good and cheap
as he can buy it, or make it freely without danger
of that patent which shall be presently revoked.
The same benefit shall they have which have cold
stomachs, both for *aquavitæ* and *aqua composita*,
and the like. And they that have weak stomachs
for their satisfaction shall have vinegar and alegar[1]
and the like set at liberty. Train-oil shall go the
same way; oil of blubber shall march in equal rank;
brushes and bottles endure the like judgment. The
patent for pouldavy,[2] if it be not called in, it shall be.
Oade,[3] which, as I take it, is not restrained either by
law, or statute, but only by proclamation (I mean
from the former sowing), though for the saving
thereof it might receive good disputation, yet for
your satisfaction the Queen's pleasure is to revoke
that proclamation; only she prayeth thus much,
that when she cometh on progress to see you
in your countries she be not driven out of your
towns by suffering it to infect the air too near them.
Those that desire to go sprucely in their ruffs may at
less charge than accustomed obtain their wish; for
the patent for starch, which hath so much been
prosecuted, shall now be repealed." This was an
important achievement of the worthy knights and

---

[1] *I.e.*, vinegar made of ale.

[2] Also written "polldavy" or "poledavy", a kind of coarse
canvas.

[3] *I.e.*, woad (*Isatis tinctoria* or *Reseda luteola*), formerly culti-
vated as a dye.

burgesses of that day ; but it surpassed their courage
to mention (or it did not come sufficiently home to
their feelings) that only ten months had elapsed since
her Majesty had granted a far vaster monopoly, and
had interdicted her liege subjects from more than
half the sea-coasts and from three-fourths of the
waters of the earth.

In 1604 James the First violated the charter of
1600 by granting a licence to persons who were not
of the Company to trade to China and Japan ; but,
on the 31st of May 1609 he granted a new charter,
which recited that of Elizabeth and granted that
the petitioners thenceforth for ever should be one
body corporate in deed and in name, with powers
and privileges for the most part similar to those
which have been mentioned to have been given by
the first charters.   But the exclusive liberty of trade
is given "for ever thereafter": and it is provided
that the East Indies shall not be visited by the
subjects of the Crown during the time that those
letters patent shall be in force and not revoked,
or repealed.

As the trade of the Company began to extend
itself to the continent of India and amongst the
Spice Islands it came into collision and open contest with the Portuguese and the Dutch, the former
of whom claimed an exclusive right to the Indian
seas on account of the discovery of the Cape of
Good Hope route by Vasco da Gama[1]; and, being

---

[1] Mentioned at p. 175 of P. della Valle's Letters.

now subject to the Spanish Crown, were involved in the wars between that State and England; while the Dutch, on the other hand, claimed an exclusive right of trade with the Spice Islands, under treaties with the native powers.

In 1612, by an agreement or treaty with the Indian Governor, confirmed by the *firmáns* of the Mogul Emperor, the English Company obtained leave to establish a factory for trade at Súrat and at other places on the continent of India. About the same time they established also a factory in Japan; and in 1615 they obtained permission for another in the Zamorin's[1] country at Kranganúr on the Malabár coast; and a Captain Keiling took upon himself to make an agreement with the Zamorin to drive the Portuguese from Kúchi (Cochin), which was to be ceded to the English.

The stations at which the Company at this time carried on trade by their agents and factors, were stated to be as follows:

Bantam	
Jacatra, afterwards Batavia... ...	in Java.
Japara	
Acheen	in Sumatra.
Jambu	
Tecoa	in the Banda Islands.
Banda	

---

[1] As he was called by the Portuguese. The title adopted by the Kings of Kálikót was "Tamurin", which was corrupted into Samorin, Zamorin and Samari, by Europeans.

Benjarmassing ...	}	in Borneo.
Socondania ...		
Firando		in Japan.
Súrat		
Amadavad[1] ...		
Agra	}	in the Mogul's dominions.
Azmere, or Agimere		
Brampore, or Bur-		
ampore[2] ...		
Calicut[3]		on the Malabar coast.
Masulipatam ...	}	on the Coromandel coast.
Petapoli		
Siam		the capital of the kingdom of Siam.
Patan		in Malacca.
Macassar		in the Island of Celebes.

In 1615 King James, at the request and expense of the East India Company, sent Sir Thomas Roe as Ambassador to the Mogul Emperor : a measure which, if for no other reason, seemed to have become necessary from the contests on the sea-coasts of the Emperor's dominions between the Company and the Portuguese.[4] A treaty was concluded by the Ambassador between King James and the Mogul Emperor, whereby it was stipulated that the English should have liberty of trade and to settle factories in any ports of the Mogul Empire, together with some other beneficial privileges. It was agreed that mutual assistance should be given against the enemies of either of the contracting parties, and

---

[1] Properly Áhmadábád. (See p. 92 of P. della Valle's Letters.)
[2] Or Barhampúr. (See p. 185 of P. della Valle's Letters.)
[3] Kálikót. (See p. 60 of P. della Valle's Letters.)
[4] See pp. 8, 10, 137, and 157 of P. della Valle's Letters.

that the Portuguese should be included in the treaty, if it should be acceded to by the Viceroy at Goa within six months ; otherwise the Portuguese were to be treated as enemies.

In 1618 Sir Thomas Roe, before his departure from India, concluded another treaty with the Mogul Emperor, by which the English subjects at Súrat were taken under the Emperor's protection, and liberty of religion and of being, to a certain extent, governed by their own laws was granted ; it being provided that in any disputes between them and the natives reference was to be made to the Mogul Governor, who should decide speedily and justly ; but disputes among themselves were to be decided by their Factors.

It has been mentioned[1] that the Dutch claimed an exclusive right to trade with the Spice Islands on the ground that they had driven out the Portuguese and had entered into treaties with the natives, by which, on condition of the Dutch defending them against the Portuguese, the natives had agreed to trade solely with the Dutch.   The English thought this claim ought to be confined to those places of which the Dutch had a prior and actual possession ; and in 1616 the Agent and Council of the Company at Bantam directed the commanders of two ships to obtain from the natives of the "Islands of Puloway,[2]

---

[1] P. xxiii.

[2] Near the N. point of Sumatra,   The word *Pulo* means "island".

Puloroone, Pulo-Lantore, and Rosengin," a surrender
of those islands to the King of England upon certain conditions ; and in 1617 some of the islands
were occupied and fortified, to the great indignation
of the Dutch, who seized the English ships.   The
Dutch Company in Holland sent complaints to the
King of England, and the English Company re-
criminated ; and in 1619 the English and Dutch
Governments at home appointed commissioners to
inquire into these differences.   In the meantime the
Dutch in India waged open war against the English,
and the superintendent of the English factory at
Bantam made a treaty of alliance with the King of
Bantam against the Dutch, and besieged and took
from them the fort of Jaccatra,[1] the modern Batavia ;
but, on the whole, the Dutch had greatly the advantage, and in the end drove the English out of
the islands they had occupied and fortified.   The
commissioners at home, however, in 1619 concluded
a treaty for twenty years between the King of England and the States-General, of which the substance
was that an amnesty was granted to the agents of both
Companies for their offences ; and it was stipulated
that both should jointly participate in the Indian
trade in specified proportions ;   that each should
furnish ships of war for their common defence, and
that all proceedings should be under the regulation
of a council of defence in the Indies, composed of
four members from each Company.   This put an

---

[1] Mentioned at p. 124 of P. della Valle's Letters.

end to war, but by no means to the disputes or
animosities of the rival Companies, which continued to exist in great bitterness, until, in April
1622, the Dutch, who continued to be much the
stronger of the two, under the pretence, or perhaps
upon a mistaken belief, of a conspiracy, after tortures
of extreme barbarity, executed ten of the English
residents at Amboyna, one of the Molucca Islands,
as malefactors, together with one Portuguese and
eleven natives.   This was the event well known in
history as the " Massacre of Amboyna".

The contests of the English with the Portuguese
continued on the west of India and in the Persian
seas ; and in 1622 some English ships assisted a
Persian armament in taking by siege one of the
principal of all the Portuguese settlements, that of
Ormuz.[1] It was, perhaps, the war which shortly
afterwards broke out between Spain and England,
and the troubled state of Portugal, which prevented
the Portuguese nation from resenting more forcibly
the irregular but fatal warfare which had been
carried on between their Asiatic settlements and
those of the English Company.   In return for the
assistance of the English the Persian monarch, Sháh
Abbas, granted to them one-half of the customs
of his port of Gombroon, otherwise called Bandar
Abbas.[2]

In 1624 representations were made by the Com-

---

[1] These are the proceedings referred to in Letter No. 1 of
P. della Valle, pp. 8, 9, and 10.

[2] Mentioned at p. 3 of P. della Valle's Letters.

pany to the English Government of the transactions at Amboyna and of other great injuries which they had sustained from the Dutch, and one of the consequences was that the Attorney-General was directed to prepare a commission for the Company, authorising them to build forts in thé East Indies for the security of their trade.

In February 1625 the English Company were induced by the unfriendly conduct of the Dutch at Masulipatám (Machlipatnám), on the coast of Koromandel, to establish a new factory on the same coast a little to the southward, at Armagon, or Durgarázpatnám, for which purpose they obtained a piece of ground from the Naik,[1] or military officer of the district ; and by the year 1628 a fortress was established here, defended by twelve pieces of cannon and twenty-three factors and soldiers.

In November 1632 the English Company obtained a *farmán* (which was confirmed and enlarged by a subsequent one in 1635) from the King of Golkonda,[2] which upon certain conditions allowed them liberty of trade in his dominions ; and in February 1633 they obtained another *farmán* from the Mogul Emperor for liberty of trade in the province of Bengal, but upon condition of their using no other port than that of Pipley (Sípali) in Balasore Bay.[3]

---

[1] See p. 168 of P. della Valle's Letters.

[2] See pp. 147 and 148 of P. della Valle's Letters.

[3] As to the facts connected with this *farmán*,. see *Diary of W. Hedges*, by Sir H. Yule, vol. iii, p. 167.

The peace concluded between Spain and England in November 1630 had not put a stop to the contests between the English factories and the Portuguese settlements in India; but in 1634 the Company's agent at Surat made a treaty, or agreement, with the Portuguese Viceroy at Goa for a cessation of hostilities until six months after it should be known in India what was the determination of their respective sovereigns; and this not having been learnt before 20th January 1635, a more formal convention to the same effect was then concluded by the same parties.

In December 1635, upon an assumption that the East India Company had not observed the conditions of their charter, but, attending only to their own interests, had disregarded those of the King and his subjects, a licence from the Crown was granted to Sir Wm. Courten and others, for the purpose of trading with the Portuguese settlements and other places in India not occupied by the East India Company.   Great inconvenience ensued to the Company, and they petitioned the Privy Council, not only for a redress of these grievances but for those also which they had sustained at the hands of the Dutch.   They were told that negotiations were going on with the Dutch, and that the grant to Courten's association should not be renewed; but nothing effectual had been obtained when the Great Rebellion broke out in England.

In 1640, the Naik of the district having been conciliated, one of the agents of the Company built Fort

Saint George at a place called Madraspatnám,[1] on the Koromandel coast, and established a factory there. This has been called the first "independent" station which was acquired by the Company on the continent of India.

In 1651 the Dutch having abandoned their settlement on the island of St. Helena it was occupied by the English Company, though not situate beyond the Cape of Good Hope, nor consequently within the limits of their trade. In 1652 war broke out between the Dutch and English in Europe; and, upon the intelligence reaching India, the English Company's agents at Surat solicited the protection of the Mogul Emperor, but did not obtain any satisfactory answer; and in England proposals were made by the Company for raising by subscription the means of making reprisals upon the Dutch; but in 1654 a treaty of peace was concluded between the two nations, by the 27th article of which it was stipulated that justice should be done on those who were partakers in the "massacre" at Amboyna, and, by the 30th article, that commissioners should be appointed to inquire into and adjust the losses and injuries which were alleged by the two Companies to have been sustained from each other; the result of which commission was an award that the island of Puloroone should be restored to the English; that the Dutch Company should pay to the English Company £85,000 sterling, and to the

---

[1] Subsequently, and at present, known as Madras.

relations of those who had suffered at Amboyna, £3,615, and these sums were subsequently paid.

The affairs of the Company both at home and abroad were greatly disturbed by the revolution in England and other contemporaneous events. The continent of India was distracted by contests between the Muhammadan sovereigns of Golkonda, Ahmadnagar, and Bíjapúr on one side, with the remnants of Hindu power in Southern India on the other,[1] by the rising force of Sívaji the Maratha chief, and by the contests between the different members of the imperial family for the throne of the Mogul; moreover, the Portuguese and Dutch lost no opportunity of vexing their rivals.

Shortly after the restoration Charles the Second granted a commission to the Company to take and possess the island of Puloroone, which had been acknowledged in the treaty between the Crown and the States-General to belong to England. The Dutch, with a wretched baseness, gave secret orders to their Governor to cut down all the spice-trees before it was delivered up, which made it worthless.

On the 3rd April 1661 the King granted to the Company a new charter, by which all that was important in the charter of King James of 1609 was granted anew and confirmed to them; and some very important additions were made. The letters patent recited that disorders had been committed

---

[1] These contests are referred to in Letter No. II of P. della Valle, pp. 144 *et seq.*

by subjects of the Crown, as well as foreigners, to
the interruption of the trade of the Company, and
granted that all plantations, forts, fortifications, factories, or colonies, where the Company's factories
or trade were, or should be, in the East Indies,
should be from thenceforth under the power and
command of the Governor and Company, their successors and assigns, and that the Governor and
Company should have full power and authority to
appoint and establish governors and officers to
govern them, and that such governors and their
councils should have power to judge all persons
belonging to the Governor and Company, or that
should live under them, in all causes, whether civil
or criminal, according to the laws of England, and
to execute judgment accordingly.

The charter further granted to the Governor and
Company and their successors, free liberty and
licence (in case they conceived it necessary) to
send ships of war, men, and ammunition, into any
of their places of trade in the East Indies, for the
security and defence of the same, and to choose
commanders and officers of the same, and to give
them power and authority, by commissions under
their common seal or otherwise, to continue or
make peace, or war, with any prince, or people,
that were not Christians, in any places of their trade,
as should be most for the advantage and benefit of
the said Governor and Company and their trade ;
and to right and recompense themselves upon the
goods, estate, or people of those parts by whom the

Governor and Company should sustain injury, loss, or damage ; or upon any other people whatsoever that should any ways interrupt, wrong, or injure them in their trade ; and also to build fortifications at St. Helena, as also elsewhere, within their limits of trade, as they in their discretion should think fit ; and to send out of the kingdom to those fortifications all kinds of clothing, victuals, ammunition, and implements free of custom or duty ; and to transport and carry over such number of men, being willing thereto, as they should think fit, and to govern them in such legal and reasonable manner as the said Governor and Company should think fit.

Power was further granted to seize any subjects of the King in the East Indies who should sail thither in any Indian, or English, vessel, or inhabit there, without licence of the Company, or should disobey their orders, and to send them to England ; and that all the King's subjects employed by the Company in India should suffer such punishment for offences committed there as the president and council for the Governor and Company there should think fit and the offence should require ; and if any person so convicted and sentenced by them, or by the factors or agents of the Company, should appeal, then it should be lawful for the president and council, factors or agents, to seize upon him and carry him home prisoner to England to the Governor and Company, there to receive such punishment as the merits of his cause should

d

require and the laws of the nation allow of; and, for the better discovery of abuses, the Governor and Company, and their presidents, chief agent, or governor in the East Indies were empowered to examine persons on oath, so as the oath and the matter therein contained should not be repugnant to the laws of the realm. This charter was subjected to the same proviso against the Company forcing their trade upon any friendly Christian State, and to the same proviso for revocation by the Crown, as that of 1609.

On the 23rd June 1661 the island of Bombay was ceded by Portugal to the Crown of England "in full property and sovereignty"; permission being reserved for the enjoyment by the inhabitants of the free exercise of the Roman Catholic religion. It would not be a very easy matter to say how the enjoyment of this new dominion and property of the Crown was to be reconciled with the exclusive rights granted by the charter so shortly before. Possession, however, was not obtained by the King's forces until 1664, and the affairs of the island were still in a very unsettled state, when (on the 27th March 1668) the King granted to the Governor and Company all the said port and island of Bombay in the East Indies, with all the rights, profits, territories, and appurtenances thereof whatsoever. There were provisos in the grant, first for securing to the inhabitants of the island the free exercise of the Roman Catholic religion and all their lawful properties and privileges; and, secondly, that the

Company should not alienate the island, or any part thereof to any person not being a subject of the British Crown.

In 1664 a French East India Company, for carrying on trade between the Cape of Good Hope and the Straits of Magellan, was established by Louis XIV and his minister Colbert.

In this period of time, from 1660 to the end of 1688 the character of the British East India Company was entirely changed. At the commencement of it they were a trading association, compelled indeed occasionally to defend themselves and their trade by force of arms, but not pretending to any portion of sovereign power. Before the end of it they had been constituted by the King's charter the "Lords" of two islands which were dominions of the Crown ; they had power given them to raise troops, equip fleets, and make peace and war ; to coin money ; to make and enforce laws ; and to try, condemn and execute the King's subjects. They had declared and waged war against a powerful monarch, with designs not merely of self defence, but of conquest, and, though they were not successful in this first attempt, they did not abandon their projects for the future of government and aggrandisement.

How far they succeeded in this project is shown by the extent at the present time of the British Empire in India. But, as we have now traced the history of the East India Company to a period when the Portuguese power in India had practically come to an end, it is beyond the scope of this dissertation

d 2

to pursue the subject further. Sufficient to say that
the Portuguese and Dutch nations having left the
field England had no rival in India except the
French, and in due course of time, the French having
also been driven out, the English East India Company became the paramount power in India until
the sovereignty was assumed by Her Majesty the
Queen in 1858.

A brief survey of the political divisions of the
continent of India at the time of P. della Valle's
visit may be useful to the reader of his letters.
The whole of the northern part of India, including
the present North-West Provinces, Oudh and the
Punjáb, together with the provinces of Bengal and
Orissa, had become subject to the kings of Delhi,
whose representative at that time was the Emperor
Jahángír, son of Akbár. To these provinces may
be added the smaller territories of Malwa, Scinde,
Guzarát, Márwár, Khándesh, and Berár. The Dakhan, or that part of the peninsula lying south of the
Vindhya mountains, was divided among the Muhammadan rulers of Áhmadnagar, or Aurangábád,
Bíjápúr and Golkonda, representing respectively
the dynasties of Nizám Sháh, 'Adil Sháh, and Kútb
Sháh, who had in the year 1565 combined together
and overthrown, at Tálikota, Rám Rájá, the representative of the Hindu dynasty, generally known
as the Narsinga dynasty, whose capital was Vijáyá-
nagar, or Vidia-nagar. On the eastern coast were
the kingdoms of Telingana and Machlipatnám, and
to the extreme south were the kingdoms of Maisúr

and Travankór. On the south-western coast were
the territories of the Samorin of Kálíkót and various
other petty chiefs, who exercised powers more or
less independent of the Muhammadan rulers of the
Dakhan. On the more northerly part of this coast
were the European settlements of the Portuguese
and Dutch, such as Damán, Cháwal, Goa, and Súrat,
and there were others as far south as Kúchí
(Cochim) and the Island of Ceylon.

BIBLIOGRAPHICAL NOTICE.

"Viaggi di Pietro della Valle il Pellegrino con minuto ragguaglio di tutte le cose notabili osseruate in essi, descritti da lui medesimo in 54 Lettere familiari da diuersi luoghi della intrapresa peregrinatione, mandate in Napoli all' erudito, e fra' più cari, di molti anni suo amico Mario Schipano, diuisi in tre parti, cioè la Tvrchia, la Persia e l' India, le quali hauran per aggiunta, se Dio gli darà vita, la quarta parte, che conterrà le figure di molte cose memorabili, sparse per tutta l' opera e la loro esplicatione." *Roma:* Mascardi, 1657. 2 vols. in 4to.

The first part only, *i.e.,* Turkey, was published in the lifetime of the author. His sons Valerio, Erasmo, Francesco and Paolo supervised the publication of the Persian letters, dedicating them to Pope Alexander VIII. These were published in Rome in 1658 by Biagio Deversino.

The letters from India, with the return journey home, were issued in 1663 under the same editorial supervision, and dedicated to Cardinal Flavio Chigi (see dedication following), nephew and namesake of the Pope. They were published by Biagio Deversino and Felice Cesaretti, and printed in the press of Vitale Mascardi.

The Dragondelli edition, published at Rome (1662-3) in two volumes 4to, is considered the best, having a life of the author by Bellori, and a portrait of Pietro della Valle, reproduced in facsimile in our frontispiece. Other editions are:

Venice, 1660 and 1667, 4 vols. in 12mo, with a life by Bonini; Bologna, Longhi, 1672, 4 vols. in 12mo, with the Bonini biography; and Venice, 1681, 4 vols. in 8vo. A much more recent edition in 2 vols. 12mo was printed in 1843 for an Italian bookseller of the name of G. Gancia, residing at Brighton, probably at the suggestion of Henry Wellesley, a great lover of Italian literature, to whom the book is dedicated. Reprints of this edition were published the same year in Turin and Milan.

Of the translations of the letters, the first to appear was a French version, Paris, 1662-4, 4 vols., 4to, translated from the Italian by the Fathers Etienne Carneau and François le Comte, and published by Gervais Clousier. A second edition appeared in 1670. The translator or translators, remarks Eyries (*Biogr. Univ.*, Venice, 1830, vol. 59), placed at the head of every letter and along the margin summaries not contained in the original work, which are emphatic to the verge of ridicule. A later French edition was published at Rouen in 1745, in 8 vols. 12mo, with portraits and engravings.

Dutch editions were published at Amsterdam in 1664-5, 1666, and 1681, in 6 vols. 4to, with plates.

The German edition, published at Genff, by Widerhold in 1674, in 4 vols. fol., with illustrations on copper, and the portrait of the author and Sitti Maani, bears the following title :

" Petri della Valle, Eines vornehmen Römischen Patritii Reiss-Beschreibung in unterschiedliche Theile der Welt nemlich in Turkey, Egypten, Palestina, Persien, Ost Indien. Samt einer ausführlichen Erzehlung aller Denck- und Merckwürdigster Sachen, so darinnen zu finden und anzutreffen ; nebenst den Sitten und Gebräuchen dieser Nationen und anderen Dingen, dergleichen zuvor niemals von anderen angemercket und beschrieben worden. Erstlich von dem Authore selbst, der diese Reisen gethan, in Italiänisher Sprach beschrieben. Nachgehends auss dieser in die Französische und Holländische ; anjetzo aber auss dem Original in die Hoch-Teutsche Sprach übersetzet, mit schönen Kupfferen geziert, und vieren wohlanständigen Registern versehen."

The title of the English edition from which our text is derived is as follows :—

" The Travels of Pietro della Valle, a noble Roman, into East-India and Arabia-Deserta, in which the several countries, together with the Customs, Manners, Traffique, and Rites both Religious and Civil of those Oriental Princes and Nations, are faithfully described : In Familiar Letters to his Friend Signior Mario Schipano."

It was published in London in 1664, in one vol. folio, together with Sir Thomas Roe's Voyage to the East Indies. Of the translator, G. Havers, no mention is made in the biographical dictionaries.

With regard to the literary style of the *Viaggi*, it should be borne in mind that their author had originally intended the letters to serve only as the raw material for a more finished work which his friend Mario Schipano, to whom they were addressed, had undertaken to prepare for the press. It was only when this friend, overtaxed with other work, failed in his promise, that Della Valle set himself to the task of editing the letters in their original form with such emendations and additions as were necessary. In this way he revised the letters from Turkey and Persia with his own hand, while those from India, judging from their context and from the diary style being preserved throughout, probably remained untouched.

Such, at all events, is the judgment of his countryman and biographer Ciampi, who adds that Della Valle was an accurate observer, and described everything he saw in his work, combining the continuity of narrative, so attractive a feature in the old records of travel, with scientific observations worthy of a more mature age. He gives us the true aspect of a country in lines and colouring reminding us of the pictures of his contemporaries Poussin and Claude Lorraine.

He himself tells us, in his preface, "I should never have presumed to write these letters to thee" (he is addressing Schipano) "in chaste and elegant Tuscan, that might serve others as a model, and be cited as an authority by the orator or by the historian, but contented myself with composing them in my mother tongue, the Roman, as commonly spoken, without any affectation."

Besides the *Viaggi*, Della Valle's *magnum opus*, the author's published and unpublished writings are as follows :—*Informazione della Georgia data alla Santità di nostro Signore Papa Urbano VIII da Pietro della Valle, il Pellegrino, l' anno* 1627. This was probably printed in Rome, though unpublished. It was first made public in a French translation in Thevenot's *Relations de divers Voyages curieux qui n'ont point esté publiés, etc.*, Paris, 1663, Part i, and in subsequent editions. A note in this work states that the translation had been made from a MS. In the same volume is published P. della Valle's oration at the funeral ceremony of Sitti Maani in the church of Ara Coeli at Rome, with a portrait of this lady, a notice of her life, and an account of her funeral from the Italian of Girolamo Rocchi, Rome (Zannetti), 1627.

Della Valle's next work was entitled *Delle Conditioni di Abbas re di Persia*, dedicated to Cardinal Francesco Barberini, nephew of Pope Urban VIII, Venice, 1628. This book was divided into three parts, and contained an Appendix, entitled *Genealogia di Abbas re di Persia*, derived, the author tells us, from the Royal books of Persia. It was translated into French by Baudoin, and printed in Paris in 1731, in 4to.

Della Valle also wrote a number of letters on Oriental philosophy and religion, and on the codices he brought home. Two of these epistles were addressed to Scipio Sgambati, a Neapolitan priest of the Jesuit order, who became professor of theology in the University of Vienna. Nine others were indited to Jean Morin, of the Congregation of the Oratory in France. Morin accompanied Queen Henrietta Maria to England, and was afterwards summoned to Rome by Pope Urban VIII, to assist him in his favourite scheme of reuniting the Greek and Latin Churches. Delle Valle's letters to Morin were included in a work published in London by George Wells in 1680, entitled *Antiquitates Ecclesiæ Orientalis Clarissimorum Virorum*, etc.

Lastly, four more of his letters addressed to Tengnagel, librarian of the Imperial library at Vienna, are contained in Lambeck's commentaries, *Petri Lambecii Hamburgensis Commentariorum de Augustissima bibliotheca Cæsarea Vindobonensi. Liber primus. Vindobonæ*, 1665.

Mention must also be made of a treatise on three new kinds of rhyme, *Verso Sdrucciolo* (or verses of twelve feet instead of eleven, having the accent on the antepenultimate), being a discourse delivered by Della Valle before the Academy of Humourists, of which he was a member, and among whom he was known as " Il Fantastico". This treatise was printed in Rome (Facciotti) in 1634, in 4to. He also composed a little work on music, published in the collection of Battista Doni (Florence, 1763), under this heading: *Della Musica dell' età nostra, che non è punto inferiore, anzi è migliore de quella dell' età passata*, dedicated to Lelio Guidiccioni, and dated 1640.

Besides his prose works, Della Valle wrote poetry, some of

which was set to music; and here we may mention that he was the inventor of two musical instruments, though they were never perfected.

Further information on P. della Valle and his works will be found in Tiraboschi's *Storia della litteratura Italiana*, vol. vii; Allaci's *Apes Urbanæ;* Ciampi's *Della vita e delle opere di P. della Valle*, 1879, to which we are indebted; the *Encyclopædia Britannica;* the *Biographie Universelle*, and the *Bolletino della Società Geografica Italiana*, serie III, vol. iii, Fascicoli XI and XII, November and December 1890.

PRINCE FLAVIO CHIGI,

OUR Valle returns to bow once more, most eminent Prince, before the high summit of the mountains, which, like so many Olympuses, leaving the clouds upon their lower slopes, reach up unto the stars; and enjoys the ambition of renewing that homage which, on a like occasion, he was fortunate enough to lay at the feet of the noble Alexander, of whom you are the most worthy and universally revered nephew.

We much regret that our Father's travels did not reach to the very furthest corners of the unknown world, that we might have greater opportunity of publishing to posterity our matchless devotion, under the shade of that oak, which must excite the jealousy of the sun's most brilliant rays. The curiosity of the Learned, which has until now only enjoyed the notices of Turkey and Persia, impatient to learn accurately the wonders of the Oriental Indies, has with reason urged us to the publication of the same.

Desirous to gain for these pages the esteem and honour which fell to the lot of the Edition of the former volumes, by means of the kind Patronage of your Eminence, who with the treasures of your own knowledge enriches the mines which embellish and ennoble these most wealthy Provinces, we have resolved to put your highly prized

name on their title-page, assured that, if with the mark of a
Cæsar a hind is safe from harm, under the auspices of a
Flavio the present Volume will be welcomed by the whole
Universe. May, therefore, your Eminence deign to accept
the recital of our Father's labours, offered to you in these
pages, honouring them with an occasional glance which,
rivalling that of Midas, will change them into gold.

Be pleased at the same time to pardon the respectful
desire which we entertain of thus satisfying in some small
measure the feeling of eternal obligation which our house
must always show for the special favours received from so
great a patron, blessing, as we do, the long absence of our
Father in his distant journeys, since his labours procure for
his sons this occasion of kissing the sacred purple of your
Eminence, and laying themselves humbly at your feet.

Your most humble, devoted and obliged Servants,

> VALERIO,
> ERASMO,
> FRANCESCO and ⎱ DELLA VALLE.
> PAOLO

LATIN EPIGRAM

(By P. S. SGAMBATI, *of the Society of Jesus)*

TO PIETRO DELLA VALLE, PATRICIAN OF ROME,

ON HIS BRINGING THE REMAINS OF HIS WIFE FROM ASIA.

ÆNEADUM soboles! Albani sanguinis hæres!
Æneæ proavi quam bene facta refers!
Ille senem ex Asiâ fertur vexisse parentem;
Ex Asiâ conjux est tibi ducta comes.
Par utrique fides esset, nisi quòd tua major
Est pietas, Italûm gloria Valliade.
Ille senem extinctum Siculâ tellure reliquit;
Tu Romam extinctæ conjugis ossa vehis.

TRANSLATION.

Æneas son! Of old Albanus' line the heir!
How well dost thou repeat thy father's fame!
From Asia he his aged sire did bear,
From Asia too with thee thy lov'd wife came.
In both alike true constancy is found,
But thine, O Valle's son! we greater see,
He left his father in Sicilian ground,
Thou bring'st to Rome thy dead wife's bones with thee.

ERRATA.

P. 2, l. 10, " 19" should be " 19th".

P. 15, l. 3 (of note), " Gujarat" should be "Guzarát".

P. 35, l. 16, " riting" should be "visiting", and note 2 should be struck
 out.

 „ l. 36, the words " of Magellan" should be omitted.

 „ l. 37, the words " by F. H. Guillemard" should be omitted.

P. 49, l. 2, " Sodianga, ancient" should be " ancient Sogdiana".

 „ l. 7, Persian-Tongue should be " Persian tongue".

 „ l. 7, comma after " handsomely" should be omitted.

 „ l. 19, a hyphen should be inserted between the words "Etymological" and " Geographical".

P. 60, l. 4, " Periah" should be " Periab".

P. 66, l. 25, " Guzerat" should be " Guzarát".

 „ l. 31, " India" should be " Indian".

P. 81, l. 12, " then" should be " than".

P. 90, ll. 5 and 25, " ribban" should be " ribbon".

P. 94, l. 9, " Tarilus" should be " Taxilus".

P. 175, l. 1 (of notes), " Zuari" should be "Tuari".

c

LETTERS OF PIETRO DELLA VALLE.

TABLE OF CONTENTS.

LETTER I.

LETTER II.

LETTER III.

LIST OF ILLUSTRATIONS.

THE RIGHT HONOURABLE

ROGER,

EARL OF ORRERY, Etc.

My Lord,

It is not more commonly then truly observ'd, That the Preeminence of Excellent Things is universally attended with a proportionable Result of Benefit to those of Inferior Degree: And the same may with equal verity be affirm'd of the Glory of Great Personages. Your Names serve, not onely to distinguish you, or, by the Addition of Titles, to give you higher rank in the State; but, like the Sun communicating Light and Life together, they animate and beautifie what ever is irradiated by them. Which general Consideration, though it could not give me any particular Right, yet it may in some sort warrant the suitableness of dedicating this Transcript to your Lordship's Name; A Name which, besides having been able to revive and support a long-depressed Interest in a Considerable Kingdom, is so highly celebrated upon the account of other Performances, as scarce to find a Parallel among those of your own, or any other Orb. Nor is it a little ground of Confidence to me that what I present is neither wholly my own in any sort, nor any of it otherwise then as an Interpreter; nor (lastly) one of those refined Pieces of Invention, which while your Protection is implored, do withall solicite your judgment; But of that kind of Writings, which, containing Descriptions of Countries and their Customs, can onely please by the Variety of the Relations and the Veracity of the Relator. He whom I have interpreted was a Noble Roman, (Persons of which Quality, as they have greater Curiosity, so they have far more Advantages in reference to making of Observations in Forreign Countries than they whose chief business is Traffick), and was carried onely by his own curious Genius into those Oriental parts of the World whereof he here gives an Account; which is so full of delightful Variety and considerable Remarks that, as after his Return his Person was dignified with an Honourable Office in the Court of his own Prince, so, since his Death, his Travels have no less happily travell'd and been naturalizd in some other Languages.

The other Piece hath been judg'd fit to be adjoyned, as one of the Exactest Relations of the Eastern parts of the World that hitherto hath been publish'd by any Writer, either Domestick, or Forreign; having been penn'd by one that attended Sir Thomas Roe in his Embassy to the Great Mogol: Than whom, t'is acknowledged by one of that Country that trades most into those parts, none ever gave a more faithful Account thereof. It remaines onely that, as by this Action I have (though with all the modesty that becomes me) assum'd an Interest in a Great Name, so I also testifie the Honour and Veneration I bear to Great Worth and Rare Accomplishments; which I shall do summarily (and yet in the utmost importance of the words) by professing myself,

Inter eos qui relationes suas de hoc Regno (sc. M. Mogolis) prodiderunt facilè fide & dignatione princeps est Thomas Roeus, Mag: Britanniæ Regis ad superiorem Indiæ Regem Legatus. Saith John de Laet.

My Lord,

Your Lordship's in all Humble

Respect and Observance.

G. Havers.

Note.—The latter part of the above dedication refers to an account of Sir Thomas Roe's embassy to the King of Delhi, which was included in the same volume with the letters of P. della Valle, published in 1664, but which has been omitted (as have also some of the letters of P. della Valle) from the present edition, which includes only the eight letters written by him from *India*.

THE TRAVELS

OF

PETER DELLA VALLE,

SIRNAMED THE TRAVELLER,

Containing a Description of the East Indies, &c.

LETTER I.

From Suràt, March 22. Anno 1623.

 N the beginning of this year, at my departure from Persia, I writ last to you from aboard the ship call'd the *Whale,* in which I was newly embarqu'd upon the coasts of that Country, and had not yet begun my Voyage. Since which time having sail'd over a good part of the Ocean, arriv'd at the famous Countries of *India,* travell'd and view'd no inconsiderable portion thereof; by conveniency of the same ship which brought me hither, and is ready to set sail speedily towards *Muchà*[1] in the Arabian Gulph, (and the rather for that a German Gentleman a friend of mine is embarqu'd in her, with an intention

---

[1] Usually spelt Mocha. The chief port of Arabia, on the Red Sea. First visited by an English fleet in 1610, under Sir H. Middleton.

to travel from thence, in case he can get passage, to see
Æthiopia) with this Letter (which I recommend to him to
get transmitted into *Italy*, if possible, from those Ports of
the Red Sea, or by the way of *Cairo*, where they trade, or
by some other conveyance) I come again to give you an
Account of my Adventures, and the Curiosities which
have hitherto afforded delicious repast to my always
hungry Intellect. To begin therefore : Upon Thursday
the 19 of January, having dispatch'd and taken order for
what was needful, a little before day, after the discharge
of some Guns as 'tis the custome at going off from any
coast, we began leisurely to display our sails, moving but
slowly, because we waited for the ship-boat which was still
at Shore ; upon whose return we unfolded all our Canvase,
and, though with a small gale, directed our course between
the Islands of *Ormuz*[1] and *Kesom*,[2] passing on the outer
side of *Ormuz* next *Arabia*, in regard the shallowness of

---

[1] Hormuz, or Ormuz ; the ancient Ormuza. An island in the
Persian Gulf, celebrated for its wealth, as the emporium of commerce,
not only between Persia and India, but also between Europe and
India, its commodities being carried up the Euphrates, and thence
across the Syrian desert. The island is merely a bare rock. It was
taken by the Portuguese fleet, under Albuquerque, in 1514, and
retaken by Shah Abbas, King of Persia, with the aid of the English,
in 1622. Described by Duarte Barbosa* (? Magellan), in his account
of East African and Malabar coasts, printed for the Hakluyt
Society, 1866, p. 41. In Linschoten's *Travels* there is the following
reference to Ormuz :—" The Ile of Ormus in summer time is so
unseasonabell, and intollerabley hotte, that they are forced to lie, and
sleepe, in wooden cesternes, made for the purpose full of water,
and all naked, both men and women, lying cleane under water, saving
only their heads."

[2] Properly Kishm. An island in the Persian Gulf. Also called
Kishmish. The ancient Oaracta, celebrated for its wine.

---

* Duarte Barbosa is stated in a recent work by Guillemard to have
been a brother-in-law of Magellan, and perhaps also a cousin. Cf.
Ferdinand Magellan, by F. H. Guillemard, pp. 87, 90.

the Channel towards *Persia* afforded not water enough for such great Ships as ours.

We were in company only two English Ships, namely, the *Whale*, which was the Captain-Ship, (in which I was embarqu'd), commanded by Captain *Nicholas Woodcock*, and another called the *Dolphin*, which had for Captain, Master *Matthew Willis*. At noon, being near *Lareck*,[1] and no wind stirring, we cast Anchor without falling our sails, and our Captain sent his long-boat ashore to Lareck, with two Grey-hounds, which the English of *Combù*[2] had given him, to catch what game they could light upon. Towards night we set sail again ; but though the wind somewhat increased, yet because the boat was not returned, we struck sail a little, and staid for it, discharging also several musket shots to the end those that were in it might hear and see where we were ; and because 'twas one o'clock in the night, and the Boat was not yet come, we doubted some disaster might have befaln it, in regard of the multitude of those Arabian thieves called *Nouteks*,[3] which rob upon that sea and frequently reside in this Island of *Lareck* : Yet at length it return'd safe and sound, and brought us abundance of Goats ; whereupon we again spread our sails freely to the wind, which was pretty stiff, although not much favourable to our course. However, we went onwards, plying to the Coast of *Arabia* from that of *Persia ;* and on Saturday morning, as we drew near the Arabian shore, we saw three small Islands,[4] situate near one another, and not far from a certain Cape,[5] the

---

[1] A small island between Hormuz, and Kishm.

[2] Properly Gombroon. The principal port of S. Persia, of which the modern name is Bandar Abbas.

[3] These pirates were attacked and destroyed by the English in 1809.

[4] Probably the Quoin islands.

[5] Probably Cape Mussendom, on the Arabian coast. Also called Selemeh, and, by Ortelius, Mocandon.

name of which, and the Islands, they could not tell me, so as that I might set it down truly ; whereby I perceiv'd how it comes to pass that many names of places in these parts are very corruptly written in Geographical Charts ; for in the Countries themselves, where commerce is had for the most part with rude and ignorant people, few of them know how to pronounce the same aright.

On Sunday we went from our Ship to recreate ourselves in the *Dolphin*, our companion, where the Captain entertain'd us liberally all day. In the meantime we had a good fresh gale, and sailing directly in the middle of the gulf, we beheld both the coasts of *Arabia Felix*, and *Persia;* and in the latter discern'd a famous white rock, which, standing in the midst of a low sandy shore, looks like a little hill made by hand. We pass'd the Cape, which they call in Persian Com barick,[1] that is, small sand, and the next night we left behind us the point, or peak, of Giasck.[2]

On Monday, the Sea being calm, the Captain, and I, were standing upon the deck of our Ship, discoursing of sundry matters, and he took occasion to show me a piece of Horn,[3] which he told me himself had found in the year 1611 in a Northern Country, whither he then sail'd, which they call Greenland, lying in the latitude of seventy-six degrees. He related how he found this horn in the earth, being probably the horn of some Animal dead there, and that, when it was intire, it was between five and six feet long, and seven inches in circumference at the root, where it was thickest. The piece which I saw (for the horn was broken, and sold by

---

[1] Written Bombarack in modern maps.

[2] That is, Jask, on the coast at the entrance of the Persian Gulf.

[3] Evidently part of the canine tooth of the " Narwhal" (*Monodon Monoceros*), which, as is well known, frequently grows to an abnormal length. In Greenland such teeth are said to be used as supports for the roofs of huts, and in the Castle of Rosenburg, in Denmark, is a throne, constructed of these teeth.

pieces in several places) was something more than half a span long, and little less than five inches thick ; the colour of it was white, inclining to yellow, like that of Ivory when it is old ; it was hollow and smooth within, but wreath'd on the outside. The Captain saw not the Animal, nor knew whether it were of the land or the sea, for, according to the place where he found it, it might be as well one as the other ; but he believed for certain, that it was of a Unicorn, both because the experience of its being good against poyson[1] argu'd so much, and for that the signes attributed by Authors to the Unicorn's horn agreed also to this, as he conceiv'd. But herein I dissent from him, inasmuch as, if I remember aright, the horn of the Unicorn, whom the Greeks call'd Monoceros, is, by Pliny, describ'd black, and not white. The Captain added that it was a report, that Unicorns are found in certain Northern parts of America, not far from that Country of Greenland ; and so not unlikely but that there might be some also in Greenland, a neighbouring Country, and not yet known whether it be Continent or Island; and that they might sometimes come thither from the contiguous lands of America, in case it be no Island.

This Country of Greenland is of late discovery, and the first Christian[2] that discover'd it, or went thither, was this Captain Woodcock, in the year above-mention'd ; and he gave it the name of Greenland upon this account, because, whereas the other Northern Countries thereabouts are destitute of grass, (whence the white Bears, and Wolves,

---

[1] A superstition which applied to the horn of the rhinoceros also. The origin of this belief is probably owing to the fact that scrapings of horn (owing, perhaps, to the ammonia contained in them) were found to be efficacious, to a certain extent, when applied to bites of venomous reptiles.

[2] Martin Frobisher was there in 1576. (*Frobisher's Three Voyages*, by Hakluyt Society.)

which inhabit them live upon dead Whales and other like
things), he found this green and full of Grass, although it
be always cover'd over with snow, so that, when the
Animals there mind to feed, they hollow the snow with
their feet, and easily find the grass, which is kept continually fresh under the same. The English now yearly
sail thither, where they take abundance of Whales, and
some so vast that, when they open the mouth, the wideness
is above three Geometrical paces, or fifteen foot over. Of
these Whales the English make Oyle, drawing it onely out
of the fat of their paunch, and they make such plenty that
out of one single Whale, they say, they often get 19, 20,
and 21 Tun of Oyl. This Greenland, by what Captain
Woodcock saw, who discover'd it, from the end of seventy-
six degrees to seventy-eight and a half, (the cold not
suffering him to go further) was uninhabited, he not having
found any person there, but only wild beasts of many sorts.
The Company of the Greenland Merchants of England
had the horn, which he found, because Captains of ships
are their stipendiaries, and, besides their salary, must make
no other profit of their Voyages ; but whatever they gain
or find, in case it be known, and they conceal it not, all
accrues to the Company that employes them. When the
Horn was intire it was sent to Constantinople to be sold,
where two thousand pounds sterling was offer'd for it : But
the English Company, hoping to get a greater rate, sold it
not at Constantinape, but sent into Muscovy, where
much about the same price was bidden for it, which, being
refus'd, it was carry'd back into Turkey, and fell of its
value, a much less sum being now proffer'd than before.
Hereupon the Company conceiv'd that it would sell more
easily in pieces then intire, because few could be found
who would purchase it at so great a rate. Accordingly
they broke it, and it was sold by pieces in sundry places ;
yet, for all this, the whole proceed amounted onely to

about twelve hundred pounds sterling.[1]   And of these
pieces they gave one to the Captain who found it, and this
was it which he shew'd me.

II.—On the 25th of January, sailing in the main Sea
with the prow of the Ship South-East and by East, and, as
I conceive, at a good distance from the Country of Macran[2]
(which I conjecture to be part either of the ancient Cara-
mania, or else of Gedrosia, and at this day having a Prince
of its own, lyes upon the Sea Coast between the States of
the Persian and those of the Moghol), we discern'd behind
us three or four Ships, which seem'd to be Frigots or
Galliots, but towards evening we lost sight of them.   The
same day, and the other before, began to be seen in the
Sea abundance of certain things, which I took to be
Snakes,[3] or at least fishes in the form of Snakes, being
exactly of the form of large Eeles, long and round, and,
according to the motion of the water, seem'd crooked as
they floated along the Sea.   Nevertheless, demanding of
intelligent persons what they were, I understood that they
were neither those Animals, nor yet living things, but
onely a kind of excrement of the Sea in that shape, void of
all motion, saving what the agitated water gave it, although,

---

[1] This seems to be an incredible sum, but it is a fact that these
teeth were sold for more than their weight in gold.

[2] Or Mekran.   This province is no doubt identical with part of the
ancient Carmania and Gedrosia.   But Carmania extended further
westwards than the present western boundary of Mekran, and the
latter name is now applied only to the maritime portion of these two
ancient provinces, of which the northern portion now constitutes the
provinces of Kirman, Kohistan and Beloochistan.

[3] Compare a passage in Langsdorff's *Travels* (vol. ii, p. 147): "We
perceived in the water, near the ship, a sort of riband-like object,
perfectly clear and transparent, which had the direct form and figure
of a snake.   It was probably composed of a number of 'salpen' or
'mollusca' of a particular species, mentioned by Forskal as hanging
to each other in so extraordinary a manner."

by reason of the motion of the ship they seem'd to move
contrary to us, whilst we saw them left behind. And they
told me that the nearer we came to India we should see
more of these things.

The next Evening our Captain, who was a little more
merry than ordinary, (because the Captain of the *Dolphin*
dining with us that day, he had drunk pretty freely)
in conversation discoursing with me, as he was wont,
after Supper, spoke very frankly to me concerning their
affairs of Ormuz. In conclusion, he told me that
their Treaty with the *Persians* stood thus : That, if they
would deliver to the English the Fortress of *Ormuz*, with
half the revenues of the Custom-house and the City, as
they desir'd from the beginning, then the English would
people Ormuz, and restore the trade as formerly, keeping
the same continually open with *Persia ;* and, that for this
purpose, and also for guarding that Sea against the
Portugals and other Enemies, they would keep four ships
in Ormuz. That, when this were agreed upon, the English
would transport a good number of people from England,
and whole Families with Wives and Children, to dwell in
Ormuz, as the Portugals did before, and then they would
prosecute the War against the Portugals at Maschat and
everywhere else. But, if these things were not agreed to,
they would make war no longer against the *Portugals ;*
nor car'd they for the Traffick of *Persia* upon any other
terms. Now, should these Treaties take effect, they would
in no wise be advantagious for the Catholick Religion ;
and, were there no more to be fear'd, the *Portugals* would
thereby be for ever excluded from recovering Ormuz.
Yea, all the rest which they possess in those parts would
be in great danger. Imanculi Beig, who was General of
the *Persians* in the late Wars, and with whom the English
treated in *Combrù* concerning this affair, Captain *Woodcock* said, inclin'd to the bargain ; but it was not known what

the *Chan* of *Sciraz*,[1] and, (which is more important), the King would do. On one side, I know, the Persians insisted much upon having *Ormuz* wholly to themselves, accounting it a small matter to have gain'd, with so much War, and loss of men, onely the half, or rather less then half, (the Fortress being deducted) which the English demanded for themselves; so that the *Persians* would have but the same interest there as the King of Ormuz had with the *Portugals*, and no more. They conceive also that they have done little, and perhaps ill, should they make no greater acquisition, in having onely chang'd the *Portugals* in *Ormuz* for the English, and Christians for Christians ; that upon easier terms it might be hop'd that perhaps the Portugals, after the loss of *Ormuz*, would agree with the *Persians* now there was no more to lose, and onely give the *Persians* that which the King of *Ormuz*, a Mahometan like themselves, injoyed. Moreover, to the *Persian*, no doubt, the friendship of the *Portugals* would be more profitable, in regard to the many States which they possess in *India*, from whence they may with more facility and certainty maintain the accustomed commerce with *Persia*. But, on the other side, to see the *Portugals* so worsted, and the English more fortunate, at least, and couragious, if not more strong, 'tis a clear case that *Ormuz* will never be reinhabited, nor Trade set on foot again, unless some nation of the *Franks* reside there, which have ships and strength at sea, (things which the *Persians* wholly want, there being neither Mariners nor Timber[2] in *Persia*, about

---

[1] Or Shiraz—a noted city of Persia, esteemed the second in the kingdom, near the ruins of the ancient city of Persepolis. The birth-place of the poet Hafiz.

[2] The scarcity of wood was so great on the coast of Persia that coasting vessels were made of pieces of wood of all sorts, and sizes, from the size of a barrel-stave, and upwards, covered over with " dammer" (a kind of resin). (Heeren's *Historical Researches*.)

that Sea, wherewith to build ships), and the loss resulting to *Persia* by the extinguishing of this Traffic, the charge of maintaining the Fortress of *Ormuz* without any profit, and the continual danger of losing it every hour, unless the English guard the Sea with their ships and help to defend it, these, and other like considerations, may not improbably induce the King of *Persia*, contented to have demonstrated his power and valour, and chastis'd his Enemies, the *Portugals*, according to his desire, to grant the English as much as they demand : For he should not yield it to them upon force, but out of his liberality and, for his own profit, give them that freely, which to retain to himself, as things now stand, would not onely be of no advantage, but of loss. Peradventure he may also imagine now, in the pride of his victory, that, as with help of the English he has driven the *Portugals* out of *Ormuz*, so 'twill be easie for him to expel the English too, either by the help of others, or else by his own Forces alone, should they not comply with him. However, because these Treaties with the *Persians* are manag'd by the Company of Merchants who also made the War, and not by the King of *England*, and hitherto 'tis not known whether their King approve the fact, or no, and will prosecute or let fall the enterprise ; therefore, for a total conclusion, besides the consent of the King of *Persia*, they also wait the determination of the King of *England*, and the greatest hope I have of the defeating of these projects so prejudicial to the Catholicks is this alone, that the English King will not meddle in them, and, perhaps also, prohibit his Subjects so to do ; as a person whom we know to be a Friend to Peace, most averse from all kind of War, especially with the King of *Spain*, while the Match of his Son with the Daughter of *Spain* is in agitation.

III.—In the mean time we began to find the Sea sufficiently rough, being got wholly out of the Persian Gulph, and enter'd into the open Sea (termed by the Ancients *Mare rubrum*,[1] and by us, at this day, the Southern Ocean), and having pass'd not onely the Cape of Giasck, but also that of Arabia, which the *Portugals* vulgarly call Rosalgate,[2] as it is also set down in the Maps, but properly ought to be call'd Ras el had, which in the Arabian Tongues signifies *Capo del fine*, or the Cape of the Confine, because 'tis the last of that Country, and it is further than any other extended into the Sea ; like that of *Galicia* in our *Europe*, which, for the same reason, we call *Finis Terræ*. On Saturday, the 28th of *January*, having taken the meridional altitude of the Sun, according to daily custom, and made such detraction of degrees as was necessary, we found ourselves twenty-three degrees five minutes distant from the Equinoctial towards the North, whence by consequence we had pass'd the Tropick of *Cancer* twenty-six minutes and a-half, according to the opinion of the Moderns, who reckon the Sun's greatest declination where the Tropicks are twenty-three degrees thirty-one minutes and a-half[3] distant from the Equinoctial. During the succeeding dayes we sail'd with a brisk but favourable wind, and with a Sea not tempestuous but something rough.

Every day, about the hour of noon, the sun's altitude was infallibly observ'd, not onely by the Pilots, as the custom is in all ships, and the Captain (who was a good Seaman and perform'd all the exercises of Art very well), but (which pleas'd me most, and which I thought worthy of great

---

[1] This name was used by the ancients to include the Indian Ocean, as well as the Red Sea, and Persian Gulf. The origin of the epithet Rubrum is uncertain, but it is generally supposed to be derived from the colour of the cliffs on both sides of the Straits of Babel Mandeb, by which the Red Sea, or Indian Ocean, is entered from the south, or north, respectively.

[2] Rosalgate, called Rifalcate by Barbosa (or Magellan). Now called Ras al Had, the S.E. point of Arabia.

[3] The latitude of the tropics is in the present day fixed at 23° 28'.

praise and imitation) there was no day, but at that hour
twenty or thirty mariners, masters, boys, young men, and
of all sorts came upon the deck to make the same observations: some with Astrolabes, others with Cross-staffs,
and others with several other instruments, particularly with
one which, they told me, was lately invented by one *David*,
and, from his name, call'd *David's Staff*.[1] This Instrument
consists of two Triangles united together, one longer then
the other, both having their base arch'd, and between them,
in the circle of their bases, containing an intire quadrant of
ninety degrees. But whereas the shortest Triangle, whose
Angles are less acute, contains sixty degrees divided by
Tens (according to custom) in the circle of its base, which
are two-thirds of a quadrant; the other, longer and of
acuter Angles, which extends much backward, and opens
in a wider circle at the base, comprehends no more then
thirty, which make the remainder of the quadrant, so that
the longer Triangle contains fewer degrees by half than
the shorter; and he that would have the degrees larger, for
the better sub-dividing them into minutes, may make the
circle or base of the lesser Triangle take up seventy
degrees, and so there will remain to the longer no more
then twenty for the complement of the quadrant. According to this distribution, the degrees in the longer Triangle
will come to be so large as to be capable of the smallest
division of minutes, a thing very important. Besides, it
hath two Fanes or Sights, in each Triangle one, which are
to be mov'd backward and forward; and with these, that
is, with that of the long Triangle, the level of the Horizon
is taken, and, with the other of the short Triangle, that of
the Sun; with this further conveniency that the Sights,
being sufficiently large, are therefore very expedient for
performing the operation with speed, notwithstanding the

---

[1] This should be " Davis-staff", the instrument referred to having
been invented by Davis, the navigator.

Figure with Davis's quadrant.

Cross-staff, and manner of using.

dancing of the ship when the Sea is rough ; in which case, if the Sights be too small, 'tis hard to make any observation. With this Instrument, and several others, many of the English perform'd their operations every day ; such as knew not how to do them well were instructed ; and if any one err'd, in computation or otherwise, his error was shew'd him, and the reason told him, that so he might be train'd to work exactly. The opinion of the skilful was heard and taken notice of ; and at length, all the observations being compar'd together, the Pilot and the Captain resolv'd, and, with mature counsel, determin'd of all ; by which means their voyages are very well manag'd, and almost always succeed prosperously to them.

In the Portugal ships, I hear, the contrary comes to pass ; because the Pilots, being extremely jealous of their affairs (an habitual humour of that Nation) will be alone to make their observations, and for the most perform them in secret, without any Associate to see them : Should any other person in the ship offer to take the altitude of the Sun, or look upon the Map or Compass, or do anything that relates to the well-guiding of the Vessel, and knowing its course, they would quarrel with him, and by no means suffer him to do it ; being averse that any other should meddle with what they say is their office and belongs to them alone. From their being so little communicative and very averse to teach others, it happens that few amongst them understand anything of the Art of Navigation, there being none that will teach it experimentally, and they understand little enough, because they have no conference about the practical part, and learn much less of the Theory. This is the reason that their ships frequently miscarry, to the incredible detriment both of particular persons and of the Kingdom. And, which is worse, 'tis said that not onely many of them are lost through the ignorance or negligence, of those that guide them, but also sometime by

malice ; For the *Portugal* Pilots have got a custom, when
they are to make a voyage, to take up great sums of
money at *Lisbon* upon interest, the most they can get to
trade withall : and they take the same by way of Venture
upon the ships,[1] which they guide.   Now when by the way
any small disaster befalls them, they not onely avoid it not,
as many times they might do, but, if they be of evil intention, they cunningly run the ships aground, either in these
coasts of *Africa*, or elsewhere ; so that though oftentimes
the people, and also the arms, and goods, especially of the
greatest value, be saved, yet so it is, that sometimes many
perish, or suffer excessive loss, and this onely to the end,
that the shipwrack may be the occasion of their remaining
gainers of the monies taken up at interest upon the hazard
aforesaid, which monies they carry not with them to trade
withall, but leave all at home in *Portugal*.   A practice
indeed very pernicious, and which ought to be most
rigorously punish'd ; but the *Portugals* have now no King[2]
in their Country to mind their affairs, and the government
depends upon *Madrid*, where perhaps they that administer
it, being more intent upon their private interests then the
publick, these and infinite other disorders pass unredress'd.
The English, on the contrary, and other Europeans, which
sail upon the Ocean, are most diligent and strict observers
of all exact discipline, and of what concernes the good
conduct of their ships ; and because they well understand
all the most exquisite points of Navigation, and are extremely curious, as well in the Practice as in the Theory,
they spare no pains, and neglect not the doing of anything,

---

[1] This was a system adopted also in England as early as the sixteenth century.   Lord Keeper Bacon, in opening Queen Elizabeth's
first Parliament (1558), said : " Doth not the wise merchant, in every
adventure of danger, give part to have the rest assured ?"   (See *Parl.
Hist.*, vol. i, p. 641.)

[2] The kingdom of Portugal having been seized by Philip II of
Spain in 1580.

whereby they may render their Navigations in all places more easie and secure : Insomuch that Captain *Woodcock*, upon occasion of his having staid a year and odd moneths with his ship in the Persian Gulph, shew'd me a Chart or Plat-form of the whole Streight of *Ormuz*, made by himself during that time with the highest exactness; for he had not onely taken the most just measures and distances of all the adjacent places, but also sounded all the Coast with a plummet, to find all the convenient places where great ships, such as theirs, might ride and cast anchor when occasion should require.

IIII.—On the Third of *February*, conceiving by our reckoning that we were near *India*, in the Evening, we let down the plummet into the Sea, as we us'd often to do, and found it not above seventeen fathom ; whereby 'twas concluded, that we were little more then six leagues distant from land, although, by reason of the darkness of the Air, none could be yet discern'd ; because that precise depth of water uses to be found in those Seas at that distance from land. The Captain, who by well observing the Sun and the Winds, had every day diligently noted the Ships way in the Map, as the custom is, hop'd that we might be near the City of *Daman*,[1] which lies within the

---

[1] On W. coast of India, in lat. 22° N., about 100 miles north of Bombay. The Portuguese town and settlement of Damán on the coast in the province of Gujarat was in Hamilton's time (1688-1723) noted for its trade. He describes the town as about half-a-mile long, and nearly as broad, with a good stone wall. For a long time it had been an eyesore to the Dutch governors of Surat, who had often picked quarrels with the Portuguese, and laid siege to it without success. With the decline of Portuguese power in India, the trade of Damán fell, and since the conquest of Sind by the British, the place has lost its transit trade in opium imported from Karáchí. The town was sacked by the Portuguese in 1531, rebuilt by the natives, and retaken by the Portuguese in 1558. (Pinkerton, viii, 327 ; Sir W. Hunter's *Gazetteer*, vol. iv, p. 101.)

Gulph of *Cambaia*, on the right hand as you enter into it, a good way inwards ; but I, without having so much minded the Maps, said, I conceiv'd we were much lower, and more without the Gulph towards Bassain, because although we had always sail'd and kept the ships prow directed to Daman by the shortest line, yet, for the two or three last dayes, we had had the Wind for that place contrary ; which, although it hinder'd us not from holding our course, because we help'd ourselves with the rudder, and siding of the sails, yet the violence of the Wind must needs have continually driven the ship something lower then we intended. Two hours after midnight, the current of the Gulph of Cambaia being contrary, against which, by reason of its impetuousness, there is no sailing for a while, but the ship must stay either for the turning of it, (which is known when it will happen, because it regularly changes according to the hours and days of the Moon) or for a strong Wind wherewith to master the current ; for this reason, and also that the day-light might resolve us in what place we were, we cast anchor, and struck sail, to wait for a more fitting time. The Sea in this place began to be very rough,[1] which happens by reason of the strong current which it hath.

The next Morning we discern'd land afar off, and, according to my conjecture, it appear'd that we were lower, that is, more to the South of *Daman* about twelve leagues, in a place a little distant from *Bassain*,[2] which

---

[1] Arrian notes the same fact in regard to this locality.

[2] A seaport, eighteen leagues from Damán, in lat. 19° 20′ N., which stands on a little island separated from the mainland by a rivulet, about half-a-mile from the island of Salsette. Bassein was included in the dowry of Catherine of Braganza on her marriage with Charles II in 1662, but was never actually delivered to the English until taken by them in 1780, from the Mahrattas, who had taken it from the Portuguese in 1765. Hamilton says the Governor of Bassein was styled

the English call *Terra di San Giovanni*, but in the Sea-Chart is noted in the Portugal Tongue with the name of *Ilhas das vaccas*,[1] or the *Islands of Cows*. About one a clock in the Afternoon, the Tide being become less contrary, we set sail again by degrees, approaching still nearer the shore of *India*. But a little before night the current turning against us, we were constrain'd to cast anchor once more; nevertheless after midnight it became favourable again, and we sail'd onwards by degrees till day. This slow course through the Gulph of Cambaia with the plummet always in hand, and sounding every hour, it was requisite for us to hold, because the place is dangerous, in regard of the many shelves or quick-sands which are in it, and especially because the current, which turns every six hours, now setting one way, and anon the other, causes great hindrance. By reason of which shelves, from the time of our entrance into the Gulph, we did not guide the ship directly towards *Surát*, which no doubt would have been the shortest way by a strait line, but keeping lower towards *Daman*, fetch'd a large compass to the South, tacking about afterwards to the North

_____

General of the North, having Diu, Damán, and Chaul, with all their territories, subordinate to him. In 1782 it was restored to the Mahrattas, but subsequently became part of the British territory on the downfall of the Mahratta dynasty. Though a port of some importance, Bassein never attained that of Broach, and some others on the west coast of India. The Portuguese town, in ruins, is on the north side of the inlet. (Pinkerton, viii, 327 ; Hunter's *Gazetteer*, *sub. v.* ; Findlay's *Sailing Directions for the Indian Ocean.*)

[1] " Ilhas dos Vacos" was the name given by the Portuguese to the archipelago of islands lying off the coast south of Bassein. See the atlases of Mercator (1633), Blaeu (1664), De Witt (1688), and Van Keulen (1726). In later charts the name disappears ; cf. *The East Indian Pilot*, compiled from Daprès de Manevillette's *Neptune Oriental* (1775) and Admiralty charts. The name of St. John (San Giovanni of our text) is applied on all the above maps to a cape north of Bassein in lat. 19° 57' N.

when we were near land, onely to avoid the many shelves and shallows, through which our great ships could not pass.

On *Sunday*, the fifth of *February*, being at anchor in the morning, we discover'd near the land, which was not very far from us, ten, or fifteen, Frigots, or Galliots, sailing Eastwards ; which probably were either *Portugal*, or *Indian*, Merchants of some Cafila, (as they call a Fleet, or Consort, of ships) coming from *Cambaia*, to go to Goa[1] ; or some other place thereabouts.

The night following, we heard the report of Artillery, which we conceiv'd to come from the City of Daman, being the place nearest us. *Wednesday* night after, the wind blew somewhat hard against us, in regard whereof, and the strength of the current which carry'd us in that narrow channel amongst shelves, and quick-sands, we sail'd for a good while very circumspectly, and not without some danger. On *Thursday* we stood right against the mouth of the River of *Suràt*,[2] which City is not situate upon the shore, but some leagues within land : And because there is no station there for great ships, we continued sailing Northwards to the place where is the Port most frequented by the ships of *Europe;* which though the best of all that coast, yet the vessels of that Country, not knowing so well how to steer, make not much use of it, because the entrance is a little difficult. On *Fryday* the tenth of *February*, in

---

[1] Goa. The chief town of the Portuguese on W. coast of India, in lat. 15° 25' N. Taken by them in 1510 under Admiral Albuquerque.

[2] Sùrat. In lat. 21ˇ 13' N. The ancient Surparaka, founded by the King of the Vidarbas. It was taken by the Emperor Akbar in 1573. The name is said to be derived from the Sanskrit *Su*, good, and *Rashtra*, country. Another derivation is from the Sanskrit *Surya*, " City of the Sun." See Sir Monier Williams' *Mod. India*, p. 267. It was called by Muhamadans the " Gate of Mecca", as they went on their pilgrimage mostly from that port. For a good account of Sùrat see *Cal. Review*, ix, 103.

the Afternoon, the favour of the current failing us, we cast anchor in sight of the Port of *Suràt* at a little distance; and, our boat going ashore, the President[1] of the English Merchants (who uses to reside in *Suràt*, and is superintendent of all their Trade in *East-India*, and *Persia*, with the other places depending on the same, now one *Mr. Thomas Rastel*) perceiving our ships near, and being at that time at the Sea-side near the landing place, came in our boat to the ships, together with one of their Ministers, (so they call those who exercise the office of Priests), and two other Merchants; and after a collation, and a supper, lodg'd with us all night. He spoke Italian very well, and made me many civil offers, and complements; shewing himself in all things a person sufficiently accomplish'd, and of generous deportment, according as his gentile, and graceful, aspect bespoke him.

He inform'd me, that Sig^r· *Alberto di Scilling*, a *German* Gentleman, known to me in *Persia*, having return'd from the Court of the Moghol, and other parts of *India*, which he had travell'd to see, was at that time in *Suràt*, from

---

[1] An English factory was established here in 1612. The Dutch factory was established in 1617, and the French factory in 1664. The use of the word "President" is here somewhat of an anachronism, as this title was not officially recognised until the year 1661. Thomas Rastell (or Rastall) went to India apparently in 1615. He returned to England in Feb. 1625, after obtaining (in Sept. 1624) a concession of the privilege of trading in Surat "and all other cities and places within the dominions of Jangere Paudshah" (*i.e.*, the Emperor Jahan Gir). This was apparently the first recognition of the East India Co.'s privilege of trade in Bengal. Rastell is frequently mentioned by Sainsbury. (See Sir H. Yule's *Hobson-Jobson*, and *Diary of Sir W. Hedges*, published by Hakluyt Soc., vol. ii, p. 175.) The noble defence of Surat by the British traders against Sivagi, the founder of the Mahratta power, in 1664, may be said to have been the first step in the path of England's military glory in India, and "to the Surat merchants belongs the honour of having quickened the first germ of our now gigantic Eastern Empire." (See M. Williams' *Mod. India*, p. 269.)

whence he was gone to see the City of *Barocci*[1] hard by, and would return speedily: with which intelligence I was much pleas'd, because Sig: *Alberto* was my great friend, and I extremely desir'd to see him.

On *Saturday* Morning we convers'd together for some time, drinking a little of hot wine, boyl'd with Cloves, Cinnamon, and other spices, which the English call *burnt wine*, and use to drink frequently in the Morning to comfort the stomack, sipping it by little, and little, for fear of scalding, as they do Cahue[2] (coffee), by me elsewhere describ'd. And they use it particularly in the Winter to warm themselves; though in India 'tis not necessary for that end, because albeit 'twas still Winter, according to our division of the seasons, yet we had more heat than cold.

After this short refection the President return'd a shore, and I remain'd in the ship, not expecting to disimbarque till we were got into the Harbour, which was a little before night, and the anchors were cast very near the land; but because 'twas now late, and the city of *Surat* was a good distance off, none of us car'd to land. Nor did I go out of the ship on *Sunday*, both because it was a sacred day, and because our Captain was pleas'd to give an Entertainment to us, and the Captain of the *Dolphin*, our companion in the voyage.

Monday, the thirteenth of the same moneth, was the day of my Ague, whereof I had had divers fits by the way at sea; nevertheless, after a collation I went on shore together with the Captain of our ship, where we continu'd under certain tents, pitch'd for convenience of the *Ton-*

---

[1] Broach, or Bharuch, in lat. 21° 44′ N. on the Gulf of Cambay, at the mouth of the Narbada river. The ancient name of this port was Barygaza. A more ancient name of the place was "Bharu-kachha", a corruption of Bhrigukachha, or "field of Bhrigu".

[2] The Arabic name is "Kahuah". Coffee was not introduced into England, and probably not into Italy, until 1652.

nellers,[1] (so the English term certain of their Mariners employ'd to fill the Casks with water) in expectation of Coaches to carry us to Suràt ; there being in those Countries subject to the *Moghol*, abundance of Coaches, made after their fashion, which I formerly describ'd when I saw some of them at *Casbin*,[2] which the Indian Ambassador gave, amongst his presents, to the King of Persia ; nor remains any thing more to be said of them, but that they are at this day much like the ancient Indian Chariots,[3] describ'd by *Strabo*, and are generally covered with crimson silk, fring'd with yellow round about the roof, and the curtains ; and that the oxen, which also, as anciently, draw the same, are fair, large, white, with two bunches[4] like those of some Camells, and run, and gallop, like Horses ; they are likewise cover'd with the same stuff, but beset with many tufts, or tassels, and abundance of bells at their necks ; so that, when they run, or gallop, through the streets, they are heard at a sufficient distance, and make a very brave show. With these kind of Coaches in *India*, they not onely go in Cities, but also for the most part travel in the Country.

To the Sea side came no Coach, and therefore the Captain went on foot to a Town a mile off, called Sohali, where he intended to spend the day in recreating himself amongst *Franks*, who have Houses there for repositing the goods, which they continually send to the Sea side to be ship'd ; but I could not accompany him, because of my Ague, and

---

[1] From the French word *tonnelle* (English "tunnel"), meaning a pipe, or tube (like our funnel), used for filling casks, or other vessels.

[2] Kasvin, or Kasbin, a town of Persia in lat. 36° N.

[3] Strabo speaks of *four*-wheeled carts, which are seldom seen in India at the present day.

[4] The Indian ox (*Taurus Indicus*) has very rarely more than one hump, though two-humped oxen are occasionally found. Ælian (*De Nat. Anim.*, xv, 24, quoted by Sir H. Yule in *Hobson-Jobson*) says that the Indian oxen run very swiftly. The smaller kinds of oxen move more quickly than those of larger and more powerful breeds.

therefore staid in a Tent, well cover'd with Clothes upon my bed, which I caus'd to be laid upon the ground, waiting till the Captain sent me a Coach, and Carts, from the City for my goods.

Whilst I was lying in this place, the violence of my fit was scarce over, when I beheld a Cavalier appear on the shore on Horse-back, cloth'd, and arm'd, after the Indian manner, with a Scemiter, and Target, who came towards our Tent, and stood still to speak with some person, as if he inquir'd for something among us : Upon his nearer approach, and my better considering him, I perceiv'd 'twas my great friend Sig : *Alberto di Scilling*, who, being return'd from Barocci, whither the President had told me he was gone, and hearing news of us, was come from *Surât* to the Sea side to meet me. Whereupon, raising myself suddenly from the bed, we received one the other with such kindnesses as are usual between two good friends, who come from far, and have not seen one another a long time ; after which, sitting down together, we recounted our adventures one to the other at length, he much condoling my misfortunes, and regretting to find me sufficiently different from what he had left me in *Persia*.

Towards Evening came two Coaches, and a Carr, with which we went together to the Town *Sohali*, where we found the two Captains of the ships, waiting for us with a Collation ready prepar'd, which immediately they gave us, entertaining us in conversation till night ; and certain Indian Women of the Town, publick dancers, gave us some pastime, by dancing to the sound of drums, Bells, and other instruments of their fashion, which were sounded by their Husbands with very great noise, and not without disturbance of my head. A little within night the Captains took leave of us, and return'd to their ships, and we betook ourselves to rest the remainder of the night in this Town, because it was necessary to stay till day before we could enter into *Suràt*, the Gates of the City being shut in the night time, at least that of the *Dogana*, or Custom-house, through which we were to pass. They told us the way to the City was seven *Cos*, or *Corrì*, (for 'tis all one) and every *Cos* or *Corrì* is half a *Fersegna*, or league of *Persia ;* so that it answers to little less then two English Miles.

V.—The next Morning very early we put ourselves on the way towards *Suràt*, and being I conceiv'd my abode there would be but short, and that when I should depart thence my way would be by Sea ; therefore to avoid greater trouble, both of conveyance, and of the *Dogana*, or Custom House, which is known to be rigorous in *Suràt*, I left all my Trunks, and gross luggage, in the ship, and carry'd with me only such few things as were requisite for daily use. The high-way from the Sea side to the City, (as 'tis also generally in this province of *Guzaràt*, wherein we were) is all very even ; the soil green all the year round, and about the town *Sohali* grow aboundance of Trees and Indian Nuts, Tamarinds, and other fruits. Beyond the Town the Trees are not so plentiful, unless near certain houses ; but the fields are every where either ploughed, or full of living creatures feeding in them.

We arrived at the City in good time, in the entrance of which there is a River call *Tapi*, or *Tapte*,[1] which was to be pass'd over by boat : On the other side of which River, something on the right hand as you go into the City, which hath no walls, stands a Castle, lately built, but very ill design'd. Moreover, near the place where the boats land stands the *Dogana*, or Custom-house, and it took us up

---

[1] Derived from Sanskrit *Tapanti*, from the root *Tap*, to be warm. Another name of this river is " Payoshni", warm as milk. (See Sir Monier Williams' *Modern India.*) Mentioned in the Mahabharata.

some time to dispatch there, because they observe very narrowly all goods that are brought in, (although they be but Clothes for change) to see whether there be anything coming to the Customes ; nor will they suffer strangers to enter till they be first known, and have license, as 'tis also practis'd in *Venice*. In all things they proceed with so great wariness, and good order, that it being known that I conducted with me the Sig^ra Mariuccia,[1] although a girl very young, the *Capo*, or President of the *Dogana*, requir'd likewise to be inform'd of her quality, and gave order that she should not be conducted with any violence, or other disorder : otherwise, in lawful things, there is no difficulty, either through diversity of Religion, or upon any other account.

We were no sooner come to the *Dogana*, but the news of our arrival was, I think, by Sig: *Alberto's* means, carried to the House of the Dutch, many of which have Wives there, which they married in *India*, purposely to go with them, and people a new colony of theirs in *Java Major*,[2] which they call *Batavia Nova ;* where very great privileges are granted to such of their Country men as shall go to live there with Wives, and Families : For which end, many of them, for want of European, have taken Indian, Armenian and Syrian, Women, and of any other race that falls into their hands, so they be, or can be made, Christians.

---

[1] This refers to an orphan girl, Maria Tinatin di Ziba, a Georgian by birth, adopted by the wife of P. della Valle, Sitti Maani, who died near Persepolis. At her death the girl was left in charge of P. della Valle. She accompanied him in his travels, and he afterwards married her at Rome. In his 12th letter he speaks of her as " the faithful companion of most of my peregrinations".

[2] The island of Java, so called to distinguish it from Sumatra, called Java Minor, though it is in fact the smaller island of the two. The town of New Batavia (so called after the ancient name of Holland) was founded in 1619, by P. Van den Broecke.

Last year the Fleet of the Portugals which went to *India* was encountred at Sea, and partly sunk, partly taken by the Hollanders ; amongst other booty, three Maidens were taken, of those poor, but well descended, Orphans,[1] which are wont to be sent from *Portugal* every year, at the King's charge, with a dowry which the King gives them, to the end they may be married in *India*, in order to further the peopling of the *Portugal* Colonies in those parts. These three virgins falling into the hands of the Hollanders, and being carry'd to Suràt, which is the principal seat of all their traffick, the most eminent Merchants amongst them strove who should marry them, being all passably handsome. Two of them were gone from Suràt, whether to the above said Colony, or elsewhere, I know not. She that remain'd behind was called *Donna Lucia*, a young woman, fair enough, and Wife to one of the wealthiest, and eminentest, Hollanders.

The President of the Hollanders, call'd by them the *Commendator*, who resides in *Suràt*, and has the general superintendency of their affairs in all these parts of the East, is at this time Sig: Pietro Vandenbroecke, a Gentleman of good breeding, and very courteous ; he speaks no Italian, but Spanish very well, as being born at *Antwerp*.[2] He lives in a goodly Palace, which hath many distinct apartments, with several entrances into a Court, like so many different houses, onely included within the same wall, which is entred into by one great Gate : Here the

---

[1] In *A Voyage to East India*, by Sir T. Roe's chaplain (published in 1665), reference is made to this custom in the mention of the arrival at the Cape of Good Hope of " Ten Portugal virgins sent to that Colony (Bantam), I suppose for husbands". (P. 329 of *A Voyage to East India*.)

[2] A proof of the ascendency of the Spanish nation in Holland at that time. A fine portrait of P. Van den Broecke, by Franz Hals, is in the possession of Lord Iveagh, and was exhibited at Burlington House this year (1891).

Commendator holds the best, and largest, apartment, to himself ; in the rest lodge some of their gravest Merchants, which are of the Council for management of affairs, in order to their better conveniency, and union, besides many others of inferior condition, which live out of this great inclosure, dispers'd elsewhere in the City, and when occasion requires, they all repair to the Palace of the Commendator. Amongst those whose habitation was in the Palace of the Commendator *Donna Lucia's* Husband has one of the principal, where he lives with his family and Wife, whom, according to the custom of *India*, he maintains with much splendor, and gallantry.

Now upon their knowledge of our arrival, *Donna Lucia* presently sent her coach to bring Sig: Mariuccia to her house, for her better accommodation with her, till we had settled our business, and provided lodgings.   I was well pleas'd with the motion, because till I had well accommodated myself with a place of residence, the Sig. Mariuccia could not be better dispos'd of than with this Portugal Gentlewoman, who is a Christian, and withal secretly a Catholick, with the privity, and connivance, of her Husband, although in publick she makes a virtue of necessity, and in appearance conformes to the unhappy mode of that Nation, into whose power the fortune of war, and the disaster of her Country-men, hath brought her.

Sig: *Alberto Scilling*, had, before we came from the Sea-side, importun'd me in the name of the Commendator to lodge at his house ; which favour I much thank'd him for, and handsomely declin'd, not thinking fit to accept it, because I had receiv'd, and wav'd the like invitation made to me before by the English President, who thought me the more oblig'd to comply with his offer, because I came in their Ships :   But I excus'd myself both to the Commendator, and the President ; partly because I was desirous to be at liberty by myself, and partly, for that it was requisite

for Sig: Mariuccia to be amongst Women, of which there
was none in the English House.

Being got quit of the Custom-house, I went to see for a
House ; and because I was a new comer, and had no
servant that knew the City, I referred myself to the direction
of Sig: *Alberto*, who took this care upon himself, and soon
after told me he had sent to get one prepar'd, and put in
good order ; But by what I found afterwards, he had
contriv'd with the Dutch Commendator onely to delude me ;
for as he was carrying me to the place where he pretended
to have taken a House for me, he made me pass by the
Palace of the Hollanders, out of the Gate whereof a Gentleman, belonging to the Commendator, step'd forth, and
invited me in his name to alight from my Horse, and at
least stay, and dine with him that day, the rather because
Sig^ra. *Mariuccia* was there; telling me it was not convenient for me to wait in the streets undecently, and
tediously, whilst a House was preparing for me elsewhere,
which could not be done so speedily. Notwithstanding
which reasons, I endeavour'd all that possibly I could to
decline this invitation, out of respect to the English
President, and with affectionate thanks desir'd the Gentleman to excuse me to the Sig^r. Commendator, straining
myself to correspond to his courtesie with the best complements I had. But this avail'd me little; for as I was hastening
to break off the discourse, and be gone, the Commendator
himself came forth into the street, half undress'd as he was
in the house, and, taking hold of my Horse's bridle, told
me that he would by no means suffer me to go any where else
now it was late without certain quarters; at least, I must
needs stay, and dine with him that day. Beholding him
thus on foot before me, I alighted in civility from my Horse,
and with the best words I could, endeavour'd to get quit
from the courteous violence which he us'd to me : But there
was no remedy, he held me prisoner, as I may say, and I

was fain to stay dinner with him as he desir'd. Moreover,
when night came, being I was resolv'd[1] to lodge in another
House of my own, under pretext that none could be got,
though sought for all day, (wherein I know not whether
Sigr. *Alberto* deluded me too) I was forc'd to accept of a
large House from the Commendator which he had taken
for himself, before his late removal to that great Palace
wherein he liv'd with the rest of his Country-men; which
former House remaining empty at his charge, and disposal,
I was by his great importunity oblig'd to accept: Wherefore I went to lodge there this night, and for the conveniency
of Sig^{ra,} Mariuccia, they sent thither one of their Wives,
a young Christian woman of Armenian race, though born
in *India*, with some other women-servants.

Now lest the English President should take this ill, I
purpos'd to prevent him with terms of courtesie, and the
next Morning after a short, and the last, fit of my Tertian,
I went to give him a visit, and make my excuses to him
by representing to him the reasons of what had pass'd
with the Hollanders, without any voluntary fault of mine :
But upon my enquiry at his House, and sending my
message to him, I was answer'd that he was not at home,
although we perceiv'd by certain signes that he was, but
fairly declin'd to receive my visit. Wherefore understanding afterwards that he was much incens'd, not onely
against me, but also against the Holland Commendator,
conceiving that he had unhandsomely stolen, and usurp'd,
me, from him, (as he said) in regard of the interest he had
in us, upon the account of our being brought thither in
their ships ; and that he had a more particular displeasure
against Sig^r. *Alberto*, knowing him to have been the prin-

---

[1] " Being" for "since" or " inasmuch as", the English rendering of
the Italian *stante che*. Beaumont and Fletcher use the word in
this sense :—" And being you have declined his means, you have
increased his malice."

cipal occasion of all, I thought it expedient to appease him by all means, and upon whatever terms of satisfaction. Nevertheless I did not judge it meet to venture another repulse by going to visit him, but sent him a Letter in justification of myself, with all the civil expressions I could devise.   At first he was something backward to receive it, doubting perchance that I had written angerly to him, in regard of my preceding visit : yet at length, upon the request of some mediators, whom I made use of, he took it, read it, and remain'd well satisfied with my proceedings, in which there was nothing but gentleness. The Commendator likewise, being one of an excellent nature, us'd all means he could to give the President satisfaction, and, to shew him that what he had done with us was to no ill end, he went purposely to visit him, carrying Sig : *Alberto* with him, to the end he might justifie himself too : both of them intreated, and both of them took the blame upon themselves ; in fine, so much was done, and said, that the President was reconcil'd with all.   And because it was insisted on my behalf that he would admit a visit from me, he consented upon this condition, that this first time should not be simply my visit, but his invitation, which accordingly he made to us to come all together that night to supper with him, where he treated us very splendidly, and everything ended in jollity and friendship as at first.   And all the while that I stay'd at Suràt, he oblig'd me continually with sundry demonstrations of his affection; particularly, by often sending his own Coach to me, with his Interpreter, who is an Armenian Christian, and a Catholick, call'd *Scander*,[1] Brother to F. *Agostino Bagiezzi*, of *Alingia*, a Dominican, my acquaintance in *Persia ;* which Interpreter being skill'd in the Country, and conversing with me in the Persian Tongue, carry'd me frequently abroad to see sundry

---

[1] For Iskandar, or Alexander.

things. As for the Hollanders, the caresses and civilities which they have done, and still continue to me, are so numerous, that I shall have them in remembrance as long as I live. But 'tis time now to speak a little of this City, and the curiosities which here, and elsewhere, I have lately seen.

VI.—The City of Suràt is of a handsome greatness, and for these Countries, of sufficiently good building : 'Tis very populous, as all other Cities and places are in *India*, which everywhere abounds with people. The Inhabitants are partly Gentiles, and partly Mahometans ; and, if I am not deceived, the former are the greater number : However, they live all mixt together, and peaceably, because the *Gran Moghel*,[1] to whom Guzaràt is now subject,[2] (having sometimes had a distinct King) although he be a Mahometan (but not a pure one, as they report) makes no difference in his Dominions between the one sort and the other ; and both in his Court, and Armies, and even amongst men of the highest degree, they are of equal account, and consideration. Yet the Mahometans, as the Masters, especially those of the Mogholian Race, which now is the Imperial in these parts, seems to have some little more of authority.

But forasmuch as I have formerly survey'd, and observ'd, the manner of the Mahometans, both in *Turkey* and *Persia*, I now turn my mind to those of the Gentile Idolaters[3] in *India*, which are more new to me ; and with such

---

[1] This was the Emperor Jahangir (whose real name was Selim), son of the Emperor Akbar. His religion was pure Deism.

[2] This province was occupied by the Emperor Humayun. It subsequently became independent, but was reconquered by Akbar in 1573.

[3] The word " Gentile" was adopted by early travellers in India to distinguish all the non-Muhamadan races from the followers of the Prophet, as was the word "Goim" applied by Jews to all non-Jewish races.

observations in reference to both, as shall seem worthy of notice, I shall not fail to acquaint you. In the first place, I shall give you the relation of a Nuptial Pomp, which I saw one day pass by my house in this manner ; A long train of men with Drums and Trumpets before them march'd in the day time first, carrying cover'd baskets, full of sundry things, which were either a present sent from the Bridegroom to the Bride, or rather the attiring of the Bride, which uses to be publickly shewn in the East. Then follow'd on foot likewise some black Women-slaves, well cloth'd, being given to the Bride either by the Father, or the Husband. Lastly, to conclude the Pomp, came a Palanchino,[1] a kind of Litter, wherein persons of quality are wont to be carry'd in *India*. It was not of the ordinary form, which hang downwards upon one pole between the bearers before, and behind ; but it was carry'd on high upon poles by four men, one at each corner, and it was cover'd all over with silk, yet no body was within it ; so that I know not what it serv'd for, unless haply it was intended to transport the Bride to her Husband ; this different fashion being for greater solemnity made use of, in such an occasion as Marriage. At night the married couples pass'd by, and, according to their mode, went round about the City with a numerous company. They were four, all very small children, two boys, and two girls ; (for in *India* most marriages take place at that age), and because they were not big enough to ride on Horse-back alone, therefore they were held up by so many well-grown men, who sat upon the saddle. Before them went many Torches, and Musical instruments, with a great troop of people on foot accompanying them. But the persons of quality follow'd in Coaches, of which there was a good

---

[1] This is a Javanese word, which has become naturalised in India as " Palki", *Anglicè* " palanquin".

number, and going one by one they made a very long
train ; whereby it was known that the married Children
were of considerable quality.

VII.—Of remarkable things without the city, there is on
one side a very large Cistern, or Artificial Pool, surrounded
with stone-work, and contriv'd with many sides, and angles
at which there are stairs, leading down to the surface of the
water. In the midst stands a little Island, which cannot be
gone to but by boat, or swimming. The Diametre of this
Artificial Lake is two good furlongs, which in our parts
would seem a competent largeness, but here 'tis not much;
and this Fish pond of *Suràt* is not accounted among the
greatest, but the least, in *India ;* where indeed they are
numerous, and the most magnificent, and goodly structures,[1]
or rather, the only structures in this Country which have
anything of magnificence, or handsomeness. They are
made in divers places by Princes, Governours of Countries,
or other wealthy persons, for the publick benefit, and as works
of Charity, because the soil, suitable to the Climate, is
sufficiently hot, and aboundeth not in water: Rivers are
not in all places ; and other running waters, and springs,
there are scarce any, especially in the more in-land parts
remote from the Sea ; Rain likewise very seldome during
the whole year, saving in that season, called by them
Pansecàl,[2] which signifies, *The time of rain*, being about

---

[1] It is a peculiarity of India that there are no natural lakes in it
of any size. Artificial reservoirs (or tanks, as they are generally
called) are common, and frequently of large extent. The largest in
India is said to be that at Dhebar, 20 miles S.E. of Udaipur in Raj-
putana. It covers an area of 21 sq. miles. The dam, of masonry, is
1,000 ft. long and 95 ft. high, and has a breadth of 50 ft. at the base
and 15 ft. at the top. Tanks are formed in two ways, viz., either by
excavation, or by constructing a dam across the mouth of a valley.

[2] Sometimes written " Parsecal ", a corruption of " Barsa-kal " or
" Rain-season ", which lasts about four months, during which the fall
of rain is so great as to amount to more than double the quantity
which falls in Europe during the whole year.

three moneths, beginning about the middle of June, and
during which time the Rain is continual, and very great ;
whence some upon this account call these three moneths
Winter, although the weather be then hottest, as well in
India as in all the rest of the northern Hemisphere. And
this, no doubt, proceeds from the Providence of God ;
since, were it not for this great rain, *India* would be in
regard of the great heat and drought at this time unhabit-
able ; as likewise the whole torrid Zone, in which most of
India lies, was believ'd to be by the Ancients, who had no
knowledge of these marvellous rains, which render it not
onlye habitable, but also fertile and most delicious.

Now, for that the Country is in some parts so scarce of
water, many Cities and inhabited places have no other but
the rain-water gather'd in these great Cisterns which are so
capacious that one of them suffices a City for a whole year
and more : And it not onely affords drink to men and
animals but also they wash clothes and beasts in it when
occasion requires, and make use of it to all purposes ;
whereby it comes to pass that in some places the water they
have is not over clear ; and the rude Indians care not for
such delicacies, but 'tis enough for them if they have what
is barely needful.

The Cistern or Lake of *Surat* hath a great trench
adjoyn'd to it on one side, long, large and deep, over which
certain small bridges are built ; and it falls into another less
Cistern a good way off, which though but small here comparatively, would yet be a very large one in our parts ; 'tis
built with many sides of stone like the former, as also the
banks of the Trench are. Between the great Lake and the
less, upon the Trench, stands a small *Cupola* or arched
Structure, made for the sepulture of some principal
Mahometans of the Country, and, as they say, of two
brethren who kill'd one the other, and of their Wives. 'Tis
no long time since this Cistern was made, according to the

D

common report, by a private man of this City, but
sufficiently wealthy, whose Daughter, they say, or rather
one descended from him, is still living, and I know not by
what sinister hap of fortune, very poor, so that she hath
scarce bread to eat. Wherein I observ'd a great ingratitude
of the Citizens of Suràt, in suffering his heir to want food,
who for their publick benefit had been at so great expense.

This poole of Suràt is called *Gopi Telau*,[1] that is, the
Poole of *Gopi*, which was his name who made it at his own
charge. And although the King, who in those dayes rul'd
over *Guzaràt*, did what he could to have it called after his
own name, yet that of the Builder has been justly retain'd
by the vulgar, and remains to this day. 'Tis not improbable
that this *Gopi*, who made this Piscina of *Suràt*, is the same
whom *Giovanni di Barros*[2] in his second Decade of Asia
frequently mentions, with the title of Melik,[3] and relates to
have been in those times, a little above a hundred years
ago, a great friend to the Portugals; styling him often Lord[4]
of *Barocci*,[5] and once in the last book, Lord of *Suràt ;*
but I rather believe that he was onely Governour of either
of these Cities, under the then Mahometan Kings of Cambaia,
(as he speaks), that is, of *Guzaràt ;* of which Province
Cambaia is the principal, and in a manner the Maritime
City, more known than the rest to the Portugals by trade ;
whence they have given its name to the whole Kingdome,
although not *Cambaia*, but *Ahmedabad*, more within land,
is properly the Royal Seat. 'Tis therefore possible that
Melik Gopi, mentioned by *Barros*, made this Cistern when

---

[1] *Talao*, a tank.

[2] A celebrated Portuguese historian, born at Visere in 1496 ; died
in 1570. He held the office of Treasurer of the Indies under King
John of Portugal, and wrote a history of Asia and the Indies, divided
into Decades, of which four are by himself and eight by other authors.

[3] *Malik*, Lord (Arabic).

[4] Lib. iv, c. 6; lib. vi, c. 2; lib. x, c. 1.

[5] Broach ; see *ante*, p. 19.

he was Governour of *Suràt*, it being the work, and expence, of such a person. Nor do the vulgar mistake in saying that he was a private man, since under the Mahometan Princes, who never allow any hereditary Lord in their Territories, the Governours of their Cities, and all other Ministers, (whom they choose indifferently out of all sorts of people, and not seldome out of the lowest plebeians, and who are always removable at pleasure) may with reason be call'd private persons, although advanc'd to whatever high dignity.

VIII.—On an other side of the City, but out of the circuit of the houses, in an open place, is seen a great and fair Tree, of that kind which I saw in the sea coasts of *Persia*, near Ormuz, called there *Lul* but here *Ber*.[1] The Gentiles of the Country hold it in great veneration for its greatness and age, riting[2] and honoring it often with their superstitious ceremonies, as dear and dedicated to a Goddess of theirs call'd Parvete,[3] whom they hold to be the Wife of Mahadeù, one of their greatest Deities. On the trunk of this tree a little above the ground, they have rudely engraven a round circle, which really hath not any feature of a humane countenance, but according to their gross application represents that of their Idol. This face they keep painted with a bright Flesh-colour, and this by a

---

[1] The " Bar" or " Banyan" tree (*Ficus Indica*), not to be confounded with the *Ficus religiosa*, or Pipal tree. The celebrated "Fig tree of Kabir" is probably here referred to, which had 3,350 branches, and was about 2,000 feet in circumference.

[2] *I.e.*, performing rites.

[3] Properly Parvati (Mountain goddess), wife of Siva, called also Mahadeo. This goddess is also called Devi, Bhavani, Durga, Gauri, Lakshmi, Kali, or Uma, and is worshipped by various aboriginal tribes under other names. (See Oppert's *Original Inhabitants of India*, part II, pp. 165, 205.) She is the object of worship to as great an extent as Siva himself, and is represented riding on a tiger, with a terrible countenance, streaming with blood, encircled with snakes, skulls, and human heads.

sacred rite of Religion ; as the Romans also dy'd the face
of Jupiter with Vermillion, as Pliny testifies. Round about
it are fastened Flowers and abundance of a plant, whose
leaves resemble a Heart, call'd here *Pan*,[1] but in other
places of India, Betle. These leaves the Indians use to
champ or chaw all day long, either for health's sake or
for entertainment and delight, (as some other Nations for
the same reasons, or rather through evil custome, continually take Tobacco). And therewith they mix a little
ashes of sea-shels and some small pieces of an Indian nut
sufficiently common, which here they call *Foufel*,[2] and in
other places *Areca ;* a very dry fruit, seeming within like
perfect wood ; and being of an astringent nature they hold
it good to strengthen the Teeth. Which mixture, besides
its comforting the stomack, hath also a certain biting taste,
wherewith they are delighted ; and as they chaw it, it
strangely dyes their lips and mouths red,[3] which also they
account gallant ; but I do not, because it appears not to be
natural. They swallow down only the juice after long
mastication and spit out the rest. In visits, 'tis the first
thing offer'd to the visitants ; nor is there any society or
pastime without it. He that is curious to know more of it
may consult the Natural Historians who have written of the

---

[1] A well-known climbing plant (*Piper Betelium*), a species of pepper, the leaves of which are much used in India for mastication.
Pepper was very early known as an article of commerce, for Theo-
phrastus mentions (*Hist. Plant.*, ix, 22) several varieties of it. See
Heeren's *Hist. Researches*, vol. ii, p. 276, and *Barbosa*, p. 73 (Hakluyt
edition).

[2] A palm tree (*Areca Catechu*), of which the nut is eaten with the
leaves of the betel-plant, and hence has acquired the name of betel-
nut. The native name is *Supari*. As to the Portuguese name, *Foufel*
or *Fofel*, the origin is uncertain. In Sir J. Maundeville's *Travels*
it is said that black pepper " is called Fulful", which is probably the
same word as " Foufel".

[3] The red colour proceeds from the juice of the betel-leaf.

exotick Simples of *India*, particularly *Garcias ab Horto*,[1] *Christopher Acosta*,[2] *Nicolaus Monardes*,[3] translated all together into Latin by *Carolus Clusius*.[4] I shall only add, that the fame I had heard in *Persia* of this Indian Masticatory, (especially from an Italian Fryer, who had been in *India*, and told us 'twas a thing not onely of great nutriment, and very good for the stomack, but moreover of an exquisite relish), made me desirous to try it. As for its other qualities I can say nothing ; but there is no great matter in the taste, nor should I make much difference of chawing these leaves of *Pan*, or those of our Cedars.

But to return to my Relation. Those flowers and leaves about the Idol's face carv'd in the Tree, are frequently chang'd, and fresh constantly supply'd ; and those which at times are taken away are given as a sacred thing to the people, who come from all parts to visit it. In the same rude sculpture of a humane face they have put certain eyes of Silver and Gold with some jewels, which were given by some persons, who foolishly believ'd themselves cur'd of maladies of the eyes by virtue of the Idol. Before whom, upon a little hillock, stands continually one of their Gioghi,[5] who among the Indians are a sort of Hermits ; and sometimes I have seen a Woman too standing there. On high, there hangs a

---

[1] Garcia de Orto, whose work on simples and drugs was published at Goa in 1563. A modern edition by Varnhagen appeared in 1872.

[2] Christoval Acosta, native of Portuguese Mozambique ; died in 1580.

[3] Native of Seville ; died in 1578. He wrote several works on medicine. That referred to in the text is entitled *De las Drogas de las Indias*, Seville, 1565, translated into Latin by Charles de l'Ecluse, and published in Antwerp in 1605. An Italian edition was published at Venice in 1585 by Guilandini.

[4] Charles de l'Ecluse, a celebrated French botanist, and one of the most learned men of his day. He was a native of Arras, and died at Leyden in 1609.

[5] Properly "Jogi" or "Yogi", a name applied to a class of Hindoo ascetics, from a word meaning "abstracted meditation".

Bell, which those that come to make their foolish devotions,
first of all ring out, as if thereby to call the Idol to hear
them ; then they fall to their adoration, which is commonly to extend both hands downwards as much as
possible, being joyn'd together in a praying posture; which
lifting up again by little and little, they bring to their
mouths as if to kiss them, and lastly, extend them so
joyn'd together, as high as they can, over their heads.
Which gesticulation is us'd only to Idols, and sacred things ;
for to men, even to Kings themselves, they make the same
Salutation (which in the *Persian* Tongue they call *Teslim*,[1]
and in their *Indian, Sumbaia*[2]) only with the right hand.
This ceremony being perform'd, some make their prayers
only standing, others prostrate themselves with their whole
body, groveling upon the earth, and then rise again ; others
only touch the ground with the head and forehead, and
perform other like acts of Humility. After which, they go
about the Tree, some once, others oftner, and then sprinkle
before the Idol either Rice or Oyle or Milk, or other such
things which are their Offerings and Sacrifices without
blood ; for to shed blood, even for Sacrifices, is not their
custome,[3] but to kill any sort of animals is counted a great
sin. Such as are of ability give moreover some Almes to
the person attending the service of the Idol ; from whom
in requital they receive the flowers and leaves, which are
about the Idol, and that with great devotion, kissing them,
and in token of reverence, laying them upon their heads.

---

[1] Properly *Taslim* (Arabic).

[2] Properly *Sambhavanam* (Sanskrit).

[3] Animal sacrifices are not by any means unknown to the Hindoo
ritual. But in the *Satapatha Brahmana* it is ordered that the
animal should be strangled, and "not stabbed behind the ear after the
manner of the fathers". See *Sat. Brah.*, iii, 8, 1, 15, vol. xxvi, p. 190,
quoted by Hewitt, *Early Hist. of Northern India*, part iv, p. 327. In
the present day blood *is* shed in some of the sacrifices.

A-side of this Tree stands a very small *cupola*, or Chappel with a very narrow window for entrance; I saw not what was within it, but I was inform'd that Women who have no Children go in there sometimes, and after they have been there become fruitful by the virtue of the place; but as in false Religions everything is imposture, so 'tis the opinion here, that the attendants of the Idol play fine pranks in this particular, either beguiling simple young Women, or satisfying the more crafty; whom indeed they sometimes cause to become pregnant, but 'tis by natural means without miracle, the Priests within the Chappel supplying the defects of their Husbands. Moreover, on another side of this Tree, stands a square low Post, on which certain figures of Idols are engraven; and at the foot thereof there is a little kind of Trench or hole, where also they pour milk, and oyle, and make divers other oblations. They are very solicitous in keeping the Tree with every bough and leaf of it, not suffering it to be injur'd by animals or men, nor in any wise violated and profan'd. They tell a story of an Elephant, who one day by chance eat but one single leaf of this Tree, for which being punish'd by the Idol, he dy'd within three dayes. Which story I understood to be thus far true, namely that the event was in this manner; but 'twas thought that for the reputation of the place, the attendants of the Idol either poyson'd or knock'd the Elephant on the head; in which Arts the *Gioghi* and Priests of the Gentiles use to be very dextrous.

IX.—The Commendator of the Dutch came one day to give me a visit, and after a competent conversation, carried me in his coach a little out of the City to see one of the fairest and famousest gardens of Suràt. The plot was level, well contriv'd and divided with handsome streight Walks; on either side whereof were planted rowes of

sundry Trees of this Climate, namely *Ambe*[1] or, as
others speak, *Manghe*, before describ'd by me in my last
Letters from *Persia*, in the maritime parts whereof I saw
some Trees of this kind: *Foufel*, whose leaves are like
those of the *Palm-tree*, but of a livelier, and fairer, green;
Narghil, like the Palm in the leaves also, and is that which
we call *Nux Indica*[2]: and others, different from what are
found in our parts. The plots between the several walks
were full of herbs and flowers, partly such as we have, and
partly not; amongst the rest they shew'd me a Flower, for
bigness and form not unlike our Gilly flower, but of a
whitish yellow, having a very sweet and vigorous scent,
and they call it Ciampà.[3]   In a convenient place there is a
square place,[4] rais'd somewhat from the ground and
cover'd with large sheds, to sit there in the shade, after the
manner of the East: and here we entertain'd our selves a
while and had a collation; and other things in the garden
worthy of remark I saw none.

As for the plants and strange simples of *India*, and the
whole Torrid Zone, (in these things very different from
ours) I shall say briefly once for all, that they are such and
so many, that to write fully of them would require express
volumes, and make them as big as those of *Dioscorides*
and *Pliny*, all of things unknown to us.   Nevertheless the
curiosity of the *Portugals* and other Europeans who trade
in these parts hath hitherto been so small that I know not

---

[1] Commonly called *Mango*, a Malay word.   The vernacular name
is "Am" (*Mangifera Indica*).   Called "Mangas" by Mandelslo.

[2] The Coco (generally incorrectly written cocoa) Nut (*Cocos nuci-
fera*).   The word *Narghil* is Arabic.

[3] Champa (*Champaca Michelia*).   A kind of Magnolia; a favourite
flower in India, the pale yellow hue of which is used as descriptive
of the most perfect female complexion.   A blue variety of the flower
is mentioned in Marsden's *Sumatra*, but is unknown in India.

[4] Called a *Baithakhana*, or sitting-room, if covered, or *Chabu-
tra* if uncovered.

any that have spoken and observ'd any thing in this kind besides the three Authors above mentioned. And they have written of very few things, although of those few they have written faithfully and well ; and I, who have read them all with diligence, have made some not unprofitable notes upon them, which I keep in manuscript by me, and you may see one day when it shall please God to bring us together.

As for the Dutch Commendator and the English President also, who came frequently in this manner to carry me abroad, I must not forbear to say that both of them live in sufficient splendor and after the manner of the greatest persons of the Country.[1] They go abroad with a great train, sometimes also of their own men on Horse-back, but especially with a great number of Indian servants on foot, arm'd according to the mode with Sword, Buckler, Bows and Arrows. For 'tis the custome of servants in *India*, whether Mahometans or Gentiles, to go alwayes arm'd, not onely upon a journey, but also in the City, and to serve in the house all day with the same weapons by their sides, and never to lay them off saving at night, when they go to sleep. Moreover these Governours of the two Frank or Christian Nations which reside in Suràt use to have carry'd before their coach or Horse when they ride a very high Bannerol or Streamer, by a man on foot, (which likewise is the custome of all men of quality here), and likewise to have a sadled Horse lead by hand before them. And not onely they who are publick persons, but any private person whatever, of whatever Country or Religion, may in these parts live with as much grandeur and equipage as he pleases ; and such is the liberty here, that everyone may do, if he will and be able, as much as the

---

[1] Sir W. Hedges, in his *Diary*, edited by Sir H. Yule (vol. i, p. 123) says, "A gawdy show, and great noise adds much to a Public Person's credit in this country."

King himself. Hence generally, all live much after a genteel way ; and they do it securely, as well because the King doth not persecute his subjects with false accusations, nor deprive them of anything when he sees them live splendidly and with the appearance of riches, (as is often done in other Mahometan Countries) as because the Indians are inclin'd to these vanities, and servants cost very little, in regard of the multitude of people and the small charge wherewith the common sort are maintained ; for a simple Servant, who is not an officer, commonly in the best houses, between wages, vituals and clothing, stands not in more than three *Rupià* a moneth, amounting to about the value of a Venetian Zecchine, or ten shillings sterling.[1]

Of Slaves there is a numerous company, and they live with nothing ; their clothing is onely white linnen, which though fine is bought very cheap ; and their dyet for the most part is nothing but Rice (the ancient food of all the Indians, according to Strabo[2]), of which they have infinite plenty, and a little fish, which is found every where in abundance. So that everybody, even of mean fortune, keeps a great family and is splendidly attended, which is easie enough, considering the very small charge, as I said, and on the other side the very considerable gains of traffick wherein most men are imploy'd, and the incomes of the Land, through its incredible fruitfulness, I dare say, unmeasurable.

Upon this occasion I must not forget, that amongst the Indian Men, both Mahometans and Pagans, agreably to what *Strabo*[3] testifies, they did of old wear onely white linnen, more or less fine according to the quality of the persons and the convenience they have of spending; which

---

[1] The words " ten shillings sterling" do not, of course, occur in the original Italian. A "zecchine" or "sequin" has an average value of about 9*s*. 5*d*.　　　[2] Lib. xv.　　　[3] *Ibid.*

linnen[1] is altogether of Bumbast[2] or Cotton, (there being no Flax in *India*[3]) and for the most part very fine in comparison of those of our Countries. The Garment which they wear next to the skin serves both for coat and shirt, from the girdle upwards being adorn'd upon the breast, and hanging down in many folds to the middle of the Leg. Under this Cassack,[4] from the girdle downwards, they wear a pair of long Drawers of the same Cloth, which cover not only their Thighs, but legs also to the Feet ; and 'tis a piece of gallantry to have it wrinkled in many folds upon the Legs. The naked Feet are no otherwise confin'd but to a slipper, and that easie to be pull'd off without the help of the Hand ; this mode being convenient, in regard of the heat of the Country and the frequent use of standing and walking upon Tapistry in their Chambers. Lastly, the Head with all the hair, which the Gentiles (as of old they did also, by the report of *Strabo*[5]) keep long, contrary to the Mahometans who shave it, is bound up in a small and very neat Turbant, of almost a quadrangular form, a little long, and flat on the top. They who go most gallant,

---

[1] Or rather cotton. Linen is not worn by natives of India. See a few lines below.

[2] Bumbast, or Bombast, is an old word for cotton, derived from the Greek *Bombyx*, a silkworm, whence the name " Bombax" was applied to the silk cotton-tree (*Bombax Pentandrum*) of India, and erroneously to the cotton-plant (*Gossypium herbaceum*), and corrupted into " Bombast". From the fact of cotton being used to swell out garments the verb "to bombast" and adjective " bombastic" arose. An interesting instance of the former word occurs in Sir Walter Scott's *Diary*, recently published (vol. ii, p. 394) : " The 3rd vol. of *Count Robert of Paris* is fairly begun, but I fear I shall want stuff to fill it, for I would not willingly bombast it with things inappropriate."

[3] The *Linum usitatissimum*, or flax-plant, is now common in India, and two species at least of it are indigenous.

[4] An old way of spelling "cassock", from the Italian *cassacca*, a loose coat. Derived from *casa*, house, or home.

[5] Lib. xv.

use to wear their Turbant[1] only strip'd with silk of several colours upon the white, and sometimes with Gold ; and likewise their girdles wrought in Silk and Gold, instead of plain white. I was so taken with this Indian dress, in regard of its cleanliness and easiness, and for the goodly show me thought it had on horse-back, with the Scemiter girt on and the buckler hanging at a shoulder belt, besides a broad and short dagger of a very strange shape, ty'd with tassell'd strings to the girdle, that I caus'd one to be made for myself, complete in every point, and to carry with me to shew it in *Italy*.

The Mahometan Women, especially of the Mogholians, and Souldiers of other extraneous descents, who yet are here esteem'd, go clad likewise all in white, either plain, or wrought with Gold-flowers,[2] of which work there are some very goodly and fine pieces. Their upper Garment is short, more beseeming a Man then a Woman, and much of the same shape with those of Men : Sometimes they wear a Turbant too upon their heads, like Men, colour'd, and wrought with Gold : Sometimes they wear onely fillets, either white or red, or wrought with Gold and Silver, for other colours they little use. Likewise their clothes are oftentimes red, of the same rich and fine linnen ; and their Drawers are also either white or red, and oftentimes of sundry sorts of silk-stuff strip'd with all sorts of colours. When they go along the City, if it be not in close Coaches, but on foot, or on horse-back, they put on white veils, wherewith they cover their faces, as 'tis the

---

[1] The word " Turbant" is an old English form of " turban," which is a corruption of the Arabic and Persian word *Dul-band* (lit. " turn-band"). This form of head-dress is said to have originated from the practice of Muhammadan warriors going to war with their winding-sheets on their heads.

[2] This is what is generally known as *Kincob*, properly *Kimk-hwab*.

custome of all Mahometan Women : Yet the Indian Gentile Women commonly use no other colour but red, or certain linnen stamp'd with works of sundry colours, (which they call Cit[1]) but all upon red, or wherein red is more conspicuous then the rest, whence their attire seems onely red at a distance. And for the most part they use no garment, but wear onely a close Wastecoat,[2] the sleeves of which reach not beyond the middle of the Arm, the rest whereof to the Hand is cover'd with bracelets of Gold or Silver or Ivory, or such other things according to the ability of the persons. From the waste downwards they wear a long coat down to the Foot, as I have formerly writ that the Women do in the Province of *Moghostan*[3] *in Persia*, near *Ormuz*. When they go abroad they cover themselves with a cloak of the ordinary shape, like a sheet, which is also us'd by the Mahometans, and generally by all Women in the East ; yet it is of a red colour, or else of *Cit* upon a red ground, that is of linnen stamp'd with small works of sundry colours upon red. Those that have them adorn themselves with many gold-works, and jewels, especially their ears with pendants sufficiently enormous, wearing a circle of Gold or Silver at their ears, the diametre whereof is oftentimes above half a span and 'tis made of a plate two fingers broad, and engraven with sundry works, which is a very disproportionate thing. The Pagan

---

[1] "Cit" would of course be pronounced as "Chit" in Italian—for chintz, from Persian *chins*, "spotted" or "stained".

[2] Old English for waistcoat.

[3] Della Valle calls Moghostan "the country of palms", and says that it was dependent on the Governor of Shiraz, and that its capital was Mina (Minab, in lat. 27° 10′ N.). It was here that his wife, the Signora Maani, died of fever. The province of Moghistan is still marked on some modern maps in the south-east of Persia along the Strait of Ormuz. (See Della Valle's letter from Shiraz, dated July 27, 1622.)

Women go with their faces uncover'd,[1] and are freely seen by everyone both at home and a broad. Nevertheless they are modest, and honor'd much more then the Mahometans; and amongst them 'tis a certain thing that there is not any publick Courtisan; but amongst the Mahometan Women there are infinite, who go every day publickly to houses, and where they please; to play Musick, sing, dance, and do what else belongs to their profession. But of these things enough for this time.

X.—I came from *Persia* with a great desire to go to *Cambaia*, in regard of what I had heard of it, being told that in that City, which is one of the ancientest of *India*, the Pagans are very numerous, and above measure observers of their Rites; so that I might probably see more remarkable Curiosities there of those Idolaters then elsewhere; Sig: *Alberto Scilling* had the same desire, so that upon my imparting to him, and his consenting thereunto, both of us desir'd the Dutch Commendator, that when any of his nation went to *Cambaia*, as they us'd to do sometimes about their affairs, he would do us the favour to advertise us thereof that we might go thither in their company. The Commendator promis'd to do us this kindness as soon as possible, nor was it long before we were advertis'd of an opportunity. The Commendator's Steward, who takes care of the like businesses, came to know of us how many Coaches we should need; Sig: *Alberto* spoke to him for one for himself, and I for two, intending to carry Sig[a] Mariuccia with me, because I thought it not fit to leave her in *Suràt* without me, although she had the company of good Women. I offer'd the Steward money for the Coaches, but he refus'd then to take it, saying that it was not the custome, and that at our return accounts should be made

---

[1] This statement shows the gradual adoption of the Muhammadan custom of veiling the face which is now prevalent in India among native women of all sects, except those of low caste, and Parsees.

up ; for so they were wont to deal with those Hackney-
men, with whom the Nation had always long account for
such matters, and, I, who understood things no otherwise
then by this information, suffer'd myself to be perswaded.

Now, on Monday the 23d of *February*, being the day for
our setting forth, besides the three Coaches for Sig : Alberto and me, and two others full of Dutch-men who were
to go this journey with us, all in very good order for
habits and arms, and also with a Trumpeter with a silver
Trumpet, to recreate the Travellers, the Commendator
himself came to my house with many others of his followers in their City-Coaches, to conduct me forth and set
me in the way. He accompany'd me to a certain place
without the City, where in the shadow of a small chappel,
we convers'd together for a good while, and were entertained with sundry fruits, particularly with Grapes, which
here in *Suràt* we have often ate ripe, sweet, and good, in
February, yet green of colour, like the *Uva-Jugliatica* or
early *July*-grape of Italy, and I believe there is plenty
enough to make Wine.

Whilst we were in this place a Post came to the Commendator from *Agra* and from the Court, with news that
Sciàh Selim,[1] King of the Country, had sent one of his
principal Chans, call'd *Asàf Chan*,[2] to Agra, to remove the
Royal Treasure thence before the arrival of Sultan *Chorròm*,[3] one of the same King's Sons, lately rebell'd against his
Father, and then reported to be upon his march with his

---

[1] Shah Selim, third son of Akbar, who adopted the name of Jahangir
(Ruler of the World). He reigned from A.D. 1605 to 1627.

[2] Asaf Khan, brother of the celebrated Queen Nurmahal (" Light
of the Palace", afterwards called Nur Jahan, or " Light of the World"),
wife of the Emperor Jahangir. His daughter married Shah Jehan,
who succeeded his father Jahangir as emperor.

[3] Or Kharram (third son of Jahangir), who became emperor under
the name of Shah Jahan (" King of the World"), and reigned from
A.D. 1627 to 1658.

Army thither. And from *Agra* it was signifi'd that things were in great danger of alterations through this war rais'd between the Father and the Son, with great danger of the whole state of *India*. This notable Passage happening in my time will give me occasion to write many things worthy of memory, usually attending the like conjunctures; and being present in the country, peradventure I shall hereafter be an eye-witness, or at least have certain intelligence of sundry occurrences. In the mean time, to the end that what I shall have occasion to speak of these Revolutions may be better understood, I shall here give such account of the State of the King and his people as may suffice to give light to all the rest.

Sciah Selim (who, as I have formerly writ to you, is King of the greater part of *India*, between *Indus* and *Ganges*, and whose Countries are extended Northwards as far as the cliffs of Mount *Taurus*[1] or *Imaus*, where it divides *India* from *Tartaria*), is that great Monarch, whom in *Europe* you commonly call the Great *Moghòl*.[2] Which Name is given him because of his being deriv'd from a Race of Tartars call'd Moghols[3] who are of the City of

---

[1] The Taurus range is, strictly speaking, distinct from that of Imaus, which denotes the Himalayan range, the word "Imaus" being obviously connected with the Sanskrit *Himavat* (snowy). But the words "Taurus" (high mountain) and "Imaus" (snowy) were applied indiscriminately to more than one range of mountains.

[2] The so-called Mogul dynasty was founded by Baber, who was, strictly speaking, a Turk, not a Mogul, except on his mother's side. The name of Mogul was applied to the Muhammadan kings of India owing to the fact that the Hindoos applied the name of Mogul to all northern Muhammadans, to distinguish them from Afghans and Turks. The name is derived from Mogul, a son of Alanza (or Alinje) Khan, chief of the Turks, originally one of the tribes on the western boundary of China. (See Gibbon's *Roman Empire*, vi, p. 138 ; Howorth's *Mongols*, part I, p. 39.)

[3] The race of Tartars proper were descended from Tatar, another son of Alanza Khan, and were originally distinct from the Moguls,

Samarcand,[1] and the Province of *Giagatà*,[2] which is the *Sodianga*, ancient as 'tis manifested by the Persian Geography, where to this day that Territory is denoted and distinguish'd by the ancient name of *Sogd*. *Teimùr Lenk*,[3] call'd by us *Tamerlane*, as *Mir Aliscir* reports, a famous author of those times, who writ his history in the Persian-Tongue handsomely, and with great exactness, descended by a collateral line from the near kindred of *Cinghiz Chan*,[4] the most puissant King of *Chataio*,[5] known also in *Europe* to our Histories, and by S. Antonino,[6] who writes largely concerning him, nam'd with a little corrup-

---

who for the first time invaded India, under Jinghiz Khan, in 1217 A.D. (See Max Müller's *Science of Language*, p. 298.)

[1] The ancient Maracanda, which is now, under the Russian Government, regaining some of its ancient importance. According to Professor Wilson (*Ariana*, p. 165), the name is derived from the Sanskrit *Samara-Khanda*, the "warlike province". (See Smith's *Ancient Geography*, vol. ii, p. 266.) Another derivation given in Egli's *Etymological Geographical Lexicon* is from "Samar", its Arab conqueror in A.D. 643.

[2] The ancient Sogdiana, lying between the rivers Oxus and Jaxartes, comprising the present Turkestan and Bokhara, and still called by the name of Sogd. The name Giagata, or Jagata, was derived from Jagatai, or Chagatai, second son of Jinghiz Khan. See Col. Yule's *Cathay*, vol. ii, p. 525, and Gibbon's *Roman Empire*, vi, p. 145.

[3] Otherwise called Amir Timur and Tamerlane. The addition of Lenk to his name was made on account of his lameness. He was born at Kesh, now Shehri Sebsz, near Samarkand, crowned in 1369, and died in 1405. His exploits are sufficiently well known to render further reference to them unnecessary here. (See Gibbon's *Roman Empire*, vi, p. 174.) The authority, Mir Aliscir, here quoted is Mir Ali Shir, a Persian historian who lived in the fifteenth century and was Wazir to Shah Hassain, King of Persia.

[4] One of the numerous names of Jinghiz Khan, whose original name was Temuchin, or Temujin, born 1162 A.D., died 1227. (See Gibbon's *Roman Empire*, vi, p. 138.)

[5] Originally Khitai, and afterwards Cathay, a name applied to the country lying N.E. of China, whose people overran northern China, and thus caused China to be subsequently also called Cathay. (See Col. Yule's *Cathay and the Way Thither*.)

[6] Part 3, Tit. 19, c. 8, and elsewhere.

E

tion *Cingis Cham*. This *Cinghiz* warring with his neighbours, and destroying many other Principalities, became at length Lord of a Vast Dominion, and in a manner of all *Tartaria*, (which comprehends both the one, and the other, *Scythia*[1]) and, at his death, divided the same between his Sons. To Giagatà, the second Son, fell the Country of *Samarcand*, with all *Sogdiana*, and sundry other adjacent Territories ; and he, from his own name called it Giagataio, and all the Nations who remain'd under his Government Giagataians : a very ancient custome of the *Scythians* to give the Prince's Name to Countries, and their Subjects, as appears by *Diodorus Siculus*.[2]

XI.—In process of time a Descendant of *Giagatà*, reigning still in these parts, *Teimùr Lenk*, though extracted from the noblest blood of the Kings, yet remote from the Royal Stock by a long series, liv'd in *Samarcand* his own Country, a man rather of valour than of great fortune. But it falling out that the King[3] at that time was slain for his evil deportments, by the Grandees of the Country, in which conjuncture *Teimùr Lenk* was elected, and placed in the Sovereignty, he, not contented with the sole kingdom of *Giagataio*, being increas'd in strength and power, made afterwards those great Expeditions which the World beheld : of which nevertheless little sincere fame arrives to us ; there being no European who hath written truly thereof, saving briefly in the *Spanish* Tongue *Ruy Gonzales de Clavigo*,[4] who was sent thither Embassador by his King, Don *Henry* the Third of *Castile*. In like manner *Teimùr* at his death left that his great acquired Empire, divided amongst many Sons and Nephews, who falling at variance afterwards, and their successors continuing the same,

---

[1] *I.e.*, East, and West.   [2] Lib. ii.

[3] Amir Hosain, slain in A.D. 1370.

[4] Ruy Gonzales de Clavijo, sent as ambassador in A.D. 1403-5. A narrative of this embassy, translated by Clements R. Markham, Esq., C.B., was published by the Hakluyt Society in 1861.

ruin'd one another with sundry warrs ; and God knows
whether in *Tartary* there be left at this day any Prince of
that Race.

A *Cadet*[1] or Younger Brother of them, who had no share
among the *Tartars*, came over the Mountains to seek his
fortune in *India*, within the court of a Prince[2] then reigning in one part of it : where being once introduc'd, by
great alliances and services, he rais'd a great House ; and
in time various Revolutions brought it to pass that one of
his Successors[3] came to be possess'd of that Kingdom, and
to found the Royal Family now regnant, of which with very
great augmentations of Dominion *Sciàh Selim*, now living,
is the fourth King,[4] as his own Seals testifie, the impression
whereof I keep by me, wherein is engraven all his pedigree
as far as *Tamerlane*, from whom *Sciàh Selim* reckons himself the eighth descendant.[5]

When *Sciàh Selim* was born, he was at first call'd
Sceichù, because the King Ekbàr his Father, having before
had no children, conceiv'd he had obtain'd him by the
prayers of a certain *Sceich*, (so they call a Religious Man)
to whom he bore great reverence.   But, after he was come

---

[1] This was the celebrated Baber, fifth in descent from Timur. He
was son of Omar Sheikh Mirza, King of Cabul, born A.D. 1482—a
Turk by paternal descent, and a Mogul on his mother's side, she
being a sister of Mahmud Khan, a descendant of Jagatai or Chagatai,
son of Jinghiz Khan.

[2] Probably this was Doulat Khan Lodi, ruler of the Panjab, at
whose invitation Baber came to India.

[3] Humayun, son of Baber, who became King of Agra, and subsequently, in 1555, King of Delhi also.

[4] Humayun, and Akbar, being the second and third.

[5] The intervening descendants between Timur and Baber being
Mirath Shah, Sultan Pir Muhammad, Abu Said, and Omar Sheikh
Mirza.

As to the seal referred to, see *Voyage to East India*, by Sir T. Roe's
chaplain, in which (p. 447) he describes it as consisting of "nine
rounds, or circles, with the names and titles of Tamerlane, and his
lineal successors, in Persian words".

to ripe age, his Father chang'd his Name, as here they sometimes do, into Sciàh Selim, which in the Arabian Dialect, the learned Language of all Mahometans, signifies *Rè Pacifico*, a Peaceable, or Peace making King ; conceiving this name to agree to his Nature. The Father dying, Sciàh Selim being advanc'd to the Kingdom chang'd his Name once again (as 'tis the custom of many Oriental Princes on such an occasion) with more Magnificent Titles, (for their proper Names are nothing but Titles, and Epithets) and would be called *Nur eddin*,[1] *Muhammèd, Gihòn ghir*,[2] which partly in *Arabick*, partly in *Persick*, signifies *the Light of the Law, Mahomet, Take the World;* in regard of the profession which he makes in publick of the Mahometan Sect ; though really in secret, by what they report, he little cares for Mahomet[3] and his Law, or any other Religion ; accounting, according to the vain opinion of some in these parts, that a man may be sav'd in every Law. Nevertheless the Name *Sciàh Selim*, tenaciously inhering in the memory of people, remains still to him, and in common discourse he is more frequently call'd by this than any other Name. He had two Brothers. One, who took a part of the Province *Dacan*, was call'd by his proper Name *Peharì*, and by sirname *Sciah Muràd*.[4] The other, who dy'd in the City *Berhampor*, was nam'd *Daniel*,[5] and sirnamed *Sombòl Sciàh*, but both dyed without Heirs ; whereupon their Dominion returned back to *Sciàh Selim*.

I know not whether by one or more Women, this King had four sons ; the first is call'd *Sultàn Chosrou*[6] ; the

---

[1] Nur-ud-Dìn, Light of the Faith.
[2] Jahàn-Gir, Conqueror of the World.
[3] See Elphinstone's *India*, p. 484, on this point.
[4] Shah Muràd, second son of Akbar.
[5] Daniel, third son of Akbar, who died of drink in his thirtieth year.
[6] Khushrù, whose melancholy history is well known. He died in imprisonment

second, *Sultàn Peruiz*[1]; the third, *Sultan Chorrom*,[2] now in rebellion, (to whom, when he return'd from a war which he had prosperously manag'd in *Dacàn*, his father gave the title of *Sciahi Gihòn*,[3] which is interpreted, *King of the World*;) and the fourth, *Sultàn Scehriah*, is yet a youth of small age. 'Tis possible others besides these have been born to him; but, being dead, either in child-hood, or long ago, there is no mention made of them at present.

He hath one Wife,[4] or Queen, whom he esteems and favours above all other Women; and his whole Empire is govern'd at this day by her counsel. She was born in *India*, but of Persian Race, that is the Daughter of a Persian, who coming as many do into *India*, to the service of the *Moghòl*, hapned in time to prove a very great man in this court, and, (if I mistake not) Chan, or Vice-roy, of a Province.[5] She was formerly Wife in *India* to another Persian Captain,[6] who serv'd the Moghòl too; but, after her Husband's death, a fair opportunity being offer'd, as it falls out many times to some handsome young Widows I know not how, *Sciàh Selim* had notice of her, and became in love[7] with her. He would have carried her into his Haram, or *Gynæceo*, and kept her there like one of his other Concubines, but the very cunning and ambitious Woman counterfeited great honesty to the King, and refus'd to go into his Palace; and, as I believe, also to comply with his desires, saying that she had been the

---

[1] Sultan Parviz.　　　　　　　　　　[2] Sultan Kharram.

[3] Shah Jahan, who succeeded his father Jahangir as Emperor.

[4] The celebrated Nur Mahàl, afterwards Nur Jahàn. She died in 1646.

[5] Asaf Khàn eventually became Prime Minister.

[6] Shir Afghan Khàn, to whom she was married by Akbar, in order to prevent her from marrying his son Selim.

[7] He had been in love with her before her marriage, and brought about the assassination of her husband in order to make her his wife.

Wife of an Honourable Captain and Daughter of an
Honourable Father, and should never wrong her own
Honour, nor that of her Father and Husband, and that
to go to the King's *Haram*, and live like one of the other
Female-slaves there, was unsuitable to her noble condition. Wherefore if his Majesty had a fancy to her he
might take her for his lawful Wife, whereby his Honour
would be not onely not injur'd, but highly enlarg'd, and
on this condition she was at his service. *Sciàh Selim* so
disdaign'd this haughty motion at first that he had almost
resolv'd in despight to give her in Marriage to one of the
Race which they call *Halàlchor*,[1] as much as to say *Eater-
at-large*, that is to whom it is lawful to eat every-thing,
and for this cause they are accounted the most despicable
people in *India*. However the Woman persisting in her
first resolution, intending rather to die than alter it, and
Love returning to make impetuous assaults on the
King's Heart; with the help, too, as some say, of Sorceries
practis'd by her upon him, if there were any other charms
(as I believe there were not) besides the conditions of the
Woman, which became lovely to the King by sympathy ;
at length he determin'd to receive her for his lawful Wife
and Queen above all the rest. And as such she commands
and governs at this day in the King's Haram with supream
authority; having cunningly remov'd out of the Haram,
either by marriage, or other handsome wages, all the other
Women who might give her any jealousie ; and having
also in the Court made many alterations by deposing, and
displacing almost all the old Captains and Officers, and by
advancing to dignities other new ones of her own creatures,
and particularly those of her blood and alliance.

This Queen is call'd at this day Nurmahàl, which sig-

---

[1] "Halalkhor," literally "eater of what is lawful", or one who regards all things as lawful eating.

nifies, *Light of the Palace ;* a Name, I believe, conferr'd on her by the King, when he made her Queen. She hath a Brother, who is still in great favour with the King, and of great power, and is the *Asàf Chan* whom I mention'd above, and one of whose Daughters is one of the Wives of *Sultan Chorròm* now in rebellion ; whence some, not without ground, suspect that the present rebellion of *Sultan Chorròm* is with some participation of *Asàf Chan,* and of *Numrahàl* herself ; perhaps upon design that the Kingdom may fall to him after the death of the Father.

Sultan Scehriàr hath also to Wife a Daughter of *Nurmahàl* by her first Husband, for by the King she hath hitherto no Children. Wherein appears the prudence of this Woman, who hath so well establish'd herself with alliances in the Royal Family.

But to return to the King's Children. *Sultan Chosrou* the eldest, who was a Prince of much expectation, wellbelov'd, and, as they say, a friend in particular of the Christians, being at the government[1] of I know not what Country, rebell'd against his Father, under pretext that the Kingdom by right belonged unto him, because indeed King *Ekbar,* his Grand-father, at his death left it to him[2] his nephew, being then born, and not to *Selim* the Father, who was his son, being displeas'd with his Son *Selim,* for that one time in his life he attempted to rebel against him. So easie are Insurrections amongst these Infidels, and so little faith can Fathers have in Sons, and they in their own Fathers. With this pretence *Sultan Chosrou* once rais'd a great Army against his Father, but, coming to a battle,

---

[1] This seems to be an error ; Sultan Khushrù was living at Agra with his father when he rebelled against him. (See Elph., *India*, p. 484.)

[2] This is an error, as Akbar at his death expressly nominated Selim as his successor. (See Elphinstone's *India*, p. 466.) "Nephew" should be "grandson".

he was routed, and forc'd to surrender himself freely to his
Father, who, chiding him with words rather gentle than
otherwise, ask'd him to what end he made these tumults,
knowing well that he held and kept the whole Kingdom
for him? Yet his deeds were sharper then his words ; for
in the first place he caus'd all the chief captains who had
follow'd him in the war to be cruelly slain, and shewing
them so slain to *Chosrou*, as in his return with Triumph he
made him to pass along with himself in the middle of a long
row of them barbarously mangled in several manners, and
to behold some of his faithfullest confidents sew'd up in
beast's skins, and be so left miserably to rot, he bade him
see in what sort of people he had confided. Moreover he
suffer'd him no longer to live freely, but committed him to
the safe but honourable custody of certain Grandees of
his Court : and, which was worse, he caus'd his eyes to be
sew'd up, as 'tis sometimes the custom here, to the end to
deprive him of sight with out excæcating him, that so he
might be unfit to cause any more commotions, which
sewing, if it continue long, they say it wholly causes loss of
sight ; but after a while the Father caused this Prince's
eyes to be unripp'd again, so that he was not blinded but
saw again, and it was only a temporal penance. Yet he
was not deliver'd from prison, in which he liv'd so closely
for two years that onely one person was suffer'd to be with
him in the prison to serve him.

Nurmahal, who had apprehended that *Sultan Chosrou*
would succeed his Father in the Kingdom, and desir'd to
establish herself well, had frequently offer'd her Daughter
to *Sultan Chosrou*, before she married her to *Sultan
Scehriar*, but he, either for that he had another Wife he
lov'd sufficiently and would not wrong her, or because
he scorn'd *Nurmahal's* Daughter, would never consent :
insomuch that whilst he was in prison, and was told by
reiterated messages that if he would marry *Nurmahal's*

Daughter he should be immediately set free, nevertheless he would not be brought to do it. His Wife on the contrary, who lov'd him as well as he lov'd her, obtain'd to be the person allotted to serve him in the prison, and accordingly went thither, and liv'd with him so long as he was there, never ceasing to persuade him to marry *Nurmahal's* Daughter, that so he might be deliver'd from those troubles ; that for her part she was content to live with him as a slave, provided she saw him free and in a good condition ; but he could never be prevailed with. Thus he liv'd in prison with his faithful and dear Wife, till the malice of his persecutors and his Father's anger being wearied, about two years after he was taken out of Prison, but still held in a more honourable custody.

For these things, *Sultan Chosrou* remained always much in the hatred of *Nurmahal*, who despairing to marry her Daughter to him, gave her to *Sultan Scehriar*, as is above said.

Sultan Peruiz, the second Son, is now Governour of the Kingdom of *Bengala* at the mouth of Ganges, and lives peaceably, nor is any news heard of him. *Sultan Chorròm*, the third son, had and hath under his Government that part of *Dacan* which is subject to the *Moghol*, but now is about to usurp the Kingdom of *Guzarat*, where I write these things. *Sultan Scehriar* hath no Government yet, but 'tis said that he is lately made Captain of eight thousand Horse.

Now touching the rebellion and the beginning of it. *Sultan Chorròm*, after the alliance that he made with *Asaf Chan*, so wrought by the means of his Father in law, and *Nurmahal*, his Aunt,[1] that the King granted him the prisoner *Sultan Chosrou* into his own power, taking him out of the hands of him that kept him, and committing

---

[1] "Aunt" should be "step-mother".

him to him to keep, yet with order to use him very well
and have great care of him ; and this because *Chorròm*
refus'd to go to his Government, and to the war whereunto
they sent him, unless he carried *Sultan Chosrou* with him,
alledging that it was not convenient that he should be
absent from the Court whilst *Sultan Chosrou*, his com-
petitor and back-friend[1] stay'd there.   When he had got
him into his hands he went to his Government, and there
kept and treated him honourably a year or two : but afterwards, out of the intention which he always had to remove
him out of his way to the succession of the Kingdom, he
being absent (as some say) sent him poyson'd meats,
appointing certain of his Captains who kept him to make
him eat those meats by any means, fair or foul.   The
Captains punctually executed this order ; but because
Sultan Chosrou, becoming suspicious by their importunity
to have him eat, would by no means taste of those meats,
saying plainly that they intended to poyson him, the
Captains, since there was no other remedy, and perhaps
having order, leap'd all upon him, and he defended himself
bravely, till at length having fell'd him to the ground they
strangled him with a Bowstring.   Others say that *Sultan
Chorròm* himself slew him with his own hand[2] publickly.
Be it as it will, *Sultan Chosrou* dy'd of a violent death,
and *Sultan Chorròm* was either by himself, or by media-
tion of others, the Murtherer.

Sciah Selim upon hearing this news, being highly dis-
pleased with *Sultan Chorròm*, calls him to Court, to give
account of the fact.   *Sultan Chorròm* would not obey the
Summons, but gathering together his Forces, which never-

---

[1] See Middleton's play of *The Roaring Girl*, published 1611.
" Back friends are sometimes good." The word usually means a
false friend. (See Shakespeare, *Comedy of Errors*, Act iv, Scene 2.)

[2] There is no good authority for this statement. The facts of the
prince's death are involved in mystery. (See Elph., *India*, p. 495.)

theless are not great, to withstand his Father, and raising
not onely those of his own jurisdiction, but also divers
other neighbouring Cities, not comprehended therein (as
Cambaia, and such, from which he hath remov'd the
Governours plac'd there by his Father, and appointed
others of his own devotion) with the assistance and counsel
of some petty Gentile Princes, remov'd his Camp towards
Agra, as is above intimated. In which commotions, and
the death of *Sultan Chosrou*, 'tis not onely suspected that
there is some conspiracy of *Asaf Chan*, and *Nurmahal*,
his ancient enemies in secret, but also that the King of
Persia is of intelligence with them, who about the same
time, or a little before, on his side made the warr of
Candahar, in which the coldness which the *Moghol* shew'd,
proceeded, no doubt, either from his not being well inform'd,
because perhaps *Nurmahal* and *Asaf Chan*, who were his
chief Counsellors, suffered not true intelligence to be signifi'd to him, or perhaps because the evil carriage of *Sultan
Chorròm* hath hitherto necessitated him to stand in sus-
pense. 'Tis true the last Advertisements from *Agra*, that
the King, as I said, sent *Asaf Chan* to remove the treasure
from thence, argue that the King still entrusts him, and
consequently either that he is not in fault, or that his
fault is not yet known. The doubt will be best clear'd
by Time. *Sultan Chosrou* left a little Son behind him,
whose name is *Sultan Bulachi*.[1] But my journey now
calls me elsewhere.

XII.—The Commendator having read the letters from
Agra, and communicated to me all the News, it being now
Evening, I took leave of him, and after sundry volleys of
muskets he return'd to the City, and I, with my company of

---

[1] His other name was Dawar Sheko. He was proclaimed king by
Asaf Khan, on the death of Jahangir, but fled to Persia, where he was
seen by the Holstein ambassadors in 1633. (See Elph., *India*, p. 506.)

five Coaches, took the way of *Cambaia*.   Having travell'd
two *Cos*, we ferried over the same River of *Suràt*, and then
proceeded four other *Cos*, which in all were six, and at
Night took up our lodging at a town called *Periah*.
But we rested little, because soon after mid-night we put
our selves upon the way again.   Our journey from *Suràt*
to *Cambaia* was always with our faces towards the North.
The next Morning early we made a Collation by the side
of a Piscina, or Lake, which we found by the way, of a long
and narrow form, of which kind there are many in these
parts.

Having travell'd sixteen *Cos*, which was from *Suràt* in
all two and twenty, before Evening we arriv'd at the City
of *Barocci*,[1] or *Behrug*, as they call it in Persian ; under the
walls whereof, on the South side, runs a River call'd
Nerbeda,[2] which we ferried over.   The City is encompass'd
with a wall of moderate bigness, built high upon a rising
hill.   For the circuit 'tis populous enough, as generally are
all the parts of *India*.   'Tis considerable for a very great
Trade of fine Cotton Cloth, or Callico,[3] made more plentifully there than in other places, and dispersed not onely
through *Asia*, but also into our *Europe*, so that the English
and Dutch (which two Nations have Houses of constant
residence here) freight five or six great ships therewith
every year ; and for the better imbarking of it, make it up

---

[1] See *ante*, p. 19.

[2] Properly Narbada, the next most sacred river in India after the
Ganges.   The name is derived from the Sanskrit *Narma-da*, or
" Giver of Bliss".   (See Sir Monier Williams' *Modern India*, p. 142.)   In
accordance with certain Hindu sacred writings, the sanctity hitherto
ascribed to the Ganges should in a few years' time be transferred to
the Narbada river, *i.e.*, at the end of the five thousandth year of the
" Kali Jug", and the Ganges will, it is said, then become dry.   (See
Sir G. Birdwood's letter to the *Times*, Feb. 1891, and that of Sir J.
Johnstone to *Spectator* of March 7th, 1891.)

[3] So called from Calicut, on the west coast of India, in lat. 11° 14'
N., whence it was first imported into Europe in the 15th century.

in very great bales, each as big as a Roman Coach ; and every piece of Cloth, little bigger than one of our Towels, being carri'd to *Aleppo*, will not be sold for less than three or four *Piastres*, and in *Italy* at least for six Crowns. Whence you may infer what wealth comes out of this small City alone, which for compass and buildings is not greater than *Siena* of *Tuscany*, although 'tis above three times as populous, and you may also consider to what summ the Prince's Costumes arise.

A few *Cos* from the City is a Mine of Calcidonies[1] and Agates, white and green ; but these stones are carry'd less into *Barocci* than to *Cambaia*, although it be further from the Mine, because there is a Sea-port, and a greater concourse of foreign Merchants ; and in *Cambaia* they are wrought into little Globes, either round or oval, to make Coronets or Neck-laces, and also little Cups and divers other curious vessels for ornament.[2]

The Sea comes not up to *Barocci* even at the highest tides, but is about as many miles distant as 'tis from *Surát*. When we pass'd over the River, our Dutch Trumpeter sounding his Instrument, gave notice of our coming to his Country men residing in *Barocci;* and they at the Summons came immediately to the bank-side to meet us ; from thence we went with them to lodge in the Dutch House there. Late in the Evening they carry'd us to see a *Patache*[3] or small Indian ship, which they were building,

---

[1] More correctly "Chalcedonies".

[2] Cambay is celebrated for the manufacture of agate, cornelian, and other stones. The cornelians come from mines in the vicinity of Ratanpur, in the native state of Rajgupta, Rewa Kantha (Hunter's *Gazetteer*, sub v.). An interesting description of the operation of preparing these stones has been written by Mr. J. Wilkinson, assistant to the Resident at Baroda.

[3] A Spanish word meaning a tender, or vessel attending a squadron, and employed in carrying men and orders from one ship or place to another. The word is used by F. Mendez Pinto in his narrative (p. 22 of edition of 1891).

and was not yet finish'd, in which they treated us till night, drinking of *Tari*,[1] which is a liquor drawn from the Nut-trees of *India*, whitish and a little troubled, of taste some-what sowrish and sweet too, not unpleasing to the palate, almost like our Poignant or Brisk-wine ; yet it inebriates as Wine doth if drunk immoderately.

The next day, which was *Wednesday, Feb.* 22, we departed from *Barocci* late in the Forenoon. Six *Cos* off, we made a Collation near a water, without lighting out of the Coach, having brought provision with us for this purpose from *Barocci.* Afterwards upon the way we met the Wife and Family of the Governour of *Cambaia*, remov'd from that charge by the Rebel *Sultan Chorròm*, who had plac'd another there at his devotion ; and this, being driven from thence, return'd to *Surdt*, where his house and usual habitation was. His Wife was carry'd upon an Elephant, in a cover'd and very convenient litter. Three other Elephants follow'd unladen, saving with the men upon their necks who guided them ; then abundance of Coaches, partly covered and full of women, partly un-cover'd with men in them ; then a great number of Souldiers, Horse and Foot ; and in brief a great train suitable to the quality of the person and the custom of *India*, which is to have a very numerous attendance who-ever it be. After this we forded a small River, which I believe was of salt water, which, they say, is called *Dilavel ;* and before night, having travell'd eighteen *Cos*, we staid to lodge in a great Town call'd *Giambaser*.[2] On *Thursday,*

---

[1] Generally known as " Toddy". Also called " Terry" by Man-delslo. As to the epithet " poignant", Dryden makes use of the expression " poignant sauce". An interesting and learned article on " Spirituous Drinks in Ancient India", by Babu Rajendralala Mitra, will be found in the *Journal of the Asiatic Society*, vol. xlii, part I, 1873.

[2] That is, Jambusir, in lat. 22° 10′ N.

two hours before day, we arose to go along with a great *Cafila*, or *Caravan*, which was there united ; nevertheless we departed not so soon, but were fain to wait in the Coach till almost day, because the City was lock'd up, and none was suffer'd to go forth without paying a Toll, as likewise was paid in many other places the same day, though of small value. The *Cafila* was so great, and the Coaches so many, that in certain narrow places we were fain to stay a good while before we could go forwards, just as it happens in the streets of *Naples* and *Rome* at solemn pomps.

Having travell'd about five *Cos*, an hour after Sun-rise we came to an arm of the Sea, or, to speak better, to the inmost part of the Gulph of *Cambaia*, directly where the River *Mehi*[1] falls into the Sea : in which place the flux and reflux of the Sea is more impetuous and violent, and with a more rapid current, than perhaps in any other part of the world, at least any whereof I have Knowledge. But before I proceed further, 'tis needful here to correct an enormous error of many of our Geographers, even Moderns, which hath likewise given occasion of mistake to many Historians. In almost all the Mapps which hitherto I have seen the River *Indus* is always describ'd falling into the Sea at the inmost recess of the Gulph of *Cambaia;* which is a grievous error, and as wide from truth as the whole Country of *Guzarat* is broad, (and 'tis no narrow one): for *Indus* which is discharged into the Sea with two very large

---

[1] Written as "Mhye" in modern maps. The present mouth of the river Indus is in long. 67° 38′ E., about sixty geographical miles from Karachi ; the gulf of Cambay is in long. 72° 20′ E., lat. 21° 40′ N. Between the Indus and Cambay there is a wide expanse of low swampy ground, where rivers like the Indus might be constantly changing their courses ; indeed, we find on old charts of the 17th century the chief arm of the Indus emptying into the gulf near the town of Cambay, not far from the mouth of the Mahi (Mehi). (Cf. Admiralty Chart, and Atlases of Mercator and Blaeu.)

mouths sufficiently distant, runs not on the East of
Guzarat, as it should do if it entered into the Sea by the
Gulph of *Cambaia*, but rather on the West, and so far
from the Gulph of *Cambaia* that all *Guzarat*, and perhaps
some other Countries, lye between. Wherefore the River
which disembogues in the inmost part of this Gulph is not
Indus, but this *Mehi* which I speak of, a River of handsome but ordinary greatness, and which hath not the least
correspondence with *Indus*. Now, being come to the side
of it, we were fain to ford over this Water, and not without
danger : for there is a plain of about five *Cos*, which is all
over-flow'd at high Tide ; and, when the water is lowest, in
three or four places there are waters sufficiently broad and
deep to be forded ; and should the Sea happen to come in
whilst a man is in that passage he would infallibly be
drown'd. And besides, even in those places which are
always fordable, when the Water is a little higher, or the
current more furious than ordinary (for 'tis not always
equal, but more or less according to the times of the
Moon) it often carries away people,[1] and sometimes with
such violence, that an Elephant cannot bear up against it,
but is swept away by the Water. Therefore they wait
certain fit hours to pass this ford, namely, when the Sea is
at the lowest Ebb, which, if I mistake not, in all other
places of the World is wont to be when the Moon is either
rising or setting in the Horizon ; as, on the contrary, when
the Moon is in the middle of Heaven, the Tide uses to be
at the highest. But in the Gulph of *Cambaia*, I know not
upon what reason, perhaps because 'tis much within the
Land, and far from the great mass of the Ocean, it happens
at another different hour, yet well known to the Country-
people. The more cautious, wait also the most fitting

---

[1] High spring-tides rise as much as 33 feet. (See Hunter's
Gazetteer.)

days in the moneth ; because at the New Moon and Full
Moon the Waters are always greater and higher ; and,
without comparison, highest and most impetuous of all
about the Æquinoxes and Solstices. In the quarters of
the Moon the Tides are moderate, and in other inter-
mediate days lower than the rest. So that we being come
to this place a few days before the New Moon, were come
in a good time and likewise in a seasonable hour, the
Cafila, or *Caravan*, having set forth from the City in such
a moment as was exactly convenient for ordering matters
right, for the owners of the Coaches, and the others
employ'd in this journey are well instructed of every
thing, and know what they have to do. So, being united
in a great troop the better to break the stream, we pass'd
over all that space of five *Cos*, which was moist yet firm
ground, saving in four places where we forded the run-
ning-water of the River, which nevertheless is salt there,
the great strength of the Sea overcoming that of the River.
Of the four streams which we waded the first was con·
siderable ; the other three came higher than the belly of the
Oxen which drew the Coaches, into which nevertheless the
water enter'd not, because their floor, and especially the
wheels are very high : and you sit, according to the manner
of the East, as upon plain ground, without hanging the
Legs downwards, but keeping them bow'd under you.
For greater security they hir'd sundry men on foot, who
held the Coaches on either side steadfast with their hands,
that so in regard of their lightness they might not float
and be carry'd away ; and also to carry our bundles high
on their heads,[1] that so the same might not be wetted if the
Water should come into the body of the Coaches. The
men who go on foot in this passage either strip themselves
naked, covering only their privities with a little cloth, or

---

[1] Palanquins with travellers in them are sometimes transported
over deep water in this fashion.

F

pulling up their coat, which, as I said, is of plain white
linnen, and serves both for garment and shirt, and also
tucking up their breeches made of the same, they care not
for wetting themselves. 'Tis certainly an odd thing to
behold in this passage, which is very much frequented,
abundance of people go every day in this manner, some in
Coaches and Chariots, others on Horseback and on foot,
men and also women naked, without being shie who sees
them[1]; a spectacle, no doubt, sufficiently extravagant.
This wet passage being over, there remain two other *Cos*,
but of firm and higher ground (which is not overflow'd,
although it be plain and the Sea-shore) to arrive at the
City of *Cambaia*, whither we came before dinner-time,
having travell'd that day in all twelve *Cos*. And here
likewise we went to lodge in the House which belongs to
the Dutch Merchants, by whom we were received with
great kindness, and treated continually with exquisite
chear; for such was the order of the Commendator concerning us in all places.

XIII.—*Cambaia*[2] is a City indifferently large, though

---

[1] See a description of a sim ilar scene in Dubois' *Mœurs des
Peuples de l'Inde*, vol. i, p. 480, who says that on such occasions the
men go in front of the women, and "jamais on n'en vit un commettre
l'indiscretion qui fit perdre à Orphée son Eurydice".

[2] Now called Cambay, in lat. 22°17' N., in the province of Guzerat.
Called Cumanes by Ptolemy and Kinbaiat by Ibn Batuta. Described
by Barbosa (Hakluyt edit., p. 64). Formerly a flourishing seaport,
but the sea considerably receded from it. Taken by the Muhammadans in the 13th century, and by the British in 1780, by whom it
was restored to the Mahrattas in 1783, and again taken from them in
1803. Sometimes called "the India Cairo". (See Sir H. Yule's
Cathay, vol. ii, p. 355, and *Marco Polo*, vol. ii, p. 389.) The city was
originally surrounded by a brick wall perforated for musketry. Only
portions of this wall remain, enclosing a circumference of not more
than three miles. Many ruins attest the former wealth of Cambay
spoken of by Masudi in 915 A.D. and by Ibn Batuta, Marco Polo (*circ.*
1293), and his contemporary, Marino Samido. It was still in high
prosperity in the early part of the 16th century. Its proper Hindu-

most of its greatness consists in Suburbs without the walls, which are sufficiently spacious. 'Tis seated on the Seashore, in a plain, almost in the utmost recess of that great Gulph whereunto it gives its name. The City, that is the inner part without the Suburbs, is incompass'd with walls, built with plain cortines[1] and round battlements. The Houses within are roofed with coverings of Tiles and Cisterns,[2] which is the custom in *India* for provision of Water, which falls in such plenty during those three moneths of the great Summer rains. In our Countries they would be ordinary Houses, but in these parts they are counted good, and perhaps the best of the whole Province; and they are made shady and cool, as the heat of the place requires. The City hath no form'd Port, because it stands in a low Plain, but 'tis call'd a Port, by reason of the great concourse of Vessels thither from several parts, which nevertheless for the most part are Frigots, Galeots, and other small ones of that make, which go either by oar or sail, because great ones cannot come near the Land by a great way.

The people of *Cambaia* are most part Gentiles ; and here, more than elsewhere, their vain superstitions are observed with rigor. Wherefore we, who came particularly to see these things, the same day of our arrival, after we had din'd and rested a while, caus'd ourselves to be conducted to see a famous Hospital of Birds[3] of all sorts,

---

stani name, according to Col. Todd, was " Khambavati", " the City of the Pillar"; a copper pillar having been erected there by one of the Hindu kings.

[1] Generally written as " curtains", the rampart between two bastions. In Italian *cortina*.

[2] This word should be " gutters". Barbosa (Hakluyt edit., p. 64) notes the roofs as being " in the Spanish fashion".

[3] Institutions of this kind are still kept up in India. They are generally founded and supported by members of the Jain religion. They are mentioned by Arrian.

which for being sick, lame, depriv'd of their mates, or otherwise needing food and care, are kept and tended there with
diligence ; as also the men who take care of them are
maintain'd by the publick alms ; the Indian Gentiles, who,
with *Pythagoras* and the ancient *Ægyptians* (the first
Authors of this opinion according to *Herodotus*) believe
in the Transmigration of Souls, not onely from Man to
Man, but also from Man to brute beast, conceiving it no
less a work of Charity to do good to beasts then to Men.
The House of this Hospital is small, a little room sufficing
for many Birds : yet I saw it full of Birds of all sorts
which need tendance, as Cocks, Hens, Pigeons, Peacocks,
Ducks and small Birds, which during their being lame, or
sick, or mateless, are kept here, but being recover'd and
in good plight, if they be wild they are let go at liberty ;
if domestick they are given to some pious person who keeps
them in his House.   The most curious thing I saw in this
place were certain little Mice, who being found Orphans
without Sire or Dam to tend them, were put into this
Hospital, and a venerable Old Man with a white Beard,
keeping them in a box amongst Cotton, very diligently
tended them with his spectacles on his nose, giving them
milk to eat with a bird's feather, because they were so
little that as yet they could eat nothing else ; and, as he told
us, he intended when they were grown up to let them go
free whither they pleas'd.

From this place we went out of the city to the Sea-side,
to see a Garden sometimes belonging to the Kings of
Guzarat. 'Tis small, adorn'd with the same Trees as that
which I saw in *Surát*, with some also of ours, as the
Figtrees and Coleworts of *Europe*, which in *India* are
accounted rare things.   There is a running water which at
the entrance falls from a great *Kiosck*, or cover'd place to
keep it cool, standing upon a great Piscina, or Lake,
contiguous to the Garden on the outside, and serving

like that of *Suràt* to the common uses of the City. Besides which, in this Garden there is nothing worth notice.

Going from hence we went to see upon the same Lake a *Meschita*,[1] or Temple of the Mahometans, whereunto there is continually a great concourse of people with ridiculous and foolish devotions, not onely Mahometans but likewise Gentiles. In the street before the Gate many persons sitting on the ground asked Alms, to whom the passers-by cast, some Rice, others certain other corn, but no Money. Within the *Meschita*, in a narrow dark place by a wall's side, is a kind of little Pyramid of Marble, and this they call *Pir*, that is *Old*, which they say is equivalent to Holy : I imagine it the Sepulchre of some one of their Sect accounted such. The people enter in with great crowds, especially Women, who use to be more forward in these things than others. All who go in strew Flowers or Rice there ; to which end stand divers persons near the Gate that sell Flowers to whoso pleases for such offerings : but this is rather a Custom of the Gentiles than Mahometans ; and the Gentiles being more numerous and ancient in Cambaia, 'tis no wonder that some Rite of theirs hath adher'd to the Mahometans.[2]

A little distant from this place we saw another Sepulchre, ador'd too of some Mahometan (for the Gentiles, who burne their dead, have no Sepulchres) built with a great roof four square, supported by divers pillars, and under it a

---

[1] Generally written Mosque. More correctly "Masjid". This was probably the Jama Masjid, erected in 1325 A.D.

[2] The Muhammadans of India have, no doubt, become Hindooized to a certain extent. Most of them are subject to caste prejudices, and the mass, who are ignorant and uneducated, have a tendency to deify Muhammad himself, or the innumerable Muhammadan saints (*Pirs*) whose tombs are scattered throughout India, to revere relics of Muhammad, and even to pay reverence to so-called impresses of his feet. (See Sir Monier Williams' *Mod. India*, p. 165.)

place open on all sides like a Porch; this also many persons. came to kiss and venerate. Beyond the above-mentioned Garden, upon the Sea-side, we saw another Sepulchre of a Mahometan of quality, having a high round Cupola, like a Tower, which is ascended by a little ladder, and there you have a most goodly prospect upon the Sea and Land to a great distance.

These things being seen, we return'd home the same way we came. The next Morning, going about the City, we saw another Hospital of Goats, Kids, Sheep and Wethers, either sick or lame, and there were also some Cocks, Peacocks and other Animals needing the same help, and kept altogether quietly enough in a great Court; nor wanted there Men and Women lodg'd in little rooms of the same Hospital, who had care of them. In another place, far from hence, we saw another Hospital of Cows and Calves, some whereof had broken Legs, others more infirm, very old, or lean, and therefore were kept here to be cur'd. Among the beasts there was also a Mahometan Thief, who having been taken in Theft had both his hands cut off. But the compassionate Gentiles, that he might not perish miserably now he was no longer able to get his living, took him into this place, and kept him among the poor beasts, not suffering him to want anything. Moreover, without one of the Gates of the City, we saw another great troop of Cows, Calves and Goats, which being cur'd and brought into better plight, or gather'd together from being dispers'd and without Masters, or being redeem'd with Money from the Mahometans who would have killed them to eat, (namely, the Goats and other Animals, but not the Cows and Calves) were sent into the field to feed by neat-herds, purposely maintain'd at the publick charge; and thus they are kept till being reduc'd to perfect health 'tis found fitting to give them to some Citizens, or others who may charitably keep them. I excepted Cows and Calves from the Animals redeem'd from slaughter, because in *Cambaia* Cows, Calves and Oxen, are not killed by any, and there's a great prohibition against it, by the instance of the Gentiles, who upon this account pay a great sum of Money to the Prince, and should any, either Mahometan or other, be found to kill them, he would be punish'd severely, even with death.

At Night we had Musick at home, made by some Mahometan Women Singers and Dancers, (for among the Gentiles none practise such Arts) who with their Indian Instruments, which are Drums, Bells ty'd to the Arms, and the like, all of great noise, gave us divertisement, playing, dancing and singing whilst we were at Supper : but their Musick being too full of noise, was to me rather distasteful then pleasing.

The next Morning we saw in the City a Temple of Idols, one of the best which the Gentiles have in *Cambaia*. The form of it is a perfect square, with walls round about supporting a flat roof, which is also upheld in the middle by four pillars dispos'd in a square too ; within which, upon the little space remaining, is advanc'd somewhat higher then the roof, and yet of a square form, a kind of *Cupoletta*, or little Chappel. In the principal part of this Temple stand in three great *Nieches* so many great Idols, made of white Marble, and naked, (as the Indians paint all their Idols). They are in a sitting posture, yet after the manner of the East, as they use to sit upon the ground with the Legs gather'd under ; but they sit in a place somewhat higher then the floare, as it were upon a large Pedestal. These *Nieches* are inclos'd with doors made with lattices, that so the Idols may be seen without opening them ; but they are open'd upon occasion for any that are minded to go in : they were so for us, but we entred not, because the *Nieches* are so small that we saw everything well enough from the doors.

The principal Idol in this Temple is that which stands in
the middle *Nieche*, call'd *Mahavir*, from whom the Temple
is denominated. Who this *Mahavir* is, and whether he be
all one with *Mahadeu*,[1] as I have some suspicion, I do not
yet know ; because the Indians who talkt with us, either
in the *Portugal* or *Persian*-Tongue, being all Factors or
Merchants, and consequently unlearned, could not give us
any account of these things ; besides they speak those Languages ill, and are not intelligible saving in buying and
selling. With other learned Gentiles, to whom alone their
Indian Speech is familiar, we could not discourse for want
of Language ; wherefore of all these things and all the
particularities of their Religion I reserve myself to be
further informed at *Goa*, if it shall please God, where I
shall have better convenience and more time, and meet
with some learned Brachman, perhaps turn'd Christian, and
able to give me a more certain Relation hereof in either
Portuguez or *Latine* ; and if he be a Christian, he will, no
doubt, give it me more truly then the Gentiles, who I
believe talk with us concerning their own matters neither
willingly nor sincerely. Wherefore referring myself to the
better intelligence which I hope to have there, I shall here
only relate what I saw with mine own eyes, and something
more which I attain'd to understand, without suspicion of
error.

Before the Idol without the *Nieche* hung a Bell, (as 'tis
the custom in all their Temples) which, as I said before, all
those who come to make their prayers ring at their first
entrance. Within this and the other *Nieches* on the sides
were one or two lighted Candles. In the other sides of the
Temple, something higher then the pavement, were in the
wall certain little *Nieches*, in each of which stood an Idolet,

---

[1] Or Mahadeo, a title of Siva, the third person of the Hindu
Triad, who is also sometimes called Mahavir.

or little Idol, some in the shape of Men, others of Women. One there was which had many Arms on a side, and many Faces, and this they said was call'd *Brachma*,[1] one of their chief false Deities. Another had the head of an Elephant, and was call'd *Ganescio*[2] : They say, he is the Son of *Mahadeu*, who finding him one day with Parveti his wife, but his own Mother, and not knowing who he was, kill'd him out of jealousie, cutting off his Head ; but afterwards understanding that he was his own Son, he repented him of his error, and resolv'd to bring him to life again. Wherefore meeting with an Elephant, (as he had purpos'd to do with what he first happen'd upon) he cut off his Head, and plac'd it on his dead Son's Shoulders. Whereupon *Ganescio* reviv'd, and thenceforward liv'd immortal with an Elephant's Head. But behold another delusion ! One there is with the Head, I know not whether of a Tyger or Lyon, probably 'tis that *Narosinha*[3] which I formerly writ that I saw in *Combru*,[4] in the maritime parts of *Persia*.

Some of these Idolets sat upon Sundry Animals, as Tygers and the like, and even upon Rats ; of which things the foolish and ignorant Indians relate ridiculous stories. But I doubt not that, under the veil of these Fables, their ancient Sages (most parsimonious of the Sciences, as all Barbarians ever were) have hid from the vulgar many secrets, either of Natural or Moral Philosophy, and perhaps

---

[1] Or Brahma, the first person of the Hindu Triad. The name is from a Sanskrit root meaning "to pervade".

[2] Or Ganesa, the god who removes difficulties, son of Siva and Parvati. As to the origin of his elephant head various fables are told.

[3] A kind of Sphinx ; literally, "Man lion", a figure common to the Egyptians, Persians, and Assyrians, as well as to the Hindus. In this instance the figure probably represented Vishnu, in his fourth incarnation, in the form of a lion with human head and hands. As to the Persian figures referred to here, see Heeren's *Historical Researches*, vol. i, p. 100.

[4] See Letter No. XVI.

also of History: and I hold for certain that all these so monstrous figures have secretly some more rational significations, though express'd in this uncouth manner; as we know in ancient time among the Gentiles of our Countries there was in the figures of quadrifronted *Janus*,[1] of Jupiter Ammon with the Head of a Ram,[2] of *Anubis* with the Head of a Dog,[3] and many other extravagances, not onely of the *Grecians* and *Ægyptians*, but also of the *Romans*.

The Ceiling, Pillars, and Walls of this Temple were adorn'd with Painting, especially red, which how dear 'tis to the *Indians* I formerly intimated. The doors of their Houses, namely the Posts, Architraves, and Barrs that fasten it, are all colour'd so; adding some mixture of white limes to the red; for of white too they are so enamour'd that all Men are generally clothed with it; a custom peradventure deriv'd to them from *Ægypt* where it was in use, as *Herodotus*[4] writes, and whence perhaps *Pythagoras* himself learnt it, who went cloth'd in white, as we find noted by *Aelian*[5] and others. And I observe that in many particulars the manners of the present *Indians* much resemble those of the ancient *Ægyptians*; but since the *Ægyptians*, who descended from *Cham* the son of *Noah*, were a very ancient people, I rather believe that the *Indians* learnt from the *Ægyptians*[6] than the *Ægyptians* from the *Indians*; and 'tis known, that from *Ægypt* there was always Navigation and Commerce into *India* by the Southern Ocean. The red colour amongst these *Indians*

---

[1] Emblematical of the four seasons.

[2] Because Jupiter is said to have appeared to Bacchus in the form of a ram.

[3] So represented because he watched by day and night.

[4] Lib. ii. [5] *Var. Hist.*, lib. xii, c. 32.

[6] On this point see Heeren's *Historical Researches*, vol. ii, p. 303, and Dubois, *Mœurs des Peuples de l'Inde*, vol. ii, p. 313. Both authors are opposed to this theory. See also *Transactions of Royal Asiatic Society*, vol. i, p. 579.

is, besides by the Women, worn also by the *Sami*,[1] who are a kind of religious persons ; with red the *Gioghi*, who live like Hermits and go about begging, sometimes paint their bodies in many parts, and also with red blended with yellow, that is with some parcel of Sanders or Saffron, almost all the Indian Gentiles dye their fore-heads, and sometimes their garments ; accordingly as *Strabo*[2] reports, from the testimony of *Onesicritus*,[3] they did likewise in the time of *Alexander* the Great. Lastly, they wear red Turbans upon their Heads, and their Girdles are oftner wrought with red then any other colour.

After having seen the Temple of *Mahavir* we went to visit an old Brachman, accounted very learned amongst them, with whom we discours'd as well as we could by an interpreter, because he understood no other Language but the *Indian*. We found him amongst many Scholars, to whom he was giving a Lecture. He shew'd us his Books written in an antique Character, which is the learned amongst them, not common to the vulgar, but known onely to the learned, and us'd by the Brachmans, who, in distinction from other vulgar Characters us'd variously in sundry Provinces of *India*, call it *Nagheri*.[4] I have and shall carry with me two small Books of it which I sometime bought in *Lar*.[5] This Brachman is call'd *Beca Azàrg;* of which words *Beca* is his proper Name and *Azarg* his Title of Honour.

Amongst other Books he shew'd us that of their sect, in which, though it was bound long ways, as 'tis the fashion of their Books, yet the lines were written across the paper, after the manner of some of our Musick-Books. He

---

[1] That is, *Swami*, or " Lords" (Sanskrit).   [2] Lib. xv.

[3] Onesicritus accompanied Alexander the Great to India, and wrote a (doubtful) history of the expedition.

[4] *I.e.*, the *Deva Nagari*, or " Divine Alphabet".

[5] Capital of Laristan in Persia.

affirm'd to us for certain that it was a work of *Pythagoras*, which well agreeth with what *Philostratus*[1] saith that *Jarchas* told *Apollonius*, namely that the Indians believ'd the same concerning the soul which *Pythagoras* had taught them, and they the *Aegyptians;* which is quite contrary to what I said before was my opinion as to which of these' two Nations first taught the other. But *Diogenes Laertius*,[2] who writes *Pythagoras's* Life copiously enough, making mention of his going into Aegypt, and how he convers'd likewise with the *Chaldæns* and *Magi*, yet speaks not a word that ever he went into *India*, or had communication with the Brachmans. Wherefore, if *Pythogoras* taught anything to the *Indians*, as *Jarchas* said, he did it not in person,[3] but by his books, which possibly were carry'd into *India*. Moreover *Beca Azarg* added that their *Brachma*, esteemed one of the chief among their false Gods, (from whom they are denominated Brachmans) is all one with *Pythagoras :* a curious notion indeed, and which perhaps would be news to hear in *Europe*, that *Pythagoras* is foolishly ador'd in *India* for a God. But this, with *Beca Azarg's* good leave, I do not believe ; either he did not expressly speak thus, and by the fault of the Interpreters we did not understand him aright ; or, if he did affirm it, perhaps he came to be mistaken by having heard *Pythagoras* nam'd by some Europeans for the author of that foolish opinion of the Transmigration of Souls. Be it as it will, I cannot believe that *Pythagoras* and *Brachma* are all one ; because though *Pythagoras* be very ancient, for he flourished in the Consul-

---

[1] *De Vita Apoll.*, lib. iii, cap. 6. Flavius Philostratus lived between 190 and 244 A.D. He wrote the Life of Apollonius Tyanæus here referred to, and other works.

[2] Lib. viii. Diogenes Laertius, author of the *Lives of the Philosophers*, lived about 200 A.D.

[3] As to the question whether Pythagoras ever personally visited India see Max Müller's *Science of Languages*, p. 86.

ship of *Brutus* who expell'd the Kings out of *Rome*, yet
I hold the Rites and opinions of the Brachmans much
more ancient. For when *Diodorus*[1] relates the contest of
the two Wives of *Ceteus*, an Indian Captain in the Army
of *Eumenes*,[2] each of whom would be burnt with her
Husband slain in battel, speaking of the Laws, Customs
and Rites of the *Indians*, he calls them, even at that time,
Ancient things. And though *Pythagoras* and the Consul-
ship of *Brutus* may precede not onely *Eumenes*, who was
one of *Alexander* the Great's successors, but *Alexander*
himself, by about two ages, according to the Chronology of
Bellarmine,[3] which to me seems good enough, yet the
space of two hundred years, or somewhat more, is not such
as that those things may be call'd Ancient which had their
beginning within so short a term ; as it should be infallibly
if *Pythagoras*, whom they take to be their *Brachma*, were
the first Author to the Indians of their Learning, and
consequently of their Rites, Customs and Laws. But
since I have already made frequent mention of the Brachmans, and perhaps shall have occasion to do the same
hereafter, to the end it may be understood what they are,
I shall here subjoyn so much as I have hitherto attain'd to
know concerning them and all the other Indians.

XIV.—The whole Gentile-people of *India* is divided into
many sects or parties[4] of men, known and distinguisht by
descent or pedigree, as the Tribes of the Jews sometimes

---

[1] Lib. xix. Diodorus Siculus lived in the reign of the Emperor
Augustus. He was a contemporary of Cicero, and author of a history
of Egypt, Persia, Syria, Media, Greece, Rome, and Carthage.

[2] One of Alexander's generals.

[3] Robert Bellarmino, a learned Italian Jesuit cardinal, lived in the
sixteenth century. Among other books, he wrote one attacking a
work written by King James I of England on the *Divine Right of
Kings*.

[4] These are generally called "castes", from the Spanish or Portuguese
word *casta*, a breed.

were ; yet they inhabit the Country promiscuously mingled together, in every City and Land several Races one with another. 'Tis reckon'd that they are in all eighty four[1] ; some say more, making a more exact and subtle division. Every one of these hath a particular name, and also a special office and Employment in the Commonwealth, from which none of the descendants of that Race ever swerve ; they never rise nor fall, nor change condition : whence some are Husbandmen, others Mechanicks, as Taylers, Shoe-makers and the like ; others Factors or Merchants, such as they whom we call *Banians*,[2] but they in their Language more correctly *Vania ;* others, Souldiers, as the *Ragia-puti*[3]*;* and thus every one attends and is employ'd in the proper Trade of his Family, without any mutation ever hap-ning amongst them, or Alliance of one Race contracted with another. *Diodorus*[4] and *Strabo*[5] (almost with the same words, as if the one had transcrib'd the other) affirm that anciently the Races of the Indians were seven,[6] each addicted to their proper profession ; and for the first of all they place that of the Philosophers, who, no doubt, are the Brachmans. Into seven kinds of men with their particular, and by Generation perpetuate, Offices, *Herodotus*[7] in like manner writes, (and *Diodorus*[8] confirms it, though he dis-

---

[1] The actual number of castes in India in the present day is said to be 1,929. Among them are castes of thieves. (See *India*, by Sir J. Strachey.)   [2] From Sanskrit *Banija*, or "trader."

[3] *Raj-pūts*, or "sons of kings".

[4] Lib. ii.   [5] Lib. xv.

[6] There is no good ground for this statement as applied to caste. The earliest known division of the people into castes is that found in the *Institutes of Menu*, who defines *four* castes only. The supposed division into *seven* classes or castes is mentioned by the early Greek authors, who confounded some distinctions occasioned by civil employ-ment with those arising from the actual division described in the *Institutes of Menu*. (See Elphinstone's *India*, p. 236, and Dubois, *Mœurs des Peuples de l'Inde*, vol. i, ch. i.)

[7] Lib. ii.   [8] Lib. viii.

agrees in the number) the people of *Ægypt* was divided in those days ; whereby 'tis manifest what correspondence there was between *Ægypt* and *India* in all things. Nor do I wonder at the division into seven Races onely, because what is observ'd at this day must then also have hapned, namely that the so many Races which they reckon are reduc'd to four principal, which, if I mistake not, are the Brachmans, the Souldiers, the Merchants and the Artificers ; from whom by more minute subdivision all the rest are deriv'd, in such number as in the whole people there are various professions of men. In the substantial points of Religion all agree together ; all believe the Transmigration of Souls,[1] which according to their merits and demerits (as they think) are sent by God into other bodies, either of Animals more or less clean, and of more or less painful life, or else of men more or less noble and handsome, and more or less pure of Race, wherein they place not a little of their vain superstition ; accounting all other Nations and Religions besides themselves unclean, and some more then others, according as they more or less differ from their Customs. All equally believe that there is a Paradise in Heaven with God, but that thereinto go onely the Souls of their own Nation, more pure and without any sin, who have liv'd piously in this world ; or in case they have sin'd, after divers Transmigrations[2] into various bodies of Animals and Men, having by often returning into the world undergone many pains, they are at length purg'd, and at last dye in the body of some man of Indian and noble Race, as the Brachmans,

---

[1] This statement is not quite accurate. (See Dubois, *Mœurs des Peuples de l'Inde*, vol. ii, ch. 2, part III.)

[2] The first reference to this doctrine among the Hindoos is said by Professor Max Müller to be found in the *Upanishad*. The doctrine is well known to have prevailed among other people also, and apparently even among the Jews. (See Gospel of St. John, ch. ix, v. 2.)

who amongst them are held the noblest and purest; because their employment is nothing else but the Divine
Worship, the service of Temples and Learning, and because they observe their own Religion with more rigor then
any others.

'Tis true the Brachmans, who amongst the Indians, in
my opinion, much resemble the Levites of the Jews, are
divided too into several sorts, one more noble than another,
and, according to nobility, more rigorous also in manner of
eating, and in their other superstitious Ceremonies; for
some of them are Astrologers, some Physicians, some
Secretaries of Princes ; and so of other sorts of scholars
which I know not well ; but the most esteem'd and most
sublime amongst the Brachmans, and consequently the
most rigorous of all in point of eating and other observ-
ances, are those who perform the Office of Priests, whom
they call *Boti*.[1] Ordinarily they never admit[2] into their
Sect any man of another Religion ; nor do they think that
they do ill herein, or contrary to the zeal of saving Souls,
since, believing the Transmigration, they conceive it not
necessary to Salvation to change Religion, although one be
of a false Sect, but judge that if this Soul shall be worthy
to have pardon from God, it shall after death, and after
being purg'd sundry ways, pass into and be born in the
body of some Indian amongst them, and live excellently,
and so by this way at last arrive at Paradise and live with
God, although in the beginning it was in the world in the
body of the worst sinner and miscreant what ever. With
people of other Religion they never eat nor will have any

---

[1] For Bhāt, or Bhūt, a common title among the Mahratta Brahmans.

[2] This assertion is not strictly true. Sir Monier Williams (*Modern
India*, p. 157) says : "It is very true that a Brahman *nascitur non fit*,
but it is equally true that Hinduism could not have extended itself
over India if it had never exerted itself to make proselytes."

communication of food, and as much as possible they
avoid even to touch them ; conceiving themselves polluted
by communication with others. And herein they are so
scrupulous that even amongst the Indians themselves one
of more noble Race not only neither eats, nor makes use
of the same Clothes or Vessels, nor communicates in anything with one less noble, but also endures not to be
touch'd by him ; which if it fall out by chance that he be,
he must purifie himself from the defilement by washings
and other arrogant Ceremonies. And hence 'tis a pretty
sight to behold the great respect which upon this account
the ignoble bear to the more noble then themselves, and
how upon meeting in the street the ignoble not onely give
place, but dance wildly up and down for fear of rushing
against the noble, and polluting them in any measure ;
which, if they should not do, the Noble, and especially
the Souldiers, would make them do it to the Musick of
blows.

From this averseness to communicate one with another,
particularly in the use of eating and drinking vessels, concerning which they are most strict, is sprung a strange
Custom, which I was delighted not only to see, but also
sometimes out of gallantry to imitate in conversation. It
happens very often during hot weather, both in Travelling
and in Towns, that people have need of refreshing themselves and drinking of a little water ; but because every
one hath not a drinking-vessel of his own ready, to avoid
defiling or being defil'd by his companion's cup, there's a
way found out whereby any person may drink in that, or
any other whatever, without scruple or danger of any either
active or passive contamination. This is done by drinking
in such manner that the vessel touches not the lips or
mouth of him who drinks ; for it is held up on high with
the hand over the mouth, and he that lifts it up highest,
and holds it furthest from his mouth, shows himself most

G

mannerly ; and thus pouring the liquor out of the cup into
the mouth, they drink round while there is any left, or so
long as they please.   So accustom'd are the Indians to
drink in this manner that they practice it almost continually with their own vessels for delight, without the
necessity of shunning communication with others ; and
they are so dextrous at it, that I remember to have seen
one of them take with both hands a vessel as big as a basin,
and lifting it up above a span higher than his mouth,
poure a great torrent of water into his throat and drink it
all off.   Having been frequently present at such occasions,
that where ever I came the Indians might not be shie of
reaching me a cup of water, I purposely set myself to learn
this manner of drinking, which I call *drinking in the Air*,
and at length have learned it ; not with cups as big as
basins, like his abovesaid, but with a handsome cruze, like
those we use, or with a little bottle or drinking glass made
on purpose.   I do it very well ; sometimes in conversation
we drink healths, *all 'Indiana*, after this fashion, with consent that all do reason in the same manner ; and he that
cannot do it right either wets himself well, or falls a
coughing and yexing,[1] which gives occasion of laughter.

But to return to the opinions of the Indians : As for
good works and sins, they all agree with the Doctrine of
Morality and the universal consent of Mankind, that there
are differences of Virtue and Vice in all the world.   They
hold not onely Adultery, but even simple Fornication,
a great sin ; nor do they account it lawful, as the
Mahometans do, to have commerce with female slaves, or
with others besides their own Wives.   Yea, slaves of either
sex they no-wise admit, but hold it a sin ; making
use of free persons for their service, and paying them
wages, as we do in *Europe*.   Which likewise was their

---

[1] An obsolete word, meaning "to hiccough".

ancient custom, as appears by *Strabo*,[1] who cites *Megasthenes* and other Authors of those times for it. They detest Sodomy above measure, and abhor the Mahometans whom they observe addicted to it.[2] They take but one Wife and never divorce her till death, except for the cause of Adultery. Indeed some, either by reason of the remoteness of their Wives, or out of a desire to have children in case the first Wife be barren, or because they are rich and potent, and are minded to do what none can forbid them, sometimes take more Wives; but 'tis not counted well done, unless they be Princes, who always in all Nations are privileged in many things. When the Wife dyes they marry another if they please ; but if the Husband dye the Woman never marries more[3] ; were she so minded, nor could she find any of her own Race who would take her, because she would be accounted as bad as infamous in desiring a second Marriage. A very hard Law indeed, and from which infinite inconveniences arise ; for not a few young Widows, who in regard of their Reputation cannot marry again and have not patience to live chastly, commit disorders in private, especially with men of other Nations and Religions, and with any they find, provided it be secret. Some Widows are burnt alive together with the bodies of their dead Husbands ; a thing which anciently not onely the Indian Women did, according to what *Strabo*[4]

---

[1] Lib. xv.

[2] Dubois, in his *Mœurs des Peuples de l'Inde*, gives a less favourable account of Hindu morality. (See vol. i, p. 434 *et seq.*)

[3] Among the benefits conferred on India by the British Government, one is the Act passed in 1856, by which Hindoo widows can be legally remarried. The word " woman" used here would be more correctly rendered " wife", for remarriage, previously to 1856, was forbidden equally to children married to husbands whom they had often never even seen, as to adult women. In a paper read at the Church Congress in October 1890, it is stated that "there are at present 79,000 widows under nine years of age in India".

[4] Lib. xv, cap. 15.

writes from the Relation of *Onesicritus;* but also the chaste Wives of the *Thracians,* as appears by *Julius Solinus.* But this burning of Women upon the death of their Husbands is at their own choice to do it or not, and indeed few practice it ; but she who does it acquires in the Nation a glorious name of Honour[1] and Holiness. 'Tis most usual among great persons, who prize Reputation at a higher rate than others do ; and in the death of Personages of great quality, to whom their Wives desire to do Honour by burning themselves quick. I heard related at my first coming that a *Ragiá,*[2] that is an Indian Prince (one of the many which are subject to the Moghol), being slain in a battle, seventeen of his wives were burnt alive together with his body ; which in India was held for great Honour and Magnificence. I have heard say (for I have not seen any Women burnt alive) that when this is to be done the Wife or Wives who are to be burnt inclose themselves in a pile of wood, which is lay'd hollow like the rafters of a house, and the entrance stop'd with great logs, that they may not get out in case they should repent them when the kindled fire begins to offend them : yea, divers men stand about the pile with staves in their hands to stir the fire, and to poure liquors upon it to make it burn faster ; and that if they should see the Women offer to come out, or avoid the flames, they would knock her on the head with their staves and kill her, or else beat her back into the fire ; because 'twould be a great shame to the Woman and all her kindred, if she should go to be burnt, and then, through fear of the fire and death, repent and come out of it. I have likewise heard it said that some Women are burnt against their own will, their Relations resolving to have it so for Honour of the Husband ; and that they have

---

[1] That is, *Sati* (commonly written " Suttee"), meaning "a virtuous woman".   [2] *I.e.*, Raja.

been brought to the fire in a manner by force, and made besides themselves with things given them to eat and drink for this purpose, that they might more easily suffer themselves to be cast into the fire ; but this the Indians directly deny, saying that force is not us'd to any, and it may be true, at least in Countries where Mahometans command, for there no Woman is suffered to be burnt without leave of the Governour of the place, to whom it belongs first to examine whether the women be willing[1] ; and for a Licence there is also paid a good sum of money. Nevertheless 'tis possible too that many Widows, being in the height of their passion taken at their word by their kindred who desire it, go to it afterwards with an ill will, not daring to deny those that exhort them thereunto, especially if oblig'd by their word, nor to discover their own mind freely to the Governour ; things which amongst Women, with their natural fearfulness and modesty, easily happen. And I would to God that in our Countries in sundry cases, as of marrying or not, and the like matters, we had not frequent examples which Women not seldom give of great Resolutions, not forc'd in appearance, but indeed too much forc'd in reality, for avoiding displeasure and other inconveniences.   In the Territories of Christians, where the *Portugals* are Masters, Women are not suffer'd to be burnt,[2] nor is any other exercise of their Religion permitted them.

---

[1] A remarkable and circumstantial account of a case of self-immolation of three wives of one husband is related in the *Journal of the Royal Asiatic Society* (vol. ix, part I, 1876), given at length in the Introduction to the *Commentaries of Afonso Dalboquerque* (Hakluyt edition, vol. ii, p. lxx).

[2] Widow-burning was prohibited by Afonso Dalboquerque when he took the city of Goa (see *Commentaries of Afonso Dalboquerque*, vol. ii, p. 94, Hakluyt edition).   It is a reproach to the British Government that not until the year 1829 was the practice of widow-burning forbidden by law in British territories.   By

Moreover the Indian-Gentiles believe that there is a Devil in the world, almost of the same conditions wherewith we conceive him ; but they think too that many wretched Souls unworthy ever to have pardon from God, as the last of the great punishments which they deserve, become Devils also ; than which they judge there cannot be a greater misery. The greatest sin in the world they account shedding of blood, especially that of men ; and then, above all, the eating of humane flesh, as some barbarous Nations do, who are therefore detested by them more then all others. Hence the strictest among them, as the *Brachmans*,[1] and particularly the *Boti*, not onely kill not, but eat not, any living thing ; and even from herbs tinctur'd with any reddish colour representing blood they wholly abstain. Others of a larger conscience eat onely

---

Reg. XVII of that year (of which the preamble was written by Sir C. E. Grey, Chief Justice of Bengal), the practice was made illegal, though the regulation was not even then passed unanimously by the Council of the Governor-General. Instances of widow-burning have occurred since that (one as recently as about 1870), even in British India. The last conspicuous instance in the native States occurred at Khatmandoo in Nepal, on the death of Maharaja Jung Bahadur, about twelve years ago, when several of his widows were burnt with his corpse. In *The Times* of Sept. 2nd, 1890, is an account of a " Suttee" which recently occurred in China, when the widow strangled herself instead of being burnt. From the printed statements of the Nizamat Adalut (Criminal Court) of Calcutta, it appears that in fourteen years (from 1815 to 1828) there were 8,134 cases (or an average of 581 annually) of widow-burning reported as having occurred within the jurisdiction of that Court. In one year (1818) the number of widows burnt in Bengal alone was 839. (See Sir M. Williams' *Modern India*, p. 315.) A case of forty-seven widows of one husband, a Mahratta Prince, being burnt is recorded.

[1] The sect which holds the strictest views on this subject is that of the Jains. In the *Vedas* the destruction of animal life and eating of flesh are expressly permitted (v. 30). As to the grounds of this antipathy to destruction of life and eating of flesh, see Dubois, *Mœurs des Peuples de l'Inde*, vol. ii, p. 315, who regards it as founded only on a dread of contamination, and a horror of death generally.

fish. Others, the most ignoble and largest of all, though they kill not, nevertheless eat, all sorts of Animals good for food, except Cows[1]; to kill and eat which all in general abhor, saying that the Cow is their Mother, for the Milke she gives and the Oxen she breeds, which plough the Earth and do a thousand other services, especially in *India*, where through the paucity of other Animals they make use of these more then any for all occasions. So that they think they have reason to say that Cows are the prop of the world, which perhaps they would signifie by that Fable, common also to the Mahometans, and by me formerly mention'd, that the world is supported upon the Horns of the Cow. Moreover, they have these creatures in great Veneration; for Cows being kept well in *India*, and living with little pains and much ease, therefore they believe that the best Souls, to whom God is pleased to give little pain in this world, pass into them.

All the Indians use many washings,[2] and some never eat without first washing the whole body. Others will not be seen to eat by any one, and the place where they eat they first sweep, wash and scowre with water and Cow-dung.[3] Which, besides cleanliness, is to them a Ceremonial Rite, which they think hath the virtue to purifie. But having observ'd it too in the houses of Christians, I find that indeed it cleanses exquisitely, and makes the floores and pavements of houses handsome, smooth and bright.

---

[1] The Egyptians held similar scruples as to killing cows, though they killed and ate bulls (*Herod.*, Bk. II, ch. xli). Even in India, however, cows were sacrificed on certain occasions. (See Colebrooke's *Asiatic Researches*, vol. vii, quoted by Mr. Elphinstone in his *History of India*, p. 186.)

[2] This is not quite correct. The Jains, for instance, are said never to bathe; other sects bathe only once in every seven days. (Elphinstone's *India*, p. 109.)

[3] The practice is prevalent at the present day, and is no doubt a beneficial one in regard to cleanliness and destruction of insect pests.

And if the Cows and Bulls whose dung they use eat grass, it gives a pretty green to the pavement ; if straw, a yellowish colour. But for the most part the floores are red, as those of *Venice* are, and I know not with what they give them that colour. But these and other Ceremonies, which I have not seen myself, and know onely by Relation, I willingly pass over. I shall conclude therefore with saying that by the things hitherto mention'd it appears that in the substance of Religion and what is most important all the Races of the Indians agree together, and differ onely perhaps through the necessity which is caus'd by the diversity of humane conditions in certain Rites and Ceremonies, particularly of eating more or less indistinctly.[1] Wherein the *Ragiaputi* Souldiers, with the wonted military licentiousness, take most liberty without thinking themselves prejudic'd as to the degree of nobility. Next to them, the meanest and most laborious Professions are more licentious in eating then others, because they need more sustenance ; some of which drink Wine too, from which the others more strict abstain to avoid ebriety[2]; and so from all other beverage that inebriates.

But those of other Races, whose employments admit more rest and a better life, are also more sparing and rigorous in the use of meats, especially the Brachmans, as I said, dedicated wholly to Learning and the Service of Temples, as the most noble of all. In testimony whereof they alone have the priviledge to wear a certain Ensign of Nobility in their Sect, whereby they are distinguisht from others ; 'tis a fillet of three braids,[3] which they put next

---

[1] For "indiscriminately".

[2] "Ebriety" is used by Browne (*Religio Medici*) and others to signify intoxication.

[3] The sacred thread (Sanskrit, *Upavita*) prescribed for the three higher castes by the *Vedas*, chap. ii, 36-40. It is composed of three cords, each of which is composed of nine threads, to which an addition

the flesh like a Neck-chain, passing from the left shoulder under the right arm, and so round. This fillet hath a mystery, and is given to that Race, and to a few of one other for a great favour, with many superstitious Ceremonies, of which I forbear to speak, because I have not yet any good information thereof. There was a long dispute in *India* between the Jesuits and other Fathers, whether this fillet, which the *Portugals* call *Linha*, was a badge of Religion, or onely an ensign of piety, and whether it was to be permitted or not to Indian Converts, who were very loth to lay it aside. Much hath been said and with great contest by both parties, and at length the cause is carried to *Rome*, and I was inform'd of it two or three years ago in *Persia*. For I remember Sig. *Matteo Galvano Gudigno*, a Canon and Kinsman to the then Archbishop of *Goa*, passed by *Spahan*, and continu'd there many days; being sent by the same Archbishop, who favour'd the side contrary to the Jesuits, purposely to *Rome* with many writings touching this affair, which he out of courtesie communicated to me. I know not whether the final determination of it be yet come from *Rome;* some say it is, and in favour of the Jesuits : but at *Goa* we shall know these things better. The truth is, the Jesuits prove, (on one side) that the honour of wearing this Ribbon is frequently granted not onely to the Indians, but also to strangers of different Nation and Sect ; as to Mahometans, who (by condescension of that King who among the Indians hath authority to do it, as Head of their Sect in Spirituals) have in recompence of great and honourable services enjoy'd this priviledge, without becoming Gentiles, or changing their Religion, but still persisting to live Mahometans ; which indeed is a strong Argument. On

---

is made on marriage. A detailed account of the ceremony of investiture with this sacred thread is given in Dubois' *Mœurs des Peuples de l'Inde*, vol. ii, part II, chap. I.

the other side, they prove that many Brachmans and others of the Race priviledg'd to wear it, intending to lead a stricter life, and abandon the world by living almost like Hermits, amongst other things, in humility lay aside this Ribban, being a token of Nobility ; which 'tis not likely they would do if it were a Cognizance of Religion ; yea, they would wear it the more. But this second argument seems not to be one so cogent, because amongst us Christians, if a Knight of the order of *Calatrava*,[1] or the like, which are ensignes of Nobility, in order to a more holy life enter into some Religion, either of Fryers, Monks or other Regulars, 'tis clear that taking the Religious Habit he lays aside the body of his Knighthood, although it be that Cross, than which there cannot be a greater cognizance of Christian Religion ; albeit 'tis worn by those Knights as a token of Nobility too. 'Tis enough that the Jesuits think their opinion abundantly confirm'd by the two above said reasons, namely that it is rather a sign of Nobility than a Cognizance of Religion. And although the same is con-ferr'd with many superstitious Ceremonies, yet they will not have it taken away, alledging for example that the Crosses of our Knights, however ensignes of Nobility, are given with many Ceremonies and Rites of our sacred Religion, the more to authorize them. Whence it appears that the use of this Ribban may be without scruple per-mitted to the Indians, provided these superstitious Cere-monies be lay'd aside, and especially the End, in which alone consists the sin, changing it in that manner as the ancient Christians chang'd many Festivals and superstitions of the Gentiles into Festivals of Martyrs, and other pious Commemorations. And this may be done by applying (*e.g.*) the signification of the three Braids to the most Holy

---

[1] A military order in Spain instituted under Sancho, third King of Castile, on the occasion of entrusting the defence of the fort of Cala-trava to Don Raymond and his companions.

Trinity, or in some such manner turning it to a pious and lawful use.

Nevertheless those of the contrary party impugn that opinion with no bad Reasons ; they say 'tis a thing in it self of its own nature wholly unlawful to Christians, as being perfectly a Gentile superstition ; which is prov'd by the Ceremonies and words us'd in conferring it ; and that for the three Braids, 'tis well known they hold and wear them in honour of three of their chief false Gods[1]; and that, although they be Ensigns of Nobility in the wearer, yet they are withall and principally a manifest Cognizance of their Religion ; as Crosses are amongst our Knights, wherewith who ever hath the same on his breast not onely ostentates his Nobility, but also firmly professes the Christian Faith. That the Gentile Kings having honour'd with this Ensign some Mahometan, their Vassal, and remaining a Mahometan, is no more than as if in our Countries we should grant to some Jew the privilege of wearing a black Hat without becoming a Christian ; which may be done by way of dispensation, yet it cannot be deny'd but that the wearing a black one, or a yellow, is, besides the matter of credit, a Cognizance also of the Religion or Sect which a man professes. Many other Reasons they alledge which I do not well remember, and which, no doubt, will be narrowly examined at *Rome.* What the determination will be I shall know more certainly at *Goa ;* and for the present thus much may suffice concerning the Opinions and Rites of the Indian Gentiles.

XV.—Now in pursuance of the Narration of my Travels, I am to tell you that after the seeing of the Temple, and visiting the Brachman abovesaid, the same day, which was *Saturday,* the 25th of *February,* upon occasion of a *Cafila*

---

[1] It was the opinion of the Abbé Dubois (see *Mœurs des peuples de l'Inde,* vol. i, p. 218) that the triple cord has reference to the Hindu Triad.

or *Caravan*, which was setting forth from *Cambaia* to *Ahme-dabàd*,[1] which is the Royal Seat and Head of the whole Kingdom of *Guzaràt*,[2] we, namely Sig. *Alberto Scilling* and my self, with our attendants, were desirous to see that City ; and since the insecurity of the wayes allow'd us not to go alone, we resolv'd to go with the *Cafila*. And because at the same time another *Cafila* was setting forth for *Surat*, in which some of the *Hollanders* residing at *Cambaia*, went with their Goods which they carry'd thither in order to be shipt, we all went out of the Town together, and in a place without the Gate and Suburbs, where the wayes divided, under the shade of certain great Trees of Tamarinds,[3] which the Indians call *Hambelé* (where also are certain Sepulchres, and a Mahometan *Meschita* or Temple, unroofed and without walls about, saving a little wall at the front, and a place markt where prayers are to be made ; of which sort of *Meschitas* many are seen in *India*, especially in the Country), we entertained ourselves a good while with the Dutch, being diverted with Musick, singing and dancing, by the same Women which we had at our house

---

[1] Ahmadabad, one of the finest towns in India, is situated due north of Cambay, in lat. 23° 10' N. It was taken by the English in 1780. Here are found a greater number of Jains than in any other part of India. The city was founded in A.D. 1413 by Ahmad Shah, on the site of ancient Ashawal, on the banks of the river Sabarmati. It is one of the best fortified cities in India, having walls of brick and stone flanked with towers, with twelve gates, and a castle. It was famous for its manufacture of chintz, brocade, velvet, and arms of various kinds.

[2] Guzarat was originally held by the "Sah", or "Sinha" dynasty, which was conquered by the "Gupta" dynasty about 250 A.D., which reigned till about A.D. 650, and was succeeded by a Rajput tribe called "Chawra", who were superseded by the "Saloukhyas" about A.D. 942.

[3] The tamarind (*Tamarindus Indica*) is called "Imlee" in the vernacular, which may perhaps be represented by "Hambele". It grows to a great size in Southern India. The word is derived from an Arabic word, *tamr*, fruit, and *Hind*, India.

the night before. At length taking leave they took their way towards *Surat*, and Sig. *Alberto* and I, with our company towards *Ahmedabad*, going a little out of the way to see another very famous Temple of *Mahadeu*.

The Fabrick is small and inconsiderable ; within there is no other Idol but that of *Mahadeu*, which is no other but a little column or pillar[1] of stone, thicker below than at top, and which, diminishing by degrees, ends at the top in a round. Whatever 'tis that they would signifie thereby, the name of *Mahadeu* in their language is properly interpreted *Great God*. But we had enough to laugh at when we heard that this Idol was held by the Country people for a worker of miracles ; and amongst other of his miracles, they relate that he grows every day, and becomes bigger hourly ; affirming that many years since he was no higher than a span, or little more, and now he is above two, and perhaps three ; and thus he continues increasing every day : a folly not to be believ'd but by such fools as themselves. Having seen this Temple, we overtook our *Cafila* at a place call'd *Saimà*, three miles distant from *Cambaia*, where we all lodg'd that night. The next Morning, being *Sunday*, the *Cafila*, which consisted of above a hundred Coaches, besides foot-men and horse-men, and great loaden Wagons, set forth three hours before day, and staying not to rest anywhere, according to the custom of the East (which is to make but one bout of a day's journey), having travell'd fifteen *Cos* by noon or little later, we lodg'd at a Town call'd *Mater*, where we saw an infinite number of Squirrels[2] leaping amongst the trees every where; they were small,

---

[1] A " Lingam", or emblem of generative power.

[2] *Sciurus flavus*, or yellow squirrel. The black stripes on the back are said to have been caused by Rama stroking it with his fingers, in reward for services rendered on his expedition to Ceylon to rescue his wife. Their colour is " flaxen", not white. The word translated as " white" should be " light-coloured".

white, and with a tail less and not so fair as those of our Countries.

On *Monday,* about two hours before day, we resum'd our Voyage. When it was day we saw upon the way every where abundance of wild Monkies, of which almost all the Trees were full. They put me in mind of that Army of Monkies, which the Souldiers of *Alexander* the Great, beholding upon certain hills afar of, and taking to be Men, intended to have charg'd had not *Tarilus* inform'd them what they were, as *Strabo*[1] relates. We found abundance of people too upon the way, begging alms with the sound of a Trumpet, which almost everyone had and sounded, and most of them were arm'd with Bows and Arrows; two things sufficiently uncouth for beggars, and indeed not to be suffer'd by Governours, since these Ruffians, under pretext of begging, rob frequently upon the way when they meet persons alone and unarm'd; which, having weapons themselves, they may easily do. This country was almost all woody, the ground unmeasureably dusty, to the great trouble of Travellers; the High-ways were all enclos'd on the sides with high hedges of a plant[2] always green and unfruitful, not known in *Europe,* and having no leaves, but instead thereof cover'd with certain long and slender branches, almost like our *Sparagus,*[3] but bigger, harder, and thicker, of a very lively green; being broken, they send forth Milk like that of immature Figgs, which is very pernicious to the flesh wherever it touches. The fields were

---

[1] Lib. xv.

[2] Probably a species of Euphorbia, which forms an almost impenetrable hedge. The acrid character of the milk exuded by plants of this species is well known.

[3] "Sparagus", though said to be a vulgar form for "asparagus", would seem to be etymologically the more correct form of spelling if (as is asserted by Webster) the name is derived from the Greek σπαράσσω or σπεῖρα.

full of Olive-trees, Tamarind-trees,[1] and other such which in *India* are familiar.

About noon, having travell'd twelve, or, as others said, fourteen Cos, we arriv'd at *Ahmedabàd*, and our journey from *Cambaia* hither was always with our Faces towards the North East. Being entred into the City, which is competently large, with Great Suburbs, we went directly to alight at the house of the English Merchants, till other lodgings were prepared for us, where also we din'd with them. After which we retir'd to one of the houses which stand in the street, which they call *Terzi*[2] *Carvanserai*, that is the *Tayler's Inn*. For you must know that the *Carvanserai*, or Inns, in *Ahmedabàd*, and other Great Cities of *India*, are not, as in *Persia* and *Turkey*, one single habitation, made in form of a great Cloyster, with abundance of Lodgings round about, separate one from another, for quartering of strangers; but they are whole great streets of the City destinated for strangers to dwell in, and whosoever is minded to hire a house; and because these streets are lockt up in the night time for security of the persons and goods which are there, therefore they call them *Carvanserai*. Notwithstanding the wearisomness of our journey, because we were to stay but a little while at *Ahmedabàd*, therefore after a little rest we went the same Evening to view the market-place, buying sundry things. It displeas'd me sufficiently that the streets not being well pav'd, although they are large, fair and strait, yet through the great dryness of the Earth they are so dusty that there's almost no going a foot, because the foot sinks very deep in the ground with great defilement; and the going on Horse-back, or in a Coach, is likewise very troublesome

---

[1] This is a mistranslation. The olive is not found in the plains of India. The words in the original are, "Trees which are called 'Ambe' (*i.e.*, Mango), which bear fruit like large olives."

[2] More correctly "Darzi".

in regard of the dust, a thing indeed of great disparagement to so goodly and great a City as this is. I saw in
Ahmedabàd Roses, Flowers of *Jasmin* and other sorts, and
divers such fruits as we have in our Countries in the
Summer; whence I imagin'd, that probably, we had re-
pass'd the Tropick of *Cancer*,[1] and re-enter'd a little into
the temperate Zone; which doubt I could not clear for
want of my Astrolabe, which I had left with my other
goods at *Suràt*.

On *Tuesday* following, which to us was the day of
Carnoval, or *Shrove-Tuesday*, walking in the Morning
about the Town, I saw a handsome street, strait, long and
very broad, full of shops of various Trades: they call it
Bezari Kelan,[2] that is, the *Great Merkat*,[3] in distinction
from others than which this is bigger. In the middle is a
structure of stone athwart the street, like a bridge with
three Arches, almost resembling the Triumphal Arches of
Rome. A good way beyond this bridge, in the middle of
the same is a great well, round about which is built a
square Piazetta, a little higher than the ground. The
water of the Well is of great service to all the City, and
there is always a great concourse of people who come to
fetch it.

Going forwards to the end of the Market, we came to the
Great Gate which stands confronting the street, and beau-
tifi'd with many Ornaments between two goodly Towers;
'tis the Gate of a small Castle, which they call by the
Persian word *Cut*.[4] Nor let it seem strange that in *India*,
in the Countries of the *Moghòl*, the *Persian* tongue is us'd
more perhaps than the *Indian* itself, since the Mogholian
Princes being originally *Tartars*, and of *Samarkand*, where

---

[1] This surmise was incorrect, as Ahmadabad is just within the
tropic.

[2] That is, *Bazaar-i-Kalan*.   [3] An old form of "market".

[4] Properly *khat*.

the *Persian* is the natural tongue of the Country, have therefore been willing to retain their native Speech in *India;* in brief, the *Persian* is the Language of the *Moghol's* Court, most spoken and us'd in all publick writings.

Near this Castle Gate, in a void place of the street are two pulpits handsomely built of stone, somewhat rais'd from the ground, wherein 'tis the Custome to read the King's Commandments publickly, when they are to be proclaim'd. Thence turning to the right hand, and passing another great Gate, and through a fair street we came to the Royal Palace ; for *Ahmedabàd* is one of the four Cities,[1] amongst all the others of his Dominions, where the *Grand Moghòl* by particular privilege hath a Palace and a Court ; and accordingly he comes sometimes to reside there. This Palace hath a great square Court, surrounded with white and well polish'd Walls. In the midst stands a high Post to shoot at with arrows, as is also usual in the Piazzas of *Persia*. On the left side of the Court as you go in are the King's Lodgings, a small and low building. What 'tis within side I know not, for I enter'd not into it ; but without 'tis as follows. Under the King's Windows is a square place inclos'd with a rail of colour'd wood, and the pavement somewhat rais'd ; within which, if the King is there, are wont to stand certain Officers of the Militia, whom they call *Mansubdàr*,[2] and they are almost the same with our Colonels : their Command extends not to above a Thousand Horse ; nor are they all equal, but from a thousand downwards some have more, some less, under them. Within this inclosure of the *Mansubdary*, under

---

[1] The other cities being Agra, Mandu, and Lahore. The present town of Delhi had not as yet been adopted as the seat of empire. The ancient city of Delhi, where the kings of India held their Court until its destruction by Teimur Leng in 1398, was eight miles south of the present city, which was built by the Emperor Shah Jahan.

[2] Persian for "holder of an office", *i.e.*, an "officer".

H

the King's Balconies, stand two carv'd Elephants of em-
boss'd work, but not large, painted with their natural
colours ; and in the front of the Royal Lodgings are
other such Ornaments, after their mode, of little consideration. Some said that a while ago in one of the
Balconies stood expos'd to publick view an Image of the
Virgin *Mary*, plac'd there by *Sciàh Selim*, who, they say,
was devoted to·her,[1] and to whom perhaps it was given by
one of our Priests, who frequent his Court out of a desire
to draw him to the Christian Faith ; but the Image was
not there now, and possibly was taken away by *Sultan
Chorròm* his Son, (reported an Enemy of the Christians
and their affairs) since his coming to the Government of
those parts of *Guzaràt*. The station of the greater Captains, and of higher dignity than the *Mansubdary*, as the
Chans and others of that rank, is in the King's Balconies,
or near hand above there within the Rooms. The inferior
Souldiers, that is such as have onely two or three Horses,
stand upon the ground in the Court without the above
mention'd inclosure. In the front of the Court is another
building, with an inclosure also before it, but less adorn'd ;
'tis the place where the King's Guard stands with all its
Captains ; and the same order, I believe, is always observ'd
in the *Moghol's* Court, in whatsoever place or City he
happens to be. Within this Court is another on the left
hand, surrounded with other buildings for necessary Offices,
but not so well built nor polish'd.

Having seen what we could of the Royal Palace, we return'd by the same way we came to the street of the Great
Market. From whence we went to see a famous Temple
of *Mahedeù*, to which there is hourly a great concourse of
people, and the street which leads to it is always full, not

---

[1] Sir T. Roe mentions that the Emperor had figures of Christ and
the Virgin at the head of his rosary.

onely of goers and comers to the Temple, but also of
beggars who stand here and there asking Alms of those
that pass by. The building of this Temple is small, the
Entrance narrow and very low, almost under ground ; for
you descend by many steps, and you would think you were
rather going into a *Grotto* than into a Temple, and hence
there is always a great crowd there. On high hung a great
number of Bells, which are rung every moment with great
noise by those who come to worship. Within the Temple
continually stand many naked *Gioghi*, having onely their
privities (not very well) cover'd with a cloth ; they wear
long Hair dishevel'd, dying their Fore-heads[1] with spots
of Sanders,[2] Saffron, and other colours suitable to their
superstitious Ceremonies. The rest of their bodies is clean
and smooth, without any tincture or impurity ; which I
mention as a difference from some other *Gioghi*, whose
Bodies are all smear'd with colours and ashes as I shall
relate hereafter. There is no doubt but these are the
ancient Gymnosophists so famous in the world,[3] and, in
short, those very Sophists who then went naked and
exercis'd great patience in sufferings, to whom *Alexander*
the Great sent *Onesicritus* to consult with them, as *Strabo*[4]
reports from the testimony of the same *Onesicritus*. Many

---

[1] As to the marks made on the forehead, see Sir Monier Williams'
Modern India, p. 193. The marks represent the soles of Vishnu's
feet on a kind of lotus throne, with a central mark symbolical of
Lakshmi, wife of Vishnu. These marks are often erroneously supposed to represent a trident.

[2] In the original "Sandalo". "Sanders" is the older form of the
name of the genus *Santalum*, of which there are several varieties—
white and yellow. Red sandal, or sanders-wood, is the produce of a
tree of the genus *Pterocarpus*, or sometimes of the *Adenanthera
Pavonina*, a kind of acacia.

[3] In one respect at least they have degenerated from their ancient
fame, for Apuleius notes as their chief characteristic that "they have
an aversion to idleness and indolence".

[4] Lib. xv.

of them stood in the Temple near the Idols, which were
plac'd in the innermost Penetral, or Chancel of it, with
many Candles and lamps burning before them. The Idols
were two stones, somewhat long, like two small *Termini*,
or Land-marks, painted with their wonted colours ; on the
right side whereof was a stone cut into a figure, and on
the left another of that ordinary form of a small pillar,[1]
according to which as I said before that they use to
shape *Mahadeù*. And before all these another like figure
of *Mahadeù*, made of Crystal, upon which the Offerings
were lay'd, as Milk, Oyle, Rice and divers such things.
The assistant *Gioghi* give every one that comes to worship
some of the Flowers, which are strew'd upon and round
about the Idols, receiving in lieu thereof good summs of
Alms.

Coming out of this Temple, and ascending up the wall
of the City which is hard by, we beheld from that height
the little River call'd *Sabermeti*,[2] which runs on that side
under the walls without the City. Upon the bank thereof,
stood expos'd to the Sun many *Gioghi* of more austere
lives, namely such as are not onely naked like those above
describ'd, but go all sprinkled with ashes, and paint their
bodies and faces with a whitish colour upon black, which
they do with a certain stone[3] that is reduced into powder
like Lime. Their Beards and Hair they wear long, un-
trim'd, rudely involv'd, and sometimes erected like horns.[4]
Painted they are often, or rather daub'd with sundry
colours and hideous figures ; so that they seem so many
Devils, like those represented in our Comedies. The ashes

---

[1] *I.e.*, the Lingam, or emblem of productive power.

[2] More correctly " Sabarmati".

[3] The powder is made from burnt shells.

[4] Another mode of wearing the hair is to form it into a long rope,
mixed with ashes, and then tie it round the head. (Ward's *Hindoos*,
vol. ii, p. 123.)

wherewith they sprinkle their bodies are the ashes of burnt Carkasses ; and this to the end they may be continually mindful of death. A great crew of these, with their Chief, or Leader, (who conducts them with an extravagant banner in his Hand, made of many shreds of several colours, and whom they all religiously obey) sat by the River's side in a round form, as their custom is ; and in the field there were many people, who came some to walk, and others to wash themselves ; the Pagan Indians holding their Rivers in great Veneration, and being not a little superstitious in bathing themselves therein. From the same place I beheld a little Chappel built upon two small figures of *Mahadeù*, not upright, but lying along upon the ground, and carv'd in basse relief, where also were Lamps burning, and people making their offerings. One of the *Gioghi*, laying aside all other care, remain'd continually[1] in this Chappel with great retiredness and abstraction of mind, scarce ever coming forth, although it was very troublesome abiding there, in regard to the heat of the lights, and inconvenient too, by reason the Chappel was so little that it could scarce contain him alone as he sat upon the pavement (which was somewhat rais'd from the Earth) with his Leggs doubled under him and almost crooked. Returning home by the same way of the great *Bazàr*, or Market, I saw *Carvanserai*, or Inns made with Cloysters like those of *Persia ;* one greater and square of the ordinary form, and another less, narrow and long. Of divers other streets, in which I saw nothing observable, I forbear to speak.

XVI.—The same day after dinner, having taken leave of certain *Armenian* and *Syrian* Christians, who live in *Ahmed-abàd* with their Wives and Families, we put ourselves upon the way to return to *Cambaia*, with the same *Cafila* with

---

[1] Self-torture of this kind is common in India even at the present day. (See Sir Monier Williams' *Modern India*, p. 77.)

which we came, and which every week departs thence at a set
day. At our setting forth we met with a little obstacle,
for by reason of the new Commotion between the *Moghòl*
and his Son, *Sultan Chorròm*, who was become Master of
these parts of *Guzaràt*, there was a fresh prohibition in
Ahmedabàd, that no Souldiers' Wives nor other person of
quality should go out of the City by Land ; and this, as I
conceive, lest the rumours of the troubles should cause the
people of the City to move into other territories, and
abandon the faction of the Rebel *Sultan Chorròm*, which
they could not do if their Wives were restrain'd, because
Husbands are in a manner necessitated to abide where
their Wives and Houses are. So that by reason of this
prohibition I could not have got away, having my Sig^{ra.}
Mariuccia with me, unless I had obtained express leave in
writing from the Governour ; in order to which it was
needful for me to make it appear that we were strangers,
and not people of the Country, and to pay some small sum
of Money, besides going backward and forward, whereby
we lost much time.

Having at length obtain'd permission, and being got out
of the City, we went a little without the walls to see a
great Artificial Lake which is there, made of stone, with
stairs at several angles about it ; its Diameter was by my
conjecture about half a mile. It hath about the middle an
Island, with a little Garden, to which they go by a handsome Bridge of many Arches very well built ; upon which,
I believe, two Indian Coaches may go a breast. Indeed
these Indian Lakes are goodly things, and may be reckon'd
amongst the most remarkable structures of the world.
Having seen this we went to overtake our Cafila, which
was arriv'd at a Town seven *Cos* distant from *Ahmedabàd*,
call'd *Barigia*, or *Bariza*[1] (for the Indians very much con-

---

[1] A small town, marked in Adm. Chart as " Barajree".

found these two Letters *g* and *z* in their speaking). We came late to the said Town by reason of our hindrances at our departure from *Ahmedabàd ;* but certain Horse-men appointed, as I conceive, to guard the way, having met us in the night, would need accompany us thither so that we might go safely ; for which service they were contented with a very small gratuity which we gave them.

XVII.—The first of *March,* being *Ash Wednesday,* we set forth by break of day, and having travell'd fifteen *Cos,* an hour or little more before night we came to lodge in a competently large Town call'd *Sozintra,*[1] where I saw Batts as big as Crows.[2] The next day, *March* the second, beginning our journey early, we travell'd twelve *Cos,* and a little after noon arrived at *Cambaia.* The Dutch Merchants there, understanding by others that we were coming with this Cafila, came to meet us a little without the Gate, and with their accustomed courtesies conducted us to lodge in their House. *March* the third we went out of the walls to the top of the Tower of that Sepulchre which I said we saw near the Garden of the King of *Guzaràt,* to behold from thence (being a great prospect upon the Sea) the coming in of the Tide, which indeed was a pleasant Spectacle. 'Twas New-Moon this day, and so a greater Tide than usual, and we went to observe it at the punctual time of its being at the height, which those people know very well ; because at that time it increases in less than a quarter of an hour to almost the greatest height it is to have, and

---

1 "Sojitra", in lat. 22° 32' N., long. 72° 46' E.

2 These were no doubt what are generally called flying foxes (*Pteropus rubricollis*), described by Friar Odoric as being "as big as pigeons". They are said to have a spread of wing extending sometimes to five feet, and are certainly as large as crows or pigeons. The word "bat" is a corruption of "back", or "backe", the old English name of the animal, derived from the word *blaka,* "to flutter". In Scotland the bat is called "bak" or "bakie bird"; and in Iceland *lethr blaka,* or "leather flapper".

flows with greatest fury[1] ; contrary to what happens in other Seas. Now at the due time we saw the Sea come roaring afar off like a most rapid River, and in a moment overflow a great space of Land, rushing with such fury that nothing could have with-stood its force ; and I think it would have overtaken the swiftest Race-Horse in the world. A thing verily strange, since in other places both the rising and the falling of the Sea in the flux and reflux is done gently in full six hours, and with so little motion that 'tis scarce perceived.

After this we went to see another goodly Cistern or Lake, without the City, formerly not seen, of a square form, and of a sumptuous marble structure, with stairs about it like the others which I had seen elsewhere. Afterwards we saw in one of the Suburbs or Hamlets near the City, call'd *Causari*, a Temple of the *Gentiles*, peradventure the goodliest that I have seen, with certain *Cupola's*, and high Balconies of tolerable Architecture, but no great model. This Temple belongs to the Race of *Indians* who shave their heads (a thing unusual to all others, who wear long hair like Women), and such are called *Vertià*.[2] The Idol in it

---

[1] This refers to the sudden influx of the tide, common in many estuaries, called a "bore" (from Norse *badra*, a wave). This rush of the tide in the Gulf of Cambay has been described by many Indian travellers. It occurs in the Severn in England, in the Ganges, and other rivers. (See *R. G. S. Journal*, vol. viii, 1838.)

[2] Or Vaishnavas, *i.e.*, worshippers of Vishnu alone as the one Supreme Being. They are adherents of two religious revivalists, Madhva and Rāmānuja, and are divided into two antagonistic parties, Tengalais and Vadagalais, maintaining different doctrines, the one of absolute faith in Vishnu, and the other of man's co-operation with Vishnu, illustrated respectively by the passive dependence of a kitten, and the strenuous clinging to its mother of a young monkey. Another great bone of contention between them is the question whether the frontal mark of their sect should include part of the nose, or not. (See Sir M. Williams' *Modern India*, p. 192, who gives illustrations of the marks adopted by each sect.)

sate on high over an Altar at the upper end, in a place somewhat dark, ascended by stairs, with lamps always burning before it. When I went in there was a Man at his Devotions, and burning Perfumes before the Idol. At some distance from this stands another Temple of like structure, but more plain and of a square form ; within it were seen abundance of Idols of several shapes, whose Names and Histories the shortness of time, and my un-skilfulness in their Language, allow'd me not to learn. Without the Gate of these Temples I beheld, sitting upon the ground in a circle, another Troop of those naked *Gioghi*, having their bodies smear'd with Ashes, Earth and Colours, like those I had seen upon the River of *Ahmedabàd;* they made a ring about their *Archimandrita*, or Leader, who was held in such Veneration not onely by the Religious of their Sect, but also by the other secular *Indians*, for Repu-tation of Holiness, that I saw many grave persons go and make low Reverence to him, kiss his Hands, and stand in an humble posture before him to hear some sentence ; and He with great gravity, or rather with a strange scorn of all worldly things, hypocritically made as if he scarce deign'd to speak and answer those that came to honour him. These *Gioghi* are not such by Descent, but by Choice, as our Religious Orders are. They go naked, most of them with their bodies painted and smear'd, as is above mention'd ; yet some of them are onely naked, with the rest of their bodies smooth, and onely their Fore-heads dy'd with Sanders and some red, yellow, or white colour ; which is also imi-tated by many secular persons, out of superstition and gal-lantry. They live upon Almes, despising clothes and all other worldly things. They marry not, but make severe profession of Chastity, at least in appearance ; for in secret 'tis known many of them commit as many debaucheries as they can. They live in society under the obedience of their Superiors, and wander about the world without having any settled abode. Their Habitations are the Fields, the Streets, the Porches, the Courts of Temples, and Trees, especially under those where any Idol is worshipt by them; and they undergo with incredible patience day and night no less the rigor of the Air than the excessive heat of the Sun, which in these sultry Countries is a thing sufficiently to be admir'd.[1] They have spiritual Exercises after their way, and also some exercise of Learning, but (by what I gather from a Book of theirs translated into *Persian*, and intitl'd, *Damerdbigiaska*,[2] and, as the Translator saith, a rare piece) both their exercises of wit and their Learning consist onely in Arts of Divination, Secrets of Herbs, and other natural things, and also in Magick and Inchantments, whereunto they are much addicted, and boast of doing great wonders. I include their spiritual exercises herein because, according to the aforesaid Book, they think that by the means of those exercises, Prayers, Fastings and the like superstitious things, they come to Revelations; which indeed are nothing else but correspondence with the Devil, who appears to and deludes them in sundry shapes, forewarning them sometimes of things to come. Yea sometimes they have carnal commerce with him, not believing, or at least not professing, that 'tis the Devil; but that there are certain Immortal, Spiritual, Invisible Women,[3] to the number of forty, known to them and distinguisht by various forms, names and operations, whom they reverence as

---

[1] They sometimes subject themselves to the heat of the "five fires", *i.e.*, of four fires lighted on the ground between which they sit, with the sun above them as the fifth fire, and sometimes suspend themselves by their feet over a fire lighted beneath. (See Dubois, *Mœurs des Peuples de l'Inde*, part II, p. 277.)

[2] In the Italian text, the words "or Kamerdbigiaska, for thus the Persian copy has it, not being accurate in consonants or vowels", are added. The book here referred to has not been identified, though efforts to do so have been made.

[3] Called "Apsaras" in the Hindoo mythology.

Deities, and adore in many places with strange worship ; so that some Moorisco Princes in *India*, as one of these three petty Kings who reign'd in *Decàn*, *Telengane*, and *Meslepaton*,[1] (*Cutbsciach*[2] as I remember) though a Moor, yet retaining some reliques of ancient Gentilism, makes Great Feasts and Sacrifices to one of these Women in certain Grottoes under high Mountains which are in his Country, where 'tis reported that this Woman hath a particular and belov'd habitation ; and he of the *Gioghi* that by long spiritual exercises can come to have an apparition of any of these Women, who foretells him future things, and favours him with the power of doing other wonders, is accounted in the degree of perfection ; and far more if he happen to be adopted by the Immortal Woman for her Son, Brother, or other Kinsman ; but above all if he be receiv'd for a Husband, and the Woman have carnal commerce with him ; the *Gioghi* thenceforward remaining excluded from the commerce of all other Women in the World, which is the highest degree that can be attain'd to ; and then he is call'd a spiritual Man, and accounted of a nature above humane, with promise of a thousand strange things, which for brevitie's Sake I pass over. Thus doth the Devil abuse this miserable people. As for anything more concerning these *Gioghi*, I refer you to what I have formerly written[3] of them, and the *Samì*, who are another sort of Religious *Indians* who wear Clothes, as I saw them in *Bender* of *Combrù*.[4] And of the Sciences of the *Gioghi*, and

---

[1] Telingaha and Masulipatam, on the east coast of India.

[2] *I.e.*, Kutb Shah. The fact here mentioned (which bears some similarity to the story of the devotion of King Numa Pompilius towards Egeria) is a striking instance of the conformity on the part of Muhammadans with Hindoo superstitions, of which many other instances might be given. (See Sir M. Williams' *Modern India*, p. 201.)

[3] See Letter No. XVI.

[4] *I.e.*, the seaport town Bandar Abbas, or Gombroon, in Persia ; 'Bandar" meaning " port". See p. 3, *note*.

their spiritual exercises, especially of a curious way, rather superstitious than natural, of Divining by the breathing of a Man,[1] wherein they have indeed many curious and subtle observations, which I upon tryal have found true, if any would know more, I refer him to the Book above mention'd, which I intend to carry with me for a Rarity into *Italy;* and, if I shall find convenience, I shall one day gratifie the Curious with a sight of it in a Translation.[2]

XVIII.—On the fourth of *March* I went out of *Cambaia* to a Town two miles off, call'd *Nagrà*,[3] to see a famous Temple, built of old by the Race of the *Banions*,[4] and which belongs to them; but yet the Brachmans possess it and have care of it, as if it were descended to them.   This Temple is dedicated to *Brahmà*, who, as I said before, they hold to be the same with Pythagoras, although of the origine of *Brahmà*, and how he was produc'd of the first Cause, or else of the first Matter, and how they take this for one of the Elements, and a thousand other extravagances, they tell long Fables which do not agree to *Pythagoras*, a meer man.   But for all this they confound the two Names, and 'tis no great matter to reconcile them herein, after the same manner that our ancient Gentiles agreed in their *Jupiter*, taken sometimes for one of the Elements, and sometimes historically for an ancient King, one of *Saturn's* Sons[5]; and in divers other

---

[1] This is a reference to the practice among religious devotees of producing a kind of ecstasy, by controlling the natural process of inspiration and expiration.   An interesting account of the process will be found in part II, chap. xxxv, of Dubois' *Mœurs des Peuples de l'Inde.*   Other magical practices are described in part II, chap. xxi, of the same book.

[2] So far as is known this translation was never made.

[3] Not marked in ordinary maps.

[4] Should be Banians, or Banyas.   See p. 78.

[5] According to Cicero there were three Jupiters, of whom one sprang from Æther, or the atmosphere; another from Cœlus, the

like names, in reference to History and Philosophy they had double, allegorical and mysterious significations. Concerning the Genealogy of *Brahmà*, and the other fabulous Indian Gods, and what belongs to their vain Theology, I refer the Reader to the Books of Father *Francesco Negrone*, or *Negraone*, as the Portugals call him, who writes fully thereof in his Chronicles of the things done by those of his Order in *India*, written in the *Portugal* Language; and I think he is the first, and perhaps the onely Modern Writer who hath given account of this Matter in *Europe;* the said Father having been assisted therein for information by most fit and sufficient Interpreters, namely the Fathers of his own Religion, good Divines, skill'd in the *Indian* Tongue, and perfectly intelligent of these matters, who also read and interpreted the very Books of the Indians to him, and were likewise his interpreters in the discourses, which he had often with the learned Indians concerning their Religion, as himself frequently told me. Besides which he wanted not other helps, because, being appointed Historiographer to his Order, he was abundantly supply'd with what was needful to that Office; he convers'd long in the Kingdom of *Bisnaga*,[1] where the Religion and Sciences of the Indians have their Principal Seat; as also in the Island of *Zeilan*,[2] which many take to be the ancient *Tabrobana*, and

---

sky; and the third from Saturn. See also Virgil's *Æneid*, viii, 352-354:—

"Arcades ipsum
Credunt se vidisse Jovem, cum sæpe nigrantem
Ægida concuteret dextrâ, nimbosque cieret."

[1] Bijanagar, or Vijayanagar, where a Hindu kingdom existed till 1565 A.D., in lat. 17° 9' N. These names denote the "City of Victory". The name was afterwards changed to Bidpur, *i.e.*, Vidya-pur, or "City of Learning", on account of the number of learned men residing there.

[2] Or Ceylon, once held to be the same as the ancient Taprobane, which is now identified as the island of Sumatra (see Sir H. Yule's

in other Countries for this very purpose. He made many peregrinations expressly to see places and things conducing thereunto, and was assisted by the Vice-Roys themselves and Governours of Provinces subject to the *Portugals*, who sent him into all places, accompany'd oftentimes with whole bands of Souldiers, where the wayes were not secure ; in brief, without sparing cost, pains, or diligence, he professedly intended[1] this business for many years together, with all kind of convenience and authority. Lastly he was some years since sent by his Order into *Europe*, in order to print his Works ; and in the year 1619, as I came through *Persia*, I saw him at *Sphahàn*, and during his short abode there by means of a Friend got a sight of his Papers, but had not time to read them, as I desir'd. He went thence directly to *Rome*, whither I gave him some Letters to certain Friends and Relations of mine to be civil to him there, as I know they were ; and after some years sojourning at *Rome*, whilst I was at *Bender* of *Combrù*, I heard that he was coming from *Rome* towards *Turkie*, in order to return to *India*, where I hope to see him again ; and if he bring his Books printed with him I shall read them, and what I find remarkable therein which may be serviceable to these writings of mine I shall make mention of the same in its proper place.

Father *Joam de Lucena*, a Jesuit, in his History of the Life of *San Francesco Xavier*, written in the *Portugal*

Marco Polo, vol. ii, p. 277). The name "Taprobane" is said to be derived from the Sanskrit *Tamraparni*, or "red-leaved". Another derivation is from *Tapobon* (Sanskrit), or "Holy forest". The Sanskrit name of Ceylon was *Sihala-dwipa*, corrupted into Sielediba and Zeilan, which signifies "the lion-dwelling island" (see Tennent's *Ceylon*, i, 525). A Hindoo name for the island is *Lanka*, or "Holy land". It was called Seilen-dibra and Serendib by Muhammadans.

[1] An obsolete use of the word for "superintended". See Bacon (quoted by Webster) : "She did with singular care and tenderness intend the education of Phillip."

Tongue, makes mention likewise of the Religion and Customs of the Indian-Gentiles, and seems to speak thereof with good grounds, although in some few particulars, if I mistake not, he is capable of a little correction. Yet that which troubles me most is that it clearly appears by his Book that he knew much more of the Customs of the *Indians* than he hath written, which perhaps he would not write, either because they were obscene and impious, or pertained not to his purpose. I saw Father Negrone since at Goa, but he brought not his Book printed, either because his Fathers, as some say, would not have it printed, or for some other reason. Yet he saith he hath sent it to be printed at *Portugal* in that Language, and expects it by the next Ship ; if it comes, I shall see it. But having in *Goa* discours'd with him more largely than I did in *Persia*, I find him very little vers'd in matters of ancient History and Geography, as generally the Fryars of *Spain*, and especially *Portugal*, are not, addicting themselves little to other Studies besides what serves to Preaching; wherefore, without good skill in ancient History, Geography and other Humane Learning, I know not how 'tis possible to write Histories well, particularly concerning the Customs of the *Indians*, of which also he hath had no other information but by interpreters ; in which way I had by experience found that many errors are frequently committed. Nevertheless we shall see what light may be had from *F. Lucena's* Book, although it be short, concerning the Religion of the *Indians*.

XIX.—In the meantime returning to my purpose I shall tell you that in the Temple dedicated to Brahmà in the Town of Naghrà, which is little considerable for building, but in great Veneration for ancient Religion, there are many Idols of white Marble. The biggest is the Chief and hath the worthiest place ; in the middle is the Statue *Brahmà*, or *Pythagoras*, with many Arms and Faces, as they

ordinarily pourtray him, namely three Faces, for I could not
see whether there were a fourth or more behind ; 'tis naked,
with a long picked Beard, but ill cut as well as the rest of
the figure, which for its bigness hath a very great Belly, I
know not whether through the Artificers fault, who seem to
have been little skilful, or else because the *Indians*, as I
have also heard of the people of Sumatra, account it a
great Beauty and perfection to have a great Belly. This
figure of *Brahmà* stands upright, and at his Feet two other
less carv'd figures, which, as they say, are his two sons,
Sunnet and *Sunnatan*.[1] On each side of *Brahmà* stand
likewise two Statues of Women, somewhat less than
Brahmà himself, and they call them his Wives, *Savetrì*
and *Gavetrì*.[2] On the left side of this narrow Temple,
stand two other figures of the same bigness, being two
naked Men with long Beards, whom they pretend to have
been two religious persons, I know not whether Doctors,
or Disciples of *Brahmà* or *Pythagoras ;* one is call'd
Chescuèr, the other *Ciavan de Chescuèr*.[3] On the same
side downwards are many other Idolets, as one with an
Elephants Head,[4] and divers others formerly by me mention'd. All which Idols are serv'd, ador'd, perfum'd,
offer'd to and washed every day as for delight (for the
Indians account it delight to wash often) by the *Brachmans*,
who assist at their service with much diligence.

I must not forget that the *Banians* say this Town

---

[1] " Sunnet" and " Sunnatan" probably represent the Sanskrit word
Santhan, " son".

[2] The word *Savitri* means " life-giver", and is generally applied to
the sun. The consort of Brahma was named Sareswati (goddess of
learning and eloquence), who is, perhaps, here referred to as Savetri,

[3] These figures probably represent servants or attendants of
Brahma. As to the derivation of the name " Brahma", see *Hibbert
Lectures* of 1878, by F. Max Müller, p. 358, *note*.

[4] Ganesa, son of Siva, also called Ganpati ; see *ante*, p. 73. Sir W.
Jones considered Ganesa to be identical with Janus.

Naghra was the King's Seat and principal City, anciently the Head of the whole Kingdom of *Cambaia*, and that the City now properly call'd *Cambaia*, and rais'd to greatness by the ruine of this old, is a modern thing ; whence I have sometimes suspected that the Indian character call'd *Naghra*,[1] us'd by the learned, was denominated from this City wherein it was anciently us'd ; but 'tis onely a Conjecture, and I have learnt by long and much experience that in the derivation and interpretation of Names, especially of Places, there is no trusting to the resemblance of Words ; because by reason of the diversity of Languages, and the casual conformity of Words which signifie things sufficiently different, according to the variety of Places, gross errors are easily admitted. *Nagher*[2] in the *Indian* Language signifies a great City.

Coming from Naghra I saw some naked and besmeared Men, of deportment almost like the incinerated Gioghi,[3] who were of a Race of *Indians* accounted by themselves the most sordid and vile Race of all in India, because they eat everything, even the uncleanest Animals, as Rats and the like; whence they are call'd in *Persian Halal-chor*,[4] which signifies a Man that accounts it lawful to eat anything. The *Indians* call them *Der*,[5] and all people in general abhor not onely to converse with, but even to touch them. Con-

---

[1] The Devanagari character, or Divine Alphabet, is here referred to. The word *nagari* is derived from the Sanskrit *nagar*, "a city", the character having been used by dwellers in towns. (See Sir H. Yule's *Hobson-Jobson.*)

[2] The word should be spelt " Nagar". There is a curious tendency on the part of Europeans to insert the letter " h" in Oriental words, all the more curious because the aspirate is seldom, if ever, pronounced when thus inserted.

[3] See *ante*, p. 37.   [4] See *ante*, p. 54.

[5] More correctly *Dher*, or *Dhed*, a word generally applied to one of the lowest castes, who act as scavengers and do other menial work, and are often entrusted with the important duty of carrying letters. (See Sir M. Williams' *Modern India*, p. 46.)

I

cerning Religion I have heard nothing particular of them, but believe them *Gentiles* as the rest, or perhaps Atheists, who may possibly hold everything for lawful, as well in believing as in eating. They are all sufficiently poor, and live for the most part by begging, or exercising the most sordid trades[1] in the Common-wealth, which others disdain to meddle with, but they, either because their Rite teaches them so, or necessity inforces them, are not at all shie of.

March the fifth. We visited the King's Garden again, and many other Gardens, where we tasted divers fruits, and beheld several Flowers of *India* unknown in *Europe ;* amongst the rest one very odoriferous, which I kept in a Paper, which they call *Ciompa*.[2] Without the City we saw the Salt-pits,[3] and also the Field by the Sea-side, where the *Indians* are wont to burn the bodies of their dead, which may be known by the reliques of many fires and pieces of bones not wholly burnt which are seen scatter'd about the same. The next Morning early we returned to this Field and saw several Bodies burnt, and particularly observed the Funeral of one Woman from the beginning to the end. They carry the Corps[4] wrapt in a cloth of *Cit*,[5] of

---

[1] Such "sordid trades" are "absolutely necessary to the comfort, if not to the very health and life, of the population". (See Sir M. Williams' *Modern India*, p. 46.)

[2] *I.e.*, Champa. See *ante*, p. 46.

[3] Or, more correctly, "salt pans", for obtaining salt by evaporation of sea-water.

[4] This spelling of the word was in use up to the end of the 17th century, if not later. The epitaph on William Prynne, who died in 1669, by S. Butler, author of *Hudibras*, commences :

> "Here lies the Corps of William Prynne,
> A Bencher, late of Lincoln's Inn."

See also in Ben Jonson's *Alchemist*, Act I, sc. I :—

> "Your conjuring . . . .
> Could not relieve your corps with so much linen
> Would make you tinder."

[5] Or chintz. See *ante*, p. 45.

a red colour for the most part, and much in use among the *Indians* for other purposes. They carry it not upon a Biere as we do, but ty'd to and hanging down like a sack from a staff lay'd across on two Men's shoulders. They make the funeral pile of wood, lay'd together in form of a bed, of equal length and breadth, and sufficient to receive the Body, upon which, beginning then to lament with a loud voice, they lay the carkass naked and supine, with the Face and Feet towards the Sea; which position is likewise adopted (where the Sea is not) towards Rivers, Lakes, and Cisterns, the *Indians* having a particular devotion to the Water; nor do I know that herein they have respect to any Region of Heaven. They cover the privities with a piece of wood, anoint the Hands and Feet, put a coal of fire in the Mouth, and then, all things being prepared, they set fire first at the Throat, and afterwards to the whole pile round about, beginning first at the Head, but with their Faces turn'd another way, as *Virgil*[1] saith our Ancestors did; then sprinkle water on the ground round about the pile, which they continually stir up with staves in their Hands, and blow with the motion of a cloth, to the end the same may not spread but burn more speedily. The Body being consum'd by degrees they reduce the fire into a round form, and when all is burnt they leave the ashes, and sometimes a piece of bone not wholly consum'd, there in the same place. The cloth, wherein the body was wrapt before it was committed to the pile, they give in charity to some poor person present. Such as have wherewithall are burnt with odoriferous and precious wood, in which the rich spend much; but they that cannot reach so high use

---

[1] It is not clear to what passage in *Virgil* reference is here made. The custom of veiling the head in religious ceremonies is mentioned in *Æneid*, lib. iii, 404, 405.

> " Et positis aris jam vota in littore solves,
> Purpureo velare comas adopertus amictu."

ordinary wood. Children under two years of age are not
burnt but buried, as we saw some in the same Field. Nor
let the Reader wonder that in the same day and hour we
hapned to see so many dead persons; for, besides that
Cambaia is a large City and very populous, as all the Cities
and Lands of *India* are, the *Gentiles* are wont to perform
this Ceremony of the dead onely in the Morning, at a set
hour and in that place; so that all that dye in the whole
City during the twenty-four hours of the day are brought
to that place at the same hour.[1]

The same day we had News of a Jesuit's coming to
Cambaia from *Goa*, with a *Cafila*[2] of *Portugal* Frigats, who
was going for *Agrà*. Whereupon· in the Evening Sig.
Alberto Scilling and I, in company of a Venetian Merchant,
went to visit him at the house where he lodged; and having
told him that we were to go the next day for *Sùrat*, I desir'd him to give me a Letter to the Jesuits of *Damàn*[3] and
Bassaim[4] where I hop'd to touch upon the way to *Goa*,
which he very courteously condescending to do, we went
again the next Morning to see him before he departed.

March the seventh. In the Morning we visited the Father
Jesuit, who was not a Priest, but one of those whom they
call Fratelli, Brothers, or young Fryars. He gave me
Letters to *F. Antonio Albertino*, an Italian, and Rector of
their Colledge in *Damàn*, and to the Father Rector of their
Colledge at *Bassaim*, desiring them that since I could not
imbarque at *Cambaia* in the *Cafila* of the *Portugals*, because
I was to return to *Sùrat*, where I had left my goods in the
Ships, they would favour me and assist me to get con-
venient passage for *Goa* in the said *Cafila*, either at *Damàn*

---

[1] An interesting account of Hindu funeral ceremonies is given in
Sir M. Williams' *Modern India*, p. 97 *et seq.*, and in Dubois' *Mœurs
des Peuples de l'Inde*, vol. ii, p. 205 *et seq.*

[2] See p. 121, *note*.   [3] See p. 15.

[4] Or more correctly Bassein. See *ante*, p. 16.

or *Bassaim*, where I intended to meet it as it return'd. I on the other side gave this Father a Letter to the Fathers Resident at *Agrà*, to whom I had written formerly from *Persia*, desiring them to send me some correct Copy of the *Persian* Books, written by the Fathers in that Court, in order to get the same printed at *Rome;* and by Sig. *Alberto Scilling* I had understood that my first Letter was receiv'd there, and that the said Fathers of *Agrà* knew me by report, and the relation of divers who had seen me in *Persia*, particularly of this Sig. *Alberto*. In this other Letter from *Cambaia* I acquainted them with my voyage to *Goa*, desiring them to write me there, and to remember to favour me with those Books.

Having dispatch'd the Father Jesuit we return'd to the Dutch[1] House to have a Collation; and here we were entertain'd a good while with good Musick by an Indian, who sung tolerably well, and play'd upon a certain odd instrument used in *India*, which pleas'd me well enough, because it was not so obstreperous Musick as the ordinary of the vulgar *Indians*, but rather low and very sweet, and the Musician was skilful according to the mode of the Country, having liv'd at the Court of *Tisapor*,[2] in the service of *Adilsiah*.[3] His Instrument[4] was made of two round Gourds, dy'd black and varnish'd, with a hole bor'd in one of them, to reverberate the Sound. Between the

---

[1] Until late in the 17th century the word "Dutch" meant generally "German", while he whom we should now term a "Dutchman" would then be named a "Hollander". (See Trench's *Select Glossary*, p. 66.)

[2] "Tisapor" seems to be a mistake for "Bíjápúr", the seat of government of the Ádil Sháh dynasty, founded in the 15th century by Eusuf Sháh, a Turk.

[3] Or Ádil Sháh. See p. 143, *note*.

[4] This was probably the "Vina", "Bina", or "Veen", a description of which will be found in *Anthropological Studies*, by W. Buckland. p. 287. It has seven strings. A specimen was exhibited in the Indian and Colonial Exhibition of 1886.

one Gourd and the other was fastned a piece of wood, about the length of three spans, upon which they both hung, and the strings, which were many, partly of brass and partly of steel, were extended, passing over many little pieces of wood like so many bridges ; and these were the frets,[1] which he touch'd with the left Hand, to diversify the sounds, and the strings with the right, not with his Fingers or Nails, but with certain iron wires[2] fastened to his Fingers by certain rings like thimbles, wherewith he did not strike the strings strongly, but lightly touched them from the top downwards, so that they render'd a sound sufficiently pleasant. When he play'd he held the Instrument at his breast by a string that went round his neck, and one of the Gourds hung over his left shoulder, and the other under his right arm, so that it was a pretty sight.

Collation and Musick ended, we were conducted about two *Cos* out of the City by the Dutch Merchants, and took the same way by which we came. We pass'd over the five *Cos* of wet ground with the four Currents of Water, of which the second was the deepest (having waited a while for a fit hour), in company of a numerous *Cafila* of Coaches, Cars, Horse-men, and Foot-men, in the same manner and circumstances as I writ before ; onely the water was now much higher than we had found it at our Coming, so that it came into all the Coaches, and we were fain to stand upright and hold fast by the roof of the Coaches, bare leg'd too, because the water came above the bottom of the Coaches to the middle of the leg. The Oxen and Horses could scarce keep their Heads above Water, and the Coaches being light, if men hir'd purposely had not gone along in the water to hold them steady, and break the course thereof

---

[1] On which the wires are pressed to regulate the pitch.

[2] Like the "plectrum", which is never found in Egyptian or Assyrian representations of musical performances, but always in those of Chinese and Japanese performers. (Buckland's *Anthropological Studies*, p. 286.)

by holding great Stumps of Wood on that side the Tide came furiously in, without doubt the water would have swept them away. In this place on the left hand towards the land in the moist ground we beheld at a distance many Fowls, as big or bigger than Turkies, go up and down rather running then flying. They told us they were the same which the *Portugals* call *Paxaros Flamencos*,[1] from their bright colour, and I think they are those of whose beaks *Mir Mahammed*, in *Spahàn*, makes bow-rings for the Kings ; although he erroneously takes it for the beak of the Cocnos,[2] or Phœnix, which good Authors describe, not as a water fowl, but rather an inhabitant of high Mountains. Having at length pass'd this dangerous ford, and following our way, we came at night to lodge at *Giambuser*,[3] the same Town where we had lodg'd formerly.

March the eighth. We put ourselves upon the way again, and forded the little salt-water *Dilàvel*, and at night arriv'd at *Barocci*,[4] and were, as formerly, entertain'd in the House of the Dutch. But upon the way, before we enter'd the City, we saw a handsome structure standing upon a famous Sepulchre of I know not well whom, but it seems to be some great person's, and is worship'd by the *Moors* as a sacred thing. This Fabrick is pleasantly seated amongst Trees, something elevated upon the side of a little Lake, or great Cistern. In the chief part of it, besides the principal

---

[1] The Spanish and Portuguese name, corrupted into "flamingo" by English writers. (*Phœnicopterus*.)

[2] The phœnix is certainly nowhere described as an aquatic bird. Mir Muhammad could hardly have meant the fabulous bird called phœnix by Herodotus and others ; but it is impossible to say what bird he really spoke of. The flamingo is common in the vicinity of the Caspian Sea, and our author is probably correct in his conjecture as to this being the bird of which the beak is used in the way mentioned, if indeed the beak of a bird was so used. Barbosa (p. 43 says that the bows used at Ormuz were made of "stiff wood and buffaloe's horn". [3] See *ante*, p. 62. See *ante*, p. 19.

Sepulchre which stands apart in the most worthy place, are many other Sepulchres of white Marble, of an oblong form, with many carvings and works tolerable enough ; 'tis likely they are the Tombs, either of the Wives and Children, or of the other kindred of the Principal, because they seem all of the same work and time. Round this greater structure stand others less, with Sepulchres of *Moors* in them, who cause themselves to be buried there out of devotion to the place ; whence I gather that the principal Sepulchre is not onely of some great person or Prince as it intimates, but also of one that dy'd with some opinion among the *Moors* of sanctity. I know not who told me that it was the Sepulchre of a famous Tartarian King,[1] who came to have dominion in those parts ; but I credit not the Relation, because I had it not from a good hand.

March the ninth. We departed from *Barocci*, ferrying over the River, and at night lodg'd at *Periab*, where we had quarter'd before as we went.

March the tenth. Having gone the short way which remain'd, and passed the River of *Sùrat* by boat, we came to that City about Noon, where I repair'd to the House before assign'd me by the Dutch Commendator, and there found the Daughter of one of the *Armenian* or *Syrian* Merchants seen by us at *Ahmedabàd*, who was come thither with a Brother of hers in order to be marry'd shortly to one Sig. *Guglielmo*, a *Hollander*, to whom she had been promis'd in Marriage at *Ahmedabàd*, and who also was in the same House, which was capable

---

[1] This was probably the mausoleum (still standing, though in a dilapidated condition) of Bâwâ Rahan Sahib, said to have been built about the end of the 11th century. It is described in Campbell's *Gazetteer of the Bombay Residency*, vol. ii, p. 558, and in Forbes' *Oriental Memoirs*, vol. ii, p. 113. There are, however, other sepulchres of former Muhammadan rulers, and one of a saint called Pir Chatar, in the vicinity.

of him and more. I understood at *Sùrat* that *Sultan Chorròm* had taken and sackt the City of *Agrà,*[1] except the Castle, and that his Army and himself had committed very great Cruelties there in spoiling, and discovering, the Goods and Money of the Citizens ; particularly that he had tortur'd, and undecently mangled many Women of quality, and done other like barbarities, whereby he render'd himself very odious to the people. Concerning *Asaf Chan* it was said that he was held in custody by the King, as suspected of Rebellion, although his affairs were spoken of with much uncertainty, and that the King was hastning[2] to come against his son, but was yet far off and mov'd slowly.

XX.—*March* the thirteenth. Conceiving the return of the *Portugal Cafila*[3] from *Cambaia* to *Goa* to be near at hand, and desiring to make a Voyage with the same, since in regard of the greatness of my luggage, and the length of the way, I could not go by Land, and 'twas not safe going by Sea, by reason of the continual incursions of the *Mahabar*[4] Pirates, I despatch'd a Messenger to *Damàn,* a City of the *Portugals,* a little way from *Sùrat,* to *F. Antonio Albertino,* Rector of the Colledge of Jesuits, with the Letter which their above mention'd Father had given me in *Cambaia ;* and giving him account of my self and my intention I desir'd him to send me from *Damàn* one of

---

[1] This rumour was false, as Prince Kharram did not succeed in getting to Agra. (See Elphinstone's *India*, p. 497.)

[2] From Lahore where he was then. As to Asaf Khan, see p. 55.

[3] The use of this word "Cafila" for a fleet is unusual and, strictly speaking, incorrect, as the Arabic word really means a crowd of *men.*

[4] Mahabar should be Malabar. The name is also written as Minibar, Manibar, Monebar, Mulebar, Malibar, Milibar, and Male, and is applied to that part of the west coast lying between 10° and 13° N. lat. The word is derived from *Mala*, "a hill" (Dravidian), and the Arabic word *bar*, or Sanskrit *bara*, denoting "territory". (See Sir H. Yule's *Hobson-Jobson.*)

those Light Vessels which they call *almadia*,[1] and are of that swiftness that they are not at all afraid of Pirates, to carry me from *Sùrat* to *Damàn* where I desired to meet the *Cafila*[2] : for I could not go by a Boat of *Sùrat*, since the Mariners of *Sùrat* would not have taken my Goods aboard which were in the English Ships, without first carrying them into the City to make them pay Custom, whereby I might have been put to a great deal of trouble of going backward and forward, as also upon the account of the Moorish Books which I had with me, and reliques of Sig^{ra.} *Maani*.[3] Wherefore to prevent these Intricacies, I pray'd the Father to send me a Boat from *Damàn* to take me in, not at the City, but at the Port where the Ships ride, and where I intended to be with my Goods ready upon the shore of *Sohali*.[4] And to the end this *Portugal* boat might come securely, and not fear, I sent him two safe Conducts, one from the English and the other from the Dutch ; although there was no necessity of them, because Boats come many times secretly from *Damàn* without such safe Conduct, to sell Commodities to the English Ships.

March the fifteenth was the first day of the Feast of the *Indian-Gentiles*,[5] which they celebrate very solemnly at

---

[1] From the Moorish *Al-Mádiya*, a raft, or canoe, a kind of vessel smaller than those called " Manchua".   [2] See p. 121, *note.*

[3] These words refer to the remains of P. della Valle's wife, Sitti Maani, who had died near Persepolis, whose corpse he carried about with him in his travels, landed in Italy concealed in a bale of cotton, and buried at Rome in the family vault. (See Latin verses immediately following the Dedication of these letters.)

[4] See *ante*, p. 21.

[5] The " Holi", or " Holika", festival, held fifteen days before the full moon of Phalgun (vernal equinox), in honour of Krishna and the spring season, at which the people dance round fires (a relic, probably, of sun-worship), sing licentious and satirical songs, and give vent to all sorts of ribaldry against their superiors. Similar to the Roman Saturnalia.

the entrance of the Spring, with dancings through the street, and casting orange water and red colours[1] in jest one upon another, with other festivities of Songs and Mummeries, as I have formerly seen the same in *Spahan,* where also reside constantly a great number of *Banians*[2] and *Indian Gentiles.* Yet the solemnity and concourse of people was greater than in *Persia,* as being in their own Country and a City inhabited in a great part by *Gentiles* and wealthier persons. Otherwise I saw nothing at *Sùrat* during these three Festival Days but what I had seen already at *Spahan,* and have mentioned in my writings from that place.

March the eighteenth. Being invited to the Dutch House we there saw the Contract of Sig^ra *Mariam,* the Daughter of the abovesaid *Armenian* or *Syrian* Merchant, Resident at *Ahmedabad,* with Sig^r *Guigliélmo* a Dutchman, which was follow'd by a sumptuous Dinner, at which were all the Christian Dames of Europe that liv'd at *Sùrat,* to attend upon the Bride; namely, one *Portugal* Woman[3] taken in one of the last Ships which were surpriz'd by the *Dutch,* and married likewise to a *Dutchman : Mary Bagdadina,* wife to another *Hollander,* and with them also my young *Mariam Tinatìn ;* and another born in *India,* and contracted to a *Dutchman ;* of which Nation many, upon the encouragement of certain priviledges granted them by the State, marry Wives in *India* of any kind, either white Women or black, and go to people New *Batavia,*[4] which

---

[1] A crimson-coloured powder, made of the Singara nut, called "Abeer". Referring to this practice, Mr. Elphinstone says (*Hist. of India,* p. 182) : "A grave prime minister will invite a foreign ambassador to play the 'holi' at his house, and will take his share in the most riotous parts of it with the ardour of a school-boy."

[2] See p. 78.   [3] Donna Lucia, already mentioned at p. 25.

[4] See *ante,* p. 24, note. Capital of Java. In lat. 6° 12' N., long. 107° 4' E. Taken by the English in 1811, and subsequently restored to the Dutch.

they have built in *Java Major*,[1] near a place which they
call *Giacatora*[2]: and they that cannot light upon Free-
women for Marriage buy Slaves and make them their
lawful Wives to transport thither. At this entertainment
were present also the President of the *English*, with all
those of his Nation, all the *Dutch* Merchants, the Bride's
Brother, Sig[r] *Alberto Scilling*, myself, and in short all the
European Christians that were in *Sùrat*.

XXI.—*March* the one and twentieth. A Post came to the
Dutch Merchants from *Agra*, with fresh News that *Sultan
Chorròm* had, besides the former, given a new[3] sack to the
said City, the Souldiers committing the like and greater
Cruelties, exasperated perhaps at their being valorously
repuls'd in assaulting the Castle with loss of many of their
Companions.

March the two and twentieth. This Morning the Messenger whom I had sent to *Damàn* returned to *Sùrat* with
the answer which I expected. *F. Antonio* writ me word
that there was but one of those Light Vessels belonging
to *Damàn*, and it was now at *Sùrat*, having lately come
thither, the Master of which was one *Sebastian Luis ;*
wherefore he advis'd me to agree with him for my trans-

---

[1] Island of Java ; see *ante*, p. 24. The name of "Jave la Grande"
is also applied in some old maps to the northern part of Australia,
Java proper being marked as "Jave le Petit" or " lytil Java". The
name of Jawa (or Java) was applied by the Arab navigators to the whole
Eastern Archipelago, and hence the titles of "Jave la Grande" and
"Jave le Petit" may naturally have been used for the great Australian
continent (as it was formerly supposed to be) and the smaller island of
Java respectively. (See a note on the subject in Yule's *Cathay*, vol. ii,
p. 519.)

[2] *I.e.*, the river Jacatra, at the mouth of which the town of Batavia
is situated.

[3] Another false rumour. On this occasion Prince Kharram did not
advance further than Belochpur, forty miles S. of Delhi, whence he was
forced to retreat towards Mandu by the advance of the Emperor
Jehangir from Lahore. (See Elphinstone's *India*, p. 497, 3rd ed.)

portation, and in case he was already gone, then I should advertise him thereof at *Damàn*, and they would speedily send him back; for which purpose they kept the safe Conducts which I had sent for Security of the Vessel. But having presently found the abovesaid *Sebastian Luis* I have agreed with him to bring his boat out of the River to the Sea-side and take me in at the Port which is some distance from the mouth of the River, where I have appointed to meet him to-morrow morning. It remains onely that I take leave of the *Dutch* Commendator and the *English* Resident, from whom I have received infinite Obligations during all my residence here, particularly from the Sig^r. Commendator; the remembrance whereof shall continue with me during Life. I hope, God willing, to write to you speedily from *Goa*, and in the mean time humbly kiss your Hands.[1]

---

[1] The phrase "Bezo las manos" (I kiss hands), represented by the abbreviation "B. L. M.", was, and is, the usual complimentary conclusion to letters in Spain, and its equivalent expression in Italian is here made use of by the writer of these letters. In Sir T. Browne's *Religio Medici* (Part I, sect. 17) he says: "Nor can I relate the History of my life . . . . with a *Bezo las manos* to Fortune, or a bare Gramercy to my good Stars." For an instance of an uncomplimentary use of the expression, see Fletcher's play of *Rule a Wife and have a Wife*, Act I, Scene 4: "I leave thee as a thing despised, baso las manos à vostra seignora."

LETTER II.

From Goa, April 27, 1623.

 Now salute you (my dear Sig. *Mario*) from *Goa*; in *India* indeed I am, but no *Indian*. Having pass'd through the *Syrian*, and afterwards the *Persian*, I am again invested with our *European* garb. In *Turkie* and *Persia* you would not have known me, but could not mistake me in *India*, where I have almost resum'd my first shape. This is the third transformation which my Beard hath undergone, having here met with an odd Barber, who hath advanced my mustachios according to the *Portugal* Mode, and in the middle of my chin, shaven after the *Persian* Mode, he hath left the *European* tuft. But to continue my Diary where I left off in my last Letter, which was about my departure from *Sùrat*.

March the three and twentieth. Having taken leave of all Friends, a little after Dinner I set forth to depart, but met with so many obstacles in the Dogana, or Custom-house, that they detain'd me till almost night before I could get away. The occasion was this : in the Pass given me (without which none can depart) the Governor three times expressly prohibited my *Persian* Servant *Cacciatùr* to go with me ; and this for no other cause but that himself (foolishly, or rather cunningly, as appear'd afterwards) out of a pretended vain fear, as he said, when we first came to *Sùrat* lest he should be known to be what he was by some of the *Persians*, who are there in the Service of the Great *Moghòl*, and not knowing that in *India* there is Liberty of Conscience, and that a Man may hold or change what Faith he pleases, not the least trouble being given to any Person touching Religion in the Dominions of the *Moghòl*,[1] not knowing these things, I say, and fearing to confess himself Christian before any that might know him in *Persia* for a *Moor*,[2] had declar'd in the *Dogàna*, when he was examin'd thereupon, that he was a *Musliman*,[3] which they interpret a *Moor*, although the word properly signifies *safe* or *saved*, that is of the right Faith : and therefore by Christians (understanding it in their own sense) when considerable respects oblige them to conceal themselves perhaps is not unlawful to be assum'd. Now *Cacciatùr* being hereupon taken for a *Moor*, and not daring to deny it, or discover himself more clearly, but, as I believe, intending to be a *Moor* really, and to do what afterwards he did, they would not suffer that he should go along with me into the jurisdiction of Christians, where they conceiv'd he would be in danger of being perverted. And although

---

[1] This spirit of toleration may be said to owe its origin to the Emperor Akbar, who abolished the tax formerly imposed on "infidels" (*i.e.*, non-Muhammadans), saying that "as all modes of worship are designed for one great Being, it was wrong to cut the devout off from their mode of intercourse with their Maker". (See Elphinstone's *India*, p. 472.)

[2] The word "Moor", which was originally used to designate a native of Mauritania, eventually became synonymous with Muhammadan.

[3] From the Arabic word *Islam*, "submission", "one who has submitted himself to the will of God", corrupted generally into " Mussulman"; as to the last syllable of which word great confusion of mind exists, a notable instance of such being found in the *Nineteenth Century* periodical of August 1890, in which the word "Mussulwomen" appears as the feminine plural of "Mussulman" !

innumerable *Moors* go daily into the neighbouring Territories of the *Portugals*, nor are they wont to be forbidden; yet my *Cacciatùr*, I know not upon what account, they prohibited very strictly, I believe by his own procurement. When I had read this prohibition in my Pass I sent him out of the City before-hand, with orders to cross the River at another place a good way off and meet me at the Seaside, where, being among the *English*, he would be out of all danger; but through the negligence of a Man of the Country whom he took to direct him, either by his own will, as is most likely, because he knew not the way, or else, not having found Boats to pass the River elsewhere, as he said, he was directed to cross it at the same place near the Custom-house where we did ; whereupon being seen by the Officers he was seiz'd upon, and they would not suffer him to come by any means. I us'd much instance, and try'd divers wayes, alledging by a writing that he was bound to serve me longer, and was to go to *Goa* to be paid his wages there, according to agreement ; but all to no purpose, they still answering (though with great courtesie indeed) that the accord[1] was good, and that *Cacciatùr* did not break it, being for his part ready to go, but that they made him stay by force, as in zeal for Religion 'twas reasonable for them to do ; that had I been going into some Territory of *Moors* as I was of *Christians* they should not have kept him from me ; and therefore, in short, I must be contented to leave him behind, and pay him for his service done at *Sùrat*, otherwise they could not give a Pass to myself.

Perceiving there was no remedy I returned to the *Dutch* House, and having consulted with the Commendator what to do I agreed with *Cacciatùr* (who was willing not to be left at *Sùrat*, after I had threaten'd to cause him to

---

[1] See Dryden, " If both are satisfied with this accord."

be slain there in case he stay'd to turn *Moor*) that he should shew himself desirous to stay at *Sùrat*, and in the Governour's own House too, if he pleas'd, assuring him under his Hand that I had fully satisfi'd him, that so my journey might not be stopt ; and that after I was gone without him the *Dutch* Commendator, who took this care upon him, should procure his escape and send him by another way to the Sea-side where I took Boat ; or, if he could not be sent timely enough to find me there, then he should come to *Damàn* by Land, where he should certainly find me. Upon this agreement we went before the Governour with the discharges of his Arrears in writing and the Governour was contented to let me go, after he had narrowly examin'd whether it was true that he was pay'd by me, and that his agreeing to stay in *Sùrat* was not a fiction. But we had laid all things so together that he did not discover the truth, or perhaps did not care much to find it out.

Wherefore, leaving *Cacciatùr* in the Governour's House, where he caus'd him to stay with sundry promises, about night I departed from the City, and cross'd the River with *Sebastian Luis* in my company, who having sent his Vessel down the River went along with me by Land. On the other side of the River we waited some hours for Coaches to carry us to the Sea-side, which we were fain to hire at a town some distance off, and which were slow in coming. But as soon as they came we got into them, and travell'd the rest of the night to the Sea-side.

II.—*March* the four and twentieth. At Day-break we got to the shore side, where we found the *English* President attended by all the Merchants of his Nation, who were giving orders for dispatching their Ships which were ready to set sail to *Muchà*,[1] or *Muchàr*, in the Red Sea, namely,

---

[1] See *ante*, p. 1.

the two Ships the *Whale* and *Dolphin*, wherewith I came into *India*, for of the other three which I left in *Bender*[1] of *Kombrù* they had sold the little Frigat[2] which was in ill plight, to the *Persians*, who design'd to make use of her in the enterprize of *Arabia*, whither they had determin'd to pass alone, now the *English* plainly refus'd to join with them in the War, and the other two great Ships, having put in likewise at *Sùrat*, were soon after sent out again with Master *Thompson*, who came with them from *Persia*, it not being known in *Sùrat* whither.

I was receiv'd by the President in his Tent, together with my *Mary Tinatìn*, and soon after came *Cacciatùr* my servant and two *Moors* of *Sùrat*, by the favour of the Commendator of the *Dutch;* but I know not whether it were with his own good liking, though to us he pretended that it was. After my departure the Commendator went to visit the Governour, and since I was gone, and, as he said, could not carry *Cacciatùr* out of *Sùrat*, he desir'd that he would give him to him, to the end he might live in his House with other Friends ; which the Governour readily granting, the same night, by the help of certain persons purposely disguised in *Indian* Habit, he sent him by a secure way to the Sea-side, where he found me in the Tent of the *English* President. The same Morning I went aboard the Ship call'd the *Whale*[3] (wherein I came) to visit the Captain and take leave of my Friends, with whom also I din'd ; afterwards I went aboard the *Dolphin*, to visit not onely the Captain, who was my Friend, but especially my good Companion Sig. *Alberto Scilling*, who was aboard there in order to go to the Red Sea, intending to pass

---

[1] See p. 107, *note.*

[2] The word "Frigat" originally meant a small *undecked* vessel, called in Italian *Fregata*, from the Greek αφρακτος, "unfortified". (Webster's *Dictionary.*)

[3] See *ante*, p. 1.

from thence into *Æthiopia*,[1] to the court of the *Abissins*,[2] in case he could get Transportation, and were not hindred in the Turkish Ports where he was to pass, upon account of being a *Christian*; the *Turks* not willingly granting passage to *Christians* (especially *Europeans*) towards *Hhabese*,[3] in regard of the suspitions they have of the intelligences and converse which our Compatriots may have to their prejudice with that Prince. Wherefore, taking leave of Sig. *Alberto* with many embraces, of Master *Rosel* (whom I had known in *Persia*, and who, being come from thence after me, was here shipt for a Trading Voyage) and of all my other Friends in the two ships, I came back to sup and lye on Land in the Tent of the President.

March the twenty-fifth. Early in the Morning, I put my Goods into the Shallop[4] of *Sebastian Luis*, and also going aboard myself, whilst the President went to his own Ships to despatch them, set sail for *Damàn*; at night we cast Anchor in a narrow arm of the Sea, which enters far into the Land, of which sort of inlets there are many all along the coast of India,[5] which encompassing good portions of Land make many little Islands; and because the said arms of the sea are long and narrow, like Rivers, and some of them have little Rivers falling into them from the continent (although the water is salt, and they have no current but

---

[1] This name was formerly used in a general way to denote the African continent, and sometimes even Asia, Persia, Chaldæa, and Assyria. In the present instance, however, the name seems to apply to the country properly known as Æthiopia, *i.e.*, Abyssinia.

[2] *I.e.*, Abyssinians, from the Arabic *Habsh*, the name applied to the country called by us Abyssinia, meaning "dark". Cf. Milton: " Nor where Abassin kings their issue guard." (*Par. Lost*, iv, 280.)

[3] Or Habsh, another conspicuous instance of the insertion of a superfluous aspirate; see *ante*, p. 113.

[4] In the original " Almadia", *q. v.*, *ante*, p. 122. The word " Shallop" is derived from the Dutch *Sloep*, through the French *chaloupe*.

[5] This remark applies only to the west coast of India. The eastern coast is singularly devoid of such inlets.

the ebbing and flowing of the Sea) the *Portugals* term them
in their language, *Rios* or Rivers, which I take notice of
that it may be understood that all the *Rios* or Rivers
which I shall name on the coast of *India*, and not specifie
that they are streams of fresh waters, are such arms of the
Sea as this, improperly called Rivers. This where we stay'd
this night is call'd *Rio di Colek*, or *Coleque*.

I have better understood[1] that all the aforesaid inlets are
not arms of the Sea, but really Rivers of fresh water ; and
the Tide of the Sea at ebbing and flowing being here very
strong, and overcoming that of the Rivers, hence it comes to
pass that 'tis hardly perceiv'd whether they have any stream
or no ; and the water going very far into the Land comes
likewise to be salt ; but indeed they are Rivers, and form
Islands by their entering into the Sea with many mouths.
They are almost innumerable upon all the coast of India,
and the *Portugals* very truly call them *Rios*, Rivers.
Wonder not at these doubts and various informations, for
I could not understand things thoroughly at first, for want
of converse with intelligent persons ; nor was it easie for
me to judge right in the beginning ; the first appearance
of things oftentimes deceiving even the wisest, as the salt-
ness of the water did me in my judgment of the Rivers,
making me take them for arms of the Sea ; which mistake
was further'd by the affirmation of most of the ignorant
Portugals, who, not knowing more of this coast than the
shore where the water is salt, think that the Rivers are salt
water ; but Time and better informations assist my diligence
in discovering the truth of things.

March the twenty-sixth. About noon we arriv'd at
Damàn, but unseasonably, the *Cafila* and Fleet of the *Portugals* being gone in the Morning, and we discern'd them
sailing afar off, but it was not possible to overtake them. I

---

[1] This paragraph appears to have been written some time after the
preceding sentence, when the writer had had greater experience.

advertis'd *F. Antonio Albertino*, Rector of the Jesuits' Colledge, of my coming, and he very courteously came forthwith to the Sea-side to receive me, and carry'd me to lodge in the Colledge, which in reference to that small City is large enough and well built. He sent *Mariam Tinatìn* in a *Palanchino*, or *Indian Litter*, (wherein people are carry'd lying along as 'twere in a Couch, and those of women are cover'd) to the House of a *Portugal* Gentlewoman, and advis'd me that since the *Cafila* was departed I should go in the same Vessel to meet it at *Bassaim*[1] where it was to touch, and for that day rest a little in *Damàn*, as I accordingly did.

III.—The City of *Damàn*[2] is small but of good building, and hath long, large and straight streets. It hath no Bishop, as neither have the other Cities of the *Portugals* upon this coast, being subject in spirituals to the Arch-Bishop of *Goa ;* but in every one of them resides a Vicar, whom they call *"da Vara"*, that is, "of the *Vièrge"*,[3] or *"Mace"*, (which is the badge of Authority) with supreme power. Besides the Jesuits and the Church of the See[4] (as they call the *Duomo* or Cathedral) here are *Dominicans, Franciscans*, and, as I remember, *Augustines* too ; all of whom have good Churches and Convents. The City is environ'd with strong walls of good fortification, and hath a large Territory and many Towns under it, and because they are frequently at

---

[1] See *ante*, p. 16.   [2] See *ante*, p. 16.
[3] Hence our word " verger". See Swift—

> " The silver verge with decent pride,
> Stuck underneath the cushion side."

The mace was adopted as an emblem of authority by ecclesiastics, as they were forbidden by a canon of the Church to use the sword.

[4] The word " see", though now generally used to denote an area of episcopal jurisdiction, formerly denoted the actual seat of authority both lay and ecclesiastical. Cf. Spenser, "Jove laughed at Venus from his soverayne see", and Wiclif's *Bible* (Exod. xii, 29), " The first gotun of Pharao that sat in his see".

war with *Nizam Sciàh*,[1] whose State (being govern'd at this
day by his famous Abissine slave *Melik Ambar*[2]) borders
upon it by Land, therefore the *Portugals* here are all horse-
men and keep many good *Arabian* Horses,[3] as they are
oblig'd to do, going frequently out to war in defence of
their Territory when occasion requires, though during my
time here they were at peace.

In *Damàn* I first tasted at the Father Rector's Table
many strange *Indian* Fruits, some of which are describ'd
by *Carolus Clusius*,[4] and others not, which, as I was told,
were after the writing of his Books brought into *East India*
from *Brasil*[5] or *New Spain*[6]; namely, *Papaia*,[7] *Casa* or

---

[1] Nizám Sháh, ruler of the kingdom of Ahmadnagar, whose dynasty
was founded by Ahmad, son of Nizám 'l Mulk (a converted Hindoo,
whose real name was Timappa, son of Bheiroo, taken prisoner by
Ahmad Sháh Báhmaní, made a Muhammadan, and brought up as a
slave). He assumed the government of Ahmadábád in 1490 A.D., and
founded the city of Ahmadnagar in 1494. (See Briggs' *Ferishta*,
vol. iii, p. 189.) This dynasty came to an end in 1633 by its submission to the Emperor Sháh Jahán. An account of this dynasty will be
found in the Appendix to Elphinstone's *Hist. of India*, p. 673.

[2] Instances of slaves attaining to high office in Oriental States are,
it is well known, by no means infrequent. Malik Ambar played a
conspicuous part in the wars in the Dakhan, and was the author of a
new revenue system which has made his name famous in southern
India. (See Grant Duff's *Hist. of the Mahrattas*, vol. i, p. 95.) He
died about 1626 A.D.

[3] According to Barbosa (Hakluyt ed., p. 90) horses were even early
in the 16th century imported from Ormúz.   [4] See *ante*, p. 37, *note*.

[5] Many so-called "Indian" plants were introduced from S. America.
The most notable modern instance, perhaps, of such an introduction
is that of the Cinchona plant, by Mr. Clements Markham, C.B., F.R.S.,
which may be regarded as one of the greatest benefits conferred by the
English Government on the people of India.

[6] New Spain was the name given by Cortez to the Mexican Empire
in 1521. Brasil, or more correctly Brazil, derived its name from the
Portuguese word *Braza*, or "glowing fire", a name applied to a red-
coloured wood (*Cæsalpina cchinata*) produced in that country. (See
Webster's *Dictionary*.)

[7] Papua, or Papaw (*Carica Papaya*), a native of S. America, now

Cagiu,[1] *Giambo*,[2] *Manga*[3] or *Amba*, and *Ananas*,[4] all which seem'd to me passably good ; and, though of different taste, not inferior to ours of *Europe*, especially *Papaia*, which is little esteem'd in *India*, and, if I mistake not, is not mentioned by the abovesaid Writer; in shape and taste it much resembles our Melons, but is sweeter, and consequently to me seem'd better. *Ananas* is justly esteem'd, being of a laudable taste, though something uncouth,[5] inclining more to sharpness, which with a mixture of sweetness renders it pleasant. And because the said Books mention it not, I shall briefly add that to the outward view it seems when it is whole, to resemble our Pine-Apple,[6]

---

common in India, of which one curious property is that of making meat tender when wrapped in its leaves. The tree grows to a height of 18 or 20 feet, and bears a fruit of about the size of a melon, with an acrid, milky juice.

[1] Commonly called Cashew or Acaju (*Anacardium occidentale*), a native of tropical America, Africa, and India, one feature of which is that the nut appears to grow outside the fruit, which is really the stalk. It yields a valuable black varnish.

[2] This name denotes the *Eugenia Jambolana*, or Jambo fruit, from which India derived one of its Sanskrit names of "Jambo-dwipa", or Jambo Island.

[3] The well-known Mango ; see *ante*, p. 40. There is no good ground for supposing that this fruit was introduced from America.

[4] The Pine Apple (*Ananassa Sativa*). Originally introduced from S. America. The first pine-apple raised in England was grown in the reign of Charles II, and its presentation to the king forms the subject of a picture described by Horace Walpole, in his *Letters*, vol. iv, p. 206. Lady Wortley Montagu, writing in 1716, speaks of "two ripe 'ananas', which to my taste are a fruit perfectly delicious", eaten by her at Hanover, and apparently the first of the kind seen by her.

[5] *I.e.*, strange or unusual. The word "uncouth" literally means "unknown", from Anglo-Saxon *cunnan*, "to know", and is used by Shakespeare in this sense :

"I am surprised with an uncouth fear."

The modern meaning of "awkward" or "ungraceful" dates from last century only. (See Trench's *Select Glossary*, p. 225.)

[6] These words probably refer to the fruit of the Stone Pine (*Pinus Pinea*), common in Italy, and frequently introduced into pictures by Italian artists, of which the seeds (as of many other pines) are edible.

both in the divisions and the colour, saving that at the top
it hath a kind of tuft of long strait leaves between green
and white,[1] which the Pine-Apple hath not, and which render
it pretty to look upon ; 'tis also different from the Pine-
Apple, in that the husks[2] are not hard, but tender like the
common skin of Fruits, nor is it needful to take them off
one by one, neither is any seed eaten, as are the Pine Nuts
which are within the husks, but the whole Fruit is all pulp,
which is cut with the knife ; and within 'tis of somewhat a
greenish colour. Of temperament,[3] 'tis held to be hot and
good to promote digestion, having, in my opinion, somewhat of a winish taste and strength ; which virtue of
helping digestion is likewise ascrib'd in a higher degree to
the *Caju*, whence it always used to be eaten with fish ; but
of this and the rest, because I suppose others have written
of them, I shall forbear further to speak.

In *Damàn*, I had from the Jesuits two considerable
pieces of News. First, that the two *English* Ships, which,
as I said, were sent from *Sùrat* before my departure thence
upon some unknown design, went to *Dabul*,[4] under pretext
of Peace and Friendship, as if to traffick in that Port, and
that the Moors of *Dabul* had spread Carpets and prepar'd
a handsome entertainment for the principals upon shore,
but the *English*, having fairly landed, suddenly got to
certain pieces of Ordnance which were there and nail'd
them up[5]; then, putting their hands to their Arms, began to

---

¹ Or pale green.   ² Or, more correctly, "scales".

³ *I.e.*, "temperature". Cf. Locke, "Bodies are denominated hot or
cold in proportion to the present temperament of our body to which
they are applied."

⁴ Dabul, or Diul, or Dewal, or Daibul (probably the same as the
ancient Tiyu of the Chinese travellers), is to the W. of the Indus
mouths. It was taken by the Muhammadans in the 7th century.
(See Elphinstone's *India*, p. 263, and Yule's *Cathay*, vol. i, lxxix and
clxxviii.)

⁵ Or, as we should say, "spiked them".

fall upon the people of the City, who upon this sudden unexpected onset betook themselves to flight, and were likely to receive great dammage ; but at length a *Portugal* Factor and some few others, making head against the *English,* and animating the Citizens to do the like, turn'd the scale of victory, and in a short time beat out all the *English,* killing many of them, and constraining the rest to fly away with their Ships ; who nevertheless in their flight took two Vessels of *Dabul,* which were in the Port richly laden but unprovided, as in a secure place ; which was no small dammage to the City, and afforded a rich booty to the *English.* This action, I conceive, was done by the *English* out of some old grudge against the City of *Dabul,* or perhaps onely to force it to permit them free Trade ; and they use to deal thus with such Ports as will not admit them thereunto. The other News was, that *Prete Janni,*[1] King of *Æthiopia* and the *Abissins,* was by means of the Jesuits reconcil'd to the Roman Church, and became a good Catholick,[2] intending that his whole Country should do the same ; which, if true, is indeed a thing of great consequence.

IV.—*March* the seven and twentieth. About noon we departed from *Damàn* towards *Bassaim,*[3] in the same Barque or *Almadia,* and sail'd all the day ; at night, in regard of the contrary current and danger of Pirats, who

---

[1] This is our old friend Prester John, as to whose history the reader is referred to Sir H. Yule's *Cathay and the Way thither,* vol. i, p. 173, and also to Selden's *Titles of Honour.* An account of an embassy sent by him to Goa will be found in the *Commentaries of A. Dalboquerque,* vol. iii, p. 251.

[2] About this time Father Jerome Lobo, a Jesuit priest of Portugal, visited Abyssinia, and may have converted the king of that country. But Barbosa (Hakluyt ed., p. 20) speaks of Prester John as a Christian in the early part of the 16th century.

[3] See *ante,* p. 16.

cannot easily be seen and avoided in the dark, we cast Anchor under a place call'd *Daniè*.[1]

March the eight and twentieth. Continuing our course in the Morning we espy'd some ships, which we suspected to be Pirats of *Malabar*, and therefore fetching a compass we made but little way forwards. At night we cast Anchor in a Bay call'd *Kielme-Mahi*, from two Towns situate upon it, one call'd *Kielme*, the other *Mahi*.[2]

On the nine and twentieth of the same moneth we sail'd forward again, but, the Tide turning contrary, we cast Anchor about noon, and stay'd a while at a little Island near the Continent. The sails being mended, and the current become favourable, we set forward again ; and having pass'd by some Vessels which we doubted to be Pirats of *Malabar*, about night we arriv'd at *Bassaim*.[3] But lest the people of the Fleet, which we found there with the *Cafila*, should molest our Boat, as sometimes 'tis usual, and take away the Sea-men for the service of the Navy, we stay'd a while without the City, casting an Anchor a little wide of the shore ; and in the mean time I sent notice to F. *Diego Rodriguez*, Rector of the Colledge of Jesuits at *Bassaim*, for whom I had Letters from the Father Rector of their Colledge at *Damàn*, and one also from others for the Brother of theirs, whom I saw in *Cambaia*.

The F. Rector sent presently to the Sea-side where I was, F. *Gaspar di Govea* their Procurator, who, because 'twas said the Fleet would depart that very night with the *Cafila* for *Goa*, immediately, without my entering into the City, procur'd me passage in a Merchants' Frigat, as more commodious for passengers in regard 'twas free from the

---

[1] A small town marked as Danu in modern maps, about half-way between Damàn and Bassein, in lat. 20° N.

[2] A small town marked as Mahim in Wyld's map, in lat. 19° 30' N.   [3] See *ante*, p. 16.

trouble of Souldiers which went in the Men of War
appointed to convoy the Merchants' Ships. The Captain
of the Vessel wherein I embark'd was call'd *Diego Car-
vaglio*, with whom having agreed for my passage I presently put my Goods aboard his Ship, together with *Mariam
Tinatin*, in the most convenient cabin, and *Cacciatùr* to
take care of them. It being now night, I went alone with
F. *Govea* to their Colledge to visit and thank the F. Rector
and the other Fathers, who very courteously retain'd me
at Supper ; which ended, to avoid the danger of being left
behind, I forthwith return'd to repose in the Ship. Of the
City of Bassaim, I cannot say anything, because it was
night both at my entrance, stay and coming away ; I can
onely intimate that it is wholly surrounded with strong
walls, and, if I took good notice, seems to me greater than
Damàn, but of late years many buildings were destroy'd
by a horrible tempest, and are not yet re-edifi'd.[1]   I found
in the Colledge of *Bassaim* F. *Paolo Giovio*, an Italian.

March the thirtieth.   In the Morning, the Fleet set sail,
and going off the shore we came to the Island where they
take in fresh water, over against a City in view at a little
distance, which they call *Salsette*[2]; and the place where we
stay'd (being a large and populous Island) is call'd in the
Portugal Tongue L'Aguada[3]; and here we stay'd all the

---

[1] The word "edify", used here in its literal sense of "to build", is
used in the same sense by Spenser :
> "Countries waste and eke well edifyde."

And by Southey :
> "Of solid diamond edified."

So also by Sir T. Browne : "That Eve was edified out of the Rib
of Adam, I believe." (*Rel. Medici*, Part I, sect. xxi.)

[2] Sálsette (Sashti) is the name of the island (not of the city) taken
by the English in 1774. The city referred to was probably Bombay,
on an adjacent island, occupied by the Portuguese in 1532, and ceded
to them by the King of Guzarát in 1534.

[3] A watering-place, from *agua* (Port.), "water".

day, because the wind was so contrary that we could not
get off that point of Land ; and for that divers of the
Galeots and new Frigats, built here to be sent and arm'd
in *Goa*, were not in order to depart, and we were forc'd
to stay their preparation.

March the one and thirtieth.   At Sun-rise we put to Sea
for *Goa*, but were slow in getting forth to the Main before
we could set sail, because the Tide was still going out, and
there was so little water left, that our Frigat ran aground.
At length, the Tide turning, we row'd out of the strait
between the City and the Island, and being come into the
broad Sea hoisted all our sails.   About midnight following
we arriv'd at *Ciaùl*,[1] but enter'd not into the Port, because
it stands much within the Land upon a precipice, where
the Sea entring far into the Bay between the Hills and the
low Shore (into which also is discharg'd the mouth of a
River) makes an ample and secure harbour : wherefore by
reason of the darkness of the night, which in this place is
no seasonable time, the Fleet would not enter, but we rode
at the River's mouth till break of day.

V.—*April* the first.   Entring into the Port in the
Morning, we cast Anchor under the City upon the shore,
where nevertheless the water is so deep, and our Galeots
came so near the bank, that we went ashore by a bridge.
In the entrance of the City and Haven, on the right hand,
almost Southwards, we saw that famous Hill which the
Portugals call *Morro di Ciaùl*, commanding the Harbour
and all the adjacent City ; on the top of it stands a strong
Castle, which was sometime possessed by the Moors of

---

[1] The modern Cháwul, a port of the Konkan, about thirty-five miles
S. of Bombay, in lat. 18° 31′ N., formerly an important commercial
port (see Barbosa, Hakluyt ed., p. 69).   A description of Cháwul
(from Sloane MS.) will be found in the Appendix to *Commentaries of
Afonso Dalboquerque* (Hakluyt ed.), vol. iv, p. 243.   The Fort was
built by the Portuguese in 1521.   It is regarded by Sir H. Yule as
identical with ancient Saimur (*Cathay*, vol. i, p. cxcii).

Dacàn,[1] namely, by *Nizàm Schiàh*,[2] to whom also the whole
Territory about it belongs ; and when the said King made
war with the *Portugals* the Moors did great mischief to
them from the top of this Mountain, and another which
stands near the Harbour, but something more inwardly,
discharging great Artillery from thence upon the City and
the mouth of the Port, so that no Ship could enter. But
at last a small number of *Portugals* having routed, with a
signal and almost miraculous victory, a very great body of
Moors, the same day they likewise took the said *Morro*[3];
whither the routed Moors flying, it hapned that in the
entrance of the Fortress an Elephant, wounded by the
Portugals in its flight, fell down in the Gate, so that the
Moors could not shut it[4]; and the victorious *Portugals* in
that fury of pursuing the Enemy had occasion and convenience of entering ; so they took it, and still hold it
(having improv'd the fortifications), and consequently
deliver'd the City of *Ciaùl* from the continual molestations
which it suffer'd from thence by the *Moors ;* and now the
Citizens live in peace, and more secure.

Having landed a little way from the *Dogàna*, or Custom-
House, which stands without the walls, the first thing I
saw was the Cathedral Church, which stands likewise
without the walls upon the shore, and is the See[5] not of a
Bishop, but of a Vicar, as *Damàn, Bassaim, Ormuz* and
other places are ; which, though they enjoy the title of

---

[1] A name (generally written as Deccan) given to the whole triangular *plateau* between the Vindhya mountains and Cape Comorin,
from the Prakrit word *Dakhin* (Sanskrit *Dakshin*), meaning "south".
Called "Dachanabades" in the *Periplus*, from the Sanskrit name
Dakhshinapatha. (See Sir M. Williams' *Modern India*, p. 182.)

[2] See *ante*, p. 134.

[3] This was in the year 1592 A.D.

[4] Readers of Sir W. Scott's *Tales of a Grandfather* will remember
a somewhat similar incident of a portcullis being arrested in its fall
by a hay-cart. [5] See *ante*, p. 133.

Cities, are nevertheless all subject to the Arch-Bishop of
Goa.   I went next into the Colledge of the Jesuits, whose
Church here, as also in *Damàn, Bassaim* and almost all
Cities belonging to the *Portugals* in *India,* is call'd *Saint
Paul's ;* whence in *India* the said Fathers are more known
by the name of *Paulists* than *Jesuits.*   Here I visited F.
Antonio Pereira who was come from *Bassaim,* where I fell
acquainted with him in our Fleet, in order to go likewise
to *Goa.*   I likewise visited the F. Rector of the said Col-
ledge, who caus'd me to stay to dinner with him; and being[1]
the Fleet departed not that day, I also lodg'd in the same
Colledge at night.

April the second.   I heard Mass early in the Jesuit Church,
and taking leave of them went to embark, but found that
my Galeot was remov'd to the other side of the Port under
the Mountain to be mended, and having found Sig.
Manuel d Oliveira, one of our Companions embark'd in
the same Galeot, and understanding that the fleet did not
depart that day neither, I went with him to hear a Sermon
in the Cathedral Church ; after which we went to dine in
the House of F. *Francesco Fernandez,* Priest and Vicar,
who liv'd sometime at *Ormùz,* and after the loss of that
Island was retir'd hither.   The *Portugals* call Secular
Priests, Fathers, as we do the Religious, or Monasticks.   In
the same House dwelt Signor . . .   . a worthy and grave
Souldier, with whom, being a Friend to my said Companion, we convers'd together till it was late, and then, our
Galeot being come back, we went to embark ; but neither
did the fleet depart this night as we suppos'd it would.

April the third.   A rumour of departing being spread
abroad about noon, we put out to Sea, and cast Anchor
at the mouth of the Harbour, where many other Galeots
were gather'd, expecting the setting forth of the whole

---

[1] As to this use of the word " being", see *ante,* p. 27, *note.*

fleet; but neither did we depart this day nor the night ensuing.

VI.—*April* the fourth. The fleet being at length in readiness, and the Sun a good height, we set sail and departed from the Port of *Ciaùl*. In the Afternoon we sail'd by a Fort, which is the onely one possessed near the Sea by the *Moors* of *Damàn*, that is by *Nizàm Sciàh*, which Fort is call'd *Danda Ragiapori*[1]; and at night we cast Anchor under a deep shore call'd *Kelsi*.[2] We did not sail in the night time because the *Cafila* was numerous, consisting, by my conjecture, of above 200 Vessels, and in the dark some unwary Ship might easily have been taken by the Rovers of *Malabar*. The next day we sail'd gently along, onely with the sail call'd the Trinket,[3] making but little way, that so we might go altogether and not leave many Ships behind, which being ill provided of Tackle could not sail fast. We cast Anchor again early in the Evening, to avoid the confusion which might arise by so many Ships casting Anchor together, besides the danger of falling foul one upon another in the dark. Our course was always Southerly, and the Coast along which we pass'd on the left hand was all mountainous; till having got out of the dominion of *Nizàm-Sciàh*,[4] we began to coast along that of *Adil-Sciàh*.[5]

---

[1] *I.e.*, Danda Rajpúr, or "King's town fort".

[2] Marked as "Quelesi" in a map of 1570.

[3] Called the Trinket, from its triangular shape, from Lat. *triquetrius;* Italian *trinchetto*. (See Hakluyt's *Voyages*, "The Trinket and the Mizzen were rent asunder.") Called *traquete* by the Portuguese. (See *Commentaries of A. Dalboquerque*, vol. iii, p. 63.)

[4] This dominion comprised the division of Aurungábád and the western part of Berár, together with a part of the sea-coast in the Konkan. As to the dynasty of Nizám Sháh, see *ante*, p. 134.

[5] Bounded on the E. by the Bima and Krishna rivers, on the N. by the river Nira, on the S. by the Tambadra river, and on the W. by the sea. The dynasty of Ádil Sháh was founded by Abdúl Muzaffar Yúsuf Ádil

Now that it may be understood who these Princes are,
I shall tell you that on the South of the States of the
Great Moghòl, in the Confines whereof *India* begins to be
distended into a great Tongue of Land like a Triangle
a great way Southwards into the Sea, between the Gulph
óf *Cambaia* and the Gulph of *Bengala,* the first Province
of *India* joining to the States of the *Moghòl* is the Kingdom of *Damàn,* whereof some part is still possess'd by the
Moghòl. Next follows the Kingdom of *Telengone,* or *Telengà,*[1]
and many other Provinces divided under several Princes
into little Kingdoms, which they say were anciently but
one or two, and that the others, who are now absolute
Princes, were sometime Captains or Ministers, who, having
by degrees pull'd down their Principals (who were, if I
mistake not, the King of *Bisnagà*[2] in the South, and the
King of *Sceherbeder,*[3]) are become equal, and all without

Sháh (said to be a son of Sultán Amurath, one of the Emperors
of Rúm, *i.e.,* Asia Minor), who landed at Dabùl in the year H. 864
(A.D. 1460). He was called " Sabayo" from his having been educated
at Sava in Persia. He was sold as a slave to Mahmúd Gawán,
Minister of Muhammad Sháh, King of Ahmadábád, and eventually
became King of Bíjápúr in 1502 A.D. (See Brigg's *Ferishta,* vol. iii,
p. 4.) The dynasty came to an end in 1686, when Bíjápúr was taken
by the Emperor Aurangzíb. An account of this dynasty will be found
in the Appendix to Elphinstone's *Hist. of India,* p. 671.

[1] *I.e.,* Telingana, in the eastern part of the Indian Peninsula ; see
ante, p. 107. It is bounded on the W. by a line extending from
Chanda, through Adoni, Anantpúr, and Nandidurg to a point near
Bengalúr ; on the E. by a line from Sohnpúr through Chicacole
(Shríkákolam) to Pulicat ; on the N. by a line from Chandá to Sohnpúr,
and on the S. by a line from Bengalúr to Pulicat.

[2] Vijayanagar, the capital of the King of Narsinga, in lat. 15° 10' N.
The king here referred to was Rám Rájá, who was attacked and de-
feated by the Muhammadan rulers of the Dekkan—viz., 'Ali Ádil Sháh,
Husain Nizám Sháh, Ibrahím Baríd, and Ibrahím Kutb Sháh—at
Tálikóta, on the river Krishna, 1565 A.D. (See Elphinstone's *India,* p.
417.) For a description of the town, see Barbosa (Hakluyt ed.), p. 85.

[3] Shahr Bídar, City of Bídar, in lat. 17° 50' N., the seat of the
Báhmaní dynasty, which lasted from 1347 A.D. to 1525 A.D., and was

superiority sovereign Princes. Amongst these the nearest to the *Moghòl* are the three *Reguli*, or petty Kings, all which yet have great dominion and strength and are at this day of the Sect of the *Moors ;* for the *Moors*, having first been brought into *India* to serve as slaves,[1] are by degrees become Masters, and by oppressing the *Gentiles* in many places have much propagated their Religion. Of these three Princes, the nearest to the *Moghòl*, whose Territory lyes towards the Sea on the West, and Confines with the *Portugals* at *Ciaùl* and other places, and who is properly styl'd King of *Dacàn*[2] (from the greatest Province), is call'd by the name, or rather sirname, hereditary to all that reign in this State, of *Nizam Sciàh*,[3] which many interpret *Rè della Lancia, King of the Lance*, alluding to the *Persian* word *Nizè*, which signifies a Lance[4] ; but I conceive they are mistaken, because his name is *Nizam Sciàh*, and not *Nizè Sciah*, as according to this interpretation it should be : wherefore I have heard others, perhaps, better interpret it *Rè dei Falconi, King of Falcons*,[5] or

---

succeeded by the Baríd dynasty founded by Amír Barid, the son of Kásim Baríd, a Turk. This dynasty lasted until A.D. 1609 (when Ferishta closed his history), but how much longer is uncertain. (See Elphinstone's *Hist. of India*, p. 676.)

[1] More usually to serve as mercenary troops. These, according to Ferishta, were composed of Persians, Turks, Georgians, Circassians, and Tartars.   [2] See *ante*, p. 141.

[3] See *ante*, p. 134. The celebrated Chánd Bíbí was a princess of this dynasty who successfully defended Ahmadnagar in 1596.

[4] This is an erroneous derivation, Nizám meaning a "deputy", or "manager", or "representative" of the king. In Barros' *History of India* (IV, 16) is the following passage : "Nizamaluco (*i.e.*, Nizám Malik) is corrupted from 'Miza Malmulco (*i.e.*, Úl Múlk)', the 'Lance of the Land'."

[5] An equally fanciful and erroneous derivation, of which the origin seems to be due to the fact that "Bheira" means a falcon, and the name of the father of Nizám úl Múlk (the founder of the dynasty) was Bheiroo. Or possibly from the employment of Nizám úl Múlk, when a slave, as falconer. (See Brigg's *Ferishta*, vol. iii, p. 189.)

L

Hawks, from the word *Nizàm,* which in the *Indian* Tongue, they say, signifies a Hawk, or other Bird of Prey. And whosoever reigns here always retains this sirname, because whilst he was not an absolute Prince, but a Minister of that other great King of *India,* this was his Title and Office under that King.

The *Nizam Sciàh* now reigning[1] is a Boy of twelve years old, who therefore doth not govern it, but an Abyssine slave of the *Moors'* Religion, call'd *Melik Amber,*[2] administers the State in his stead, and that with such authority that at this day this Territory is more generally known and call'd by the name of *Melick's* Country than the Kingdom of *Nizam-Sciàh.* Nevertheless this *Melik Amber* governs not fraudulently and with design to usurp, by keeping the King shut up, as I have sometimes heard ; but, according as I have better understood since from persons inform'd nearer hand, he administers with great fidelity and submission towards the young King; to whom, nevertheless, they say, he hath provided, or already given to Wife, a Daughter of his own, upon security that himself shall be Governour of the whole State as long as he lives. This *Melik Amber* is a Man of great parts, and fit for government, but, as they say, very impious, addicted to Sorcery ; whereby 'tis thought that he keeps himself in favour with his King, and that for works of Inchantments (as to make prodigious buildings, and with good luck, that the same may last perpetually and succeed well) he hath, with certain Superstitions used in those Countries, committed most horrid impieties and cruelties, killing[3] hun-

---

[1] *I.e.,* Murtaza Nizám Sháh II, son of Sháh 'Ali, a military chief, who was placed on the throne by Malik Ambar.

[2] See *ante,* p. 134.

[3] The superstitious belief that the construction of any large building is facilitated by the sacrifice of a number of children still exists in India, and frequently causes a panic among the people when a large railway bridge, or other such work, is constructed.

dreds of his Slaves, Children and others, and offering them as in Sacrifice to the invok'd Devils, with other abominable stories which I have heard related ; but because not seen by myself I affirm not for true. The Ambassador of this *Nizam-Sciàh* in *Persia* is that *Hhabese Chan*,[1] an Abyssine also, whom I saw at my being there.

Of strange things they relate that *Nizam-Sciàh* hath, I know not where in his Country, a piece of Ordnance[2] so vast, that they say it requires 15,000 pounds of Powder to charge it ; that the Ball it carries almost equals the height of a Man ; that the metal of the piece is about two spans thick ; and that it requires I know not how many thousand Oxen, besides Elephants, to move it ; which therefore is useless for war, and serves onely for vain pomp. Nevertheless this King so esteems it that he keeps it continually cover'd with rich cloth of Gold, and once a year comes in person to do it reverence, almost adoring it ; and indeed, although these Kings are *Moors*, yet they still retain much of the ancient Idolatry of the Countries wherein Mahometism is little, or not yet universally, setled.[3]

The second of the three petty Kings, whose Country joyns to that of the *Moghòl*, but borders upon the Sea Eastward in the Gulph of *Bengala*, is he who (for the same reasons mention'd concerning *Nizam-Sciàh*) is call'd by the hereditary sirname *Cutb-Sciàh*,[4] which some erroneously ex-

---

[1] *I.e.*, Habshi Khán, or Abyssinian chief.

[2] This, no doubt, refers to the famous cannon at Bíjápúr described in Brigg's *Ferishta*, vol. iii, p. 243, and by modern writers (Grant Duff's *Hist. of Mahrattas*, vol. i, p. 112, and *Bombay Transactions*, vol. iii, p. 62). It is said to be 4 ft. 6 in. in diameter at the muzzle, with a calibre of 2 ft. 4 in. Nizám Sháh is said to have lost upwards of 600 guns in one campaign. (See Elphinstone, p. 674.)

[3] See *ante*, p. 69, *note*.

[4] The dynasty of Kutb Sháh was founded by Sultán Kuli, a Turkumán from Hamadan in Persia, at Golkonda, about the year 1512 A.D.

L 2

pound *Polo dei Rè, the Pole of Kings*,[1] being deceiv'd by the Arabick word *Cutb*, which signifies the Pole, and is us'd by the *Arabians* and *Persians* to denote supream excellency and understanding, *(e.g.)* by *Polo dei Sávii, ò di Sapienza, The Pole of Wise men, or of Wisdom*, the wisest Man in the world ; by *Polo di Santita, o della Legge, The Pole of Sanctity and the Law*,[2] the greatest pitch and the highest observer of the divine Law ; and so in all other like cases ; but I say I believe they are mistaken ; and there seems to me more truth in the exposition of others, who interpret *Rè dei Cani, King of Dogs*,[3] from *Cutb*, which in the Language of *India* signifies a Dog, because he was Master of the Dogs[4] to that supream King. Under his jurisdiction[5] is *Gulcondalàr*,[6] where, I think, he hath his Royal Seat, and *Mislipatan*,[7] a famous Port in the Gulph of *Bengala*.

Lastly the third of the three *Reguli* is he who hath his seat in *Visapor*,[8] and reigns in the Country of *Telengone*,[9]

The dynasty came to an end in 1687, on the capture of Golkonda by the Emperor Aurangzíb.

[1] *Kutb* means "Pole", in the sense of "Guiding light". The title was conferred on Sultán Kuli by Muhammad Sháh, King of Bídar.

[2] So Chaucer has been called the "Lode Star of our Language".

[3] Of course erroneous. The word "Kuttá" means dog in Persian, but "Kutb" is, of course, quite unconnected with it.

[4] There is here probably some confusion with the derivation of "King of Falcons", previously referred to.

[5] The territory of this dynasty originally extended from the Godávari river, beyond the Krishna river, and from the sea to a line drawn west of Haidarábád, about long. 78° E., but it was subsequently considerably enlarged by the addition to it of Rájámahendri, Gandikota Kadapa, etc. (See Elphinstone's *Hist. of India*, p. 675, and Brigg's *Ferishta*, vol. iii, p. 324.)

[6] *I.e.*, Golkonda, near Haidarábád, in lat. 17° 24′ N.

[7] *I.e.*, Masulipatám (Machlípatnam), on the east coast of the Indian Peninsula, in lat. 16° 10′ N. (See *ante*, p. 107.) *Pattanám* is "town" in the Tamil language.

[8] Or Bíjapúr, in lat. 16° 49′ N. (See *ante*, p. 117.)

[9] Telingana. (See *ante*, pp. 107 and 144.)

bordering upon the *Portugal* Territory of *Goa*, more Southwards than the two before mention'd. Some will have *Visapor* and *Goa* belong to the Province of *Dacàn*, and that *Telenga* lies much more remote toward the South. The truth is *India* with the Provinces thereof is very confus'd ; forasmuch as the *Indians* themselves being illiterate cannot distinguish it aright, and the *Portugals* have all their knowledge thereof from the vulgar sort of the ignorant *Indians*, whose Language they understand not well and who are extreamly corrupt in pronunciations; therefore I cannot speak any thing certain concerning the same, as neither have the *Portugal* writers been able to do, though persons very exact and sufficient.

But to return to my purpose, the proper name of him that now reigns is *Ibrahim*,[1] but his hereditary sirname (as of the others) is *Adil-Sciàh*, or *Idal-Sciàh*, which signifies not *Giusto Rè*, a *Just King*, as some think from the *Arabick* word *Adil* denoting *Just*, but rather, in my opinion, as some others say, *Rè delle Chiave*, *King of the Keys*,[2] from *Adil* or *Idal*, an *Indian* word importing *Keys*, he having been in times pass'd Superintendent of the Keys (of the Treasury perhaps, or Archives) under the supream King. Sometimes these Princes have been call'd *Nizam-Maluk*,[3] *Adil-Chan*, and so the others with the words either *Melek* or *Chan*, instead of *Sciàh*, which is all one ; for *Melek* or *Maluk*[4] (as some corruptly read) signifies a *King* in *Arabick*, as *Chan*[5] doth also in *Turkish*, and *Sciàh*[6] in

---

[1] *I.e.*, Ibrahim the Second, who began to reign in 1579 A.D.

[2] Another fanciful derivation, the word "Ádil" meaning "just".

[3] More correctly "Úl Múlk". [4] More correctly "Malik".

[5] More correctly "Khán". This title must not be confused with that of Káan (or Qáan), adopted by the Mongol chiefs, and which is identical with Kháqán, the Χαγάνος of the Byzantine historians, and has been translated by old travellers as "Magnus Canis", and thence into German as "Der grosse Hund". (See Yule's *Cathay*, vol. i, pp. cxvii and 128.) [6] More correctly "Sháh".

Persian. And because these three Languages are sufficiently familiar and almost common to the *Moors*, therefore they have us'd sometimes one word sometimes
another[1]; but in later times it seems that those who now
rule, rejecting the words *Melek* and *Chan*, are better
pleas'd with the *Persian* Title *Sciàh*, as being, perhaps,
more modern to them[2]; whence they are ordinarily call'd
now *Nizam-Sciàh, Cutb-Sciàh,* and *Adil-Sciàh,* which are
the three Princes of whom I undertook to give an account,
as persons whom I shall have frequent occasion to mention
in these Writings ; and to leave nothing unsaid, I shall
add that *Nizam-Sciàh,* or rather his Governour *Melek-
Ambar,* makes war frequently and bravely against the
Great Moghòl, upon whom he borders.[3] As to *Cutb-Sciàh,*
I know not whether he actually makes publick war against
him, but at least he fails not to assist his Neighbour,
Nizam-Sciàh, with money. The same doth also *Adil-
Sciàh,* but secretly and by under-hand : not daring
(through I know not what mean fear) to declare himself
an enemy to the *Moghòl ;* I say mean fear, because not
bordering upon him (for the two other Princes lye
between them) and being able, as they say, upon occasion
to bring into the field a hundred thousand men, he seems
justly chargeable with timorousness and cowardice, since,
me-thinks, he that hath a hundred thousand men at his
command ought not to fear the whole world ; or, if he
doth, he is a very Poltron.[4]

---

[1] In the *Commentaries of Afonso Dalboquerque* 'Ádil Shah is invariably styled " Hidalcão" or " Idal (for Adil) Khan".

[2] The use of the Persian title " Shah", and others, was owing to the
fact that the civil administration of India fell into the hands of Persians,
and their language became the official language. (See Elphinstone's
India, p. 302.)

[3] This war commenced in 1610 A.D. and lasted until 1637 A.D. For
an account of it see Elphinstone's *Hist. of India,* p. 486 *et seq.*

[4] This is the old way of spelling the word adopted by Shakespeare

But indeed *Adil-Sciàh* fears the *Moghòl*, yea he fears
and observes him so much that he pays him an annual
Tribute[1]; and when the Moghòl sends any Letter to him,
which is always brought by some very ordinary common
Souldier, or Slave, he goeth forth with his whole Army to
meet the Letter and him that brings it, who being conducted to the Palace sits down there, whilst *Adil-Sciàh*
stands all the time, and the Letter being lay'd upon a
Carpet on the pavement, before he offers to put forth his
hand to take it up, he bows himself three times to the
earth, doing reverence to it after their manner.   Moreover,
I have heard that this *Ibrahim Adil-Sciàh*, who now reigns,
some years ago poyson'd his own eldest Son, as suspected
of being likely to become one day a disturber of the
Common-wealth and the publick quiet, being displeas'd
with him onely because he once with too much freedom
perswaded him to deny the *Moghòl* the accustom'd Tribute,
saying that with the Tribute alone which he pay'd volun-
tarily he durst undertake to make a mighty war upon him
and never pay him Tribute more ; which, if true, was certainly in this Prince a strange effect of fear.

This *Adil-Sciàh* hath marry'd one of his Daughters to
Cutb-Sciàh,[2] and with *Nizam-Sciàh* he constantly maintains, and frequently renews alliance ; so that they are all
three fast friends, and firmly united together.[3]   I have also
heard that *Adil-Sciàh*, uses to wear his Beard very long,
contrary to the other two, who are shaven after the mode

and Sir T. Browne. The original word is the Italian *poltrone*, or
poltro, a lazy, good-for-nothing, fellow.

   [1] According to Mr. Elphinstone (*Hist. of India*, p. 513) it was not
until 1636 A.D. that 'Ádil Sháh became a tributary of the King of
Delhi (Sháh Jahán).

   [2] A princess of this dynasty was married to Prince Daniál, third
son of the Emperor Akbár. (See Elphinstone's *India*, p. 461.)

   [3] They had formed a league in 1565 A.D. (See Elphinstone's *India*,
p. 416.)

of *Persia* and *India*.[1]   They say the present *Ibrahim Adil-Sciàh* is infirm, by reason of a great hurt receiv'd by a Wolf in his hips, so that he cannot ride on Horse-back ; and hence perhaps it is that he is so peaceable and timorous, infirmities undoubtedly much dejecting the spirits of Men.   All these three Princes are *Moors*, as I said before, although their Countries abound with innumerable *Gentiles*.   *Cutb-Sciàh* alone, as I have heard, is *Sciani*, of the Sect of the *Persians;* but the other two, I conceive, are *Sonni*,[2] as the *Turks* and the *Moghòl;* which yet I affirm not, because I have not perfect certainty thereof.[3]   The King of *Persia* cherishes all these three Princes sufficiently, and they have great correspondence by interchangeable Embassies and Presents ; all which is onely in order to make greater opposition to the Moghòl upon whom they border, and whose greatness is equally prejudicial to them all.   And so much may suffice concerning them.

----

[1] The practice of shaving the beard was one of the reforms introduced by the Emperor Akbár about the year 1580 A.D.   (See Elphinstone's *India*, p. 472.)

[2] Or Shi'as and Sunnís, the two great rival sects of Muhammadans, between whom great enmity exists.   Quite recently a fierce fight took place between them at Delhi, on the question as to the precise way in which the word " Amen" should be pronounced.   The word " Shi'a" means "heresy", and the adherents of this sect reject the first three khalifs and regard Ali as the first and rightful successor of Muhammad.   They also reject the Sunna, or body of traditions, as forming part of the Law, which is accepted by the Sunnís (or orthodox sect), who also accept the first three khalifs as rightful successors of Muhammad.   Most of the Indian Muhammadans are " Sunnís"; those of Persia are " Shi'as".

[3] As to Nizám Sháh, it is true that the founder of the dynasty was a Sunní, but his successors were Shi'as.   Under the king Ismael the Sunní religion was introduced.   (Elphinstone's *India*, pp. 673, 674.) As to 'Ádíl Sháh, the first three kings of this dynasty were Shi'as, and the fifth also.   In the minority of the sixth king (Ibrahím the Second) the Sunní religion was introduced.   (See Elphinstone's *India*, p. 672.)

VII.—*April* the fifth, we set sail again, and in the afternoon pass'd by the City of *Dabùl*,[1] which belongs to the Dominions of *Adil-Sciàh*, and stands hid amongst Hills in a low Plain, so that 'tis scarcely seen. After which we pass'd within two Leagues of a Point or Promontory which the *Portugals* call *Dabùl falso*, because it deceives such as come from far by Sea, making them take it for the Point of *Dabùl* which it resembles. At Night we cast Anchor near another shore which they call the Gulph or Bay, or, as the *Portugals* speak, *Enceada dos Bramanes*, because the Country thereabouts is inhabited by many *Brac'hmans*.

April the sixth, we set sail, and first pass'd by *Ragiapùr*, then by *Carapetan*.[2] About two hours before night, we cast anchor in an *Enceada*, or Bay, which they call *Calosì*, or *Calosà*,[3] not far from the Point of *Carapetan*.[4] *April* the seventh, in the Morning we passed by *Tambona*, which was the Country of the Mariners of our Ship, and toward Evening by the Rocks which the *Portugals* call *Los Illeos*[5] *quemados*,[6] that is *The burnt Rocks*, because they appear such by their colour and inequality ; and we continu'd sailing all Night, every Ship going as they pleas'd, without caring for the company of the Fleet, now that by reason of the great nearness of *Goa* we were in safety.

April the eighth. Arriving before Day at the shore of *Goa*

---

[1] See *ante*, p. 136.

[2] Two small towns a little way inland, marked on Wyld's map (1857) as " Rájápoor" and " Kareeputlan".

[3] Called " Quereci" in Dourado's map of 1546.

[4] This place and Calossi will be found marked in the map included in this volume of letters, but they do not appear in most modern maps.

[5] Or more correctly " Ilheos", a word used for small uninhabited islands, as distinguished from " Ilha", an island, as generally understood, corresponding to our "islet" and " island".

[6] Called Vingorla rocks in modern maps, and I. Qeimado in Dourado's map, and Σησκριενοι by the Greeks.

we began to enter into the salt River, or *Rio*, as they speak, of salt water which the *Portugals* call *Barra*[1] *di Goa;* upon the mouth of which River, which is sufficiently broad, stand two Forts,[2] one on each side, with good pieces of Artillery planted upon them to defend the Entrance.

VIII.—'Tis to be known that the City of *Goa*,[3] at this day the Head of all the Dominion of the *Portugals* in *India*, is situate here in one of these Islands,[4] of which, as I said before, there are innumerable upon all the Coast of *India*, made by the several Rivers which divide them from the main-land. The City is built in the inmost part of the Island toward the Continent, and therefore the whole Island is plentifully inhabited with Towns and places of Recreation, and particularly upon the River, which is on either side adorn'd with Buildings and Houses, surrounded with Groves of Palm-Trees and delightful Gardens. The greatest part of the Island is

---

[1] This is not the name of the river (which is the Mandavi), but is the Bar at its mouth.

[2] The forts of Marmagaon and Aguado, on the south and north sides of the entrance. The former is now a ruin. (See Fonseca, pp. 40, 42.)

[3] This is the old city, now called Goa Velha, to distinguish it from Panjím, or New Goa, the modern town, which was formally raised to the position of capital by royal edict in 1843, though it was occupied as the capital in 1765 A.D. The old town is now quite deserted. An interesting account of its present state is given in *Murray's Magazine* for November 1890, by a recent traveller in that part of India. It was built in 1479 A.D., about two miles north of the *original* town of Goa, which was in existence in the 14th century. A good account of the history of Goa, and of the authorities on the subject, will be found in the Introduction to the *Commentaries of Afonso Dalboquerque* (Hakluyt ed.), vol. ii, p. xcvi *et seq.* An article in the *Indian Church Quarterly Review*, of June 1891, may also be referred to, and *An Historical Sketch of Goa*, by J. N. da Fonseca.

The Island of Goa, which gave its name to the city. It is called "Tis Vadi" (thirty villages) by the natives (vulg. Tissuary).

A FIGURATIVE PLAN C

Taken on the Spot, comprehending a Space of Gr
to West and three quarters of a

built part of the town or private houses.	Waste land.	Gardens or spaces of ground planted with cocoanut trees.	Sides of Hills.

References and E

1 Cathedral.
2 Archiepiscopal palace.
3 Palace of the Viceroy in ruins.
4 Church and Convent of St Francis.
5 Chapel of St Catherine.
6 Arsenal.
7 Chapel of the 5 wounds in the Arsenal.
8 Archbishops Prison or Aljuvar.
9 Senate house.
10 Old Senate house, now an hospital.
11 Inquisition in ruins.
12 3 Churches & houses of Misericordia.
13 Church and house of Bom Jesus.

— with the shrine of St Francis Xavier.
14 Church & convent of St Augustine.
15 College of the Augustinians.
16 Noviciate of the same.
17 Chapel of St Antony of Padua.
18 College of St Roc in ruins.
19 Collegiate and parochial church of the Rosary.
20 Nunnery of St Monica.
21 Convent & church of St John of God.
22 Landing Stairs.
23 Collegiate & parochial church of Luz.
24 Church of the miraculous cross.

Wharf or landing plac

| | Churches and other buildings in ruins. | + + + | Altars in the Churches. | | Churches and buildings in good repair. |

the Island.

The River or channel surrounding

xplanations.

belonging to & adjoining the convent
of the priests of the congregation.

25 *paroch.ᵊ church of the B.ᵈ Trinity in ruins*

26 *Old city Hospital almost abandoned.*

27 *Ch. & college of S.ᵗ Paul in ruins.*

28 *parochial ch. of S.ᵗ Thomas Ap.*

29 *Hospital of S.ᵗ Lazarus.*

30 *Church & house of N.ᵃ Senhora del me.ᵗᵉ*

31 *parochial church of S.ᵗ Lucia*

32 *Church & convent of S.ᵗ Dominic*

33 *Old Custom house in ruins.*

34 *Church & convent of S.ᵗ Cajetan.*

35 *and.ᵉ ch & convent of the Carmelites.*

now college of the priests of the congregation.

36 *paroch.ᵊ ch. of S.ᵗ Alexius in ruins.*

37 *Slaughter house.*

38 *Bazaar.*

39 *Colleg.ᵊ of S.ᵗ Bonaventure bel.ᵍ to*
the order of the Franciscans.

40 *College of S.ᵗ Thomas Aquinas*
belonging to the Dominicans
in the suburb of Pannely.

41 *parochial Church of S.ᵗ Peter*
in the suburb of Pannely.

42 *Bridge over the ditch, the waters*
of which flow from the hills.

W. Jervis Sculp.ᵗ Madras.

inclos'd with a Wall,[1] with Gates at the places for passage, continually guarded for security against the attempts of Neighbours, and also to prevent the flight of Slaves and thieves ; since onely that River being cross'd, you enter presently into the Territory of *Adil-Sciàh*[2] and the *Moors;* but 'tis otherwise toward the Sea-side, for all the Coast which is beset with other small Islands and Peninsulas for a good space belongs to the *Portugals*, being inhabited with Towns and divers Churches. The City which lyes on the right hand of the River,[3] as you enter into the inmost recess, is sufficiently large, built partly on a Plain and partly upon certain pleasant Hills,[4] from the tops whereof the whole Island and the Sea are discover'd, with a very delightful prospect. The buildings[5] of the City are good, large and convenient, contriv'd for the most part for the benefit of the wind and fresh Air, which is very necessary in regard of the great heats, and also for reception of the great Rains of the three Moneths of *Pansecal*,[6] which are *June, July,* and *August;* which, not upon account of the heat (although it be very great in that time, but greatest of all in *May*, when the Sun is in the Zenith), but of the great Rain, the *Portugals* call the Winter of the Earth.[7]

Nevertheless the buildings have not much ornament or exquisiteness of Art, but are rather plain, and almost all without beautifyings. The best are the Churches, of which many are held here by several Religions, as

---

[1] *I.e.*, on the eastern shore only.

[2] See *ante*, p. 143.

[3] *I.e.*, the river Mandavi, on which the old town stands, five miles inland from its mouth.

[4] Spurs of the Sahyadri range.

[5] They are said to be built mostly of laterite. (See *Proceedings of the Asiatic Society of Bengal*, for June 1874, by T. W. H. Tolbort.)

[6] See *ante*, p. 32.

[7] This should be more correctly translated "of this Land'.

Augustines,[1] *Dominicans*,[2] *Franciscans*,[3] discalceated[4] *Car-melites* and *Jesuits*,[5] with double[6] and very numerous Convents, and, indeed, half the Religions that are here would suffice for a City bigger then *Goa*.[7] But besides these there are also many of Secular Priests and Parishes, and Chappels[8]; and lastly the See or Cathedral,[9] which nevertheless is neither the fairest, nor the greatest Church of that City, there being many others that exceed it. The See of Goa[10] at the time of my being there was not finish'd, but scarce above half built,[11] and thence seem'd to me small and less stately; but, having since seen the intire design of the structure, I conceive that when 'tis finish'd 'twill be a very goodly Church.[12]

---

[1] Founded in 1256. They were suppressed at Goa in 1835.

[2] Founded in 1216. By members of this Order the atrocities of the Inquisition were perpetrated. Expelled from Goa in 1841.

[3] Founded in 1209. The Order was suppressed at Goa in 1835.

[4] Or less pedantically, "bare-footed". This Order was founded about 1185. They were expelled from Goa in 1707.

[5] As to the Jesuits, see *post*, p. 162. The Theatines (a religious Order founded by John Peter Caraffa, Bishop of Theate, or Chieti, in the kingdom of Naples, in 1524) were added in 1640. Suppressed in 1835.

[6] For monks and nuns. That of St. Monica was the chief.

[7] It is said that there were 200 churches in Goa. The inordinate number and wealth of the religious Orders in this and other Portuguese settlements is one of the causes which are said to have led to the decadence of the Portuguese power in India. (Harris' *Travels*, p. 698.)   [8] Or collegiate churches.

[9] This was the Church of St. Catherine, raised to the dignity of cathedral in 1534, now styled Sé Primacial.

[10] The name of Goa (or *Gomant*, as it is called by the 'Hindus) is derived from the Sanskrit *Govaráshtra* (or district of cowherds), the ancient appellation of the southern Konkan.

[11] It was commenced in 1562 and finished in 1631.

[12] In the account of Goa, in *Murray's Magazine* of November 1890, already referred to, is to be found a description of this cathedral, with a graphic account of the proceedings of the Grand Inquisition which formerly took place in it. (See also C. de Kloguen's *Historical Sketch of Goa*, p. 92, and Fonseca's *Sketch of Goa*, pp. 198 and 219.)

The people is numerous,[1] but the greatest part are slaves,[2] a black and lewd[3] generation, going naked for the most part, or else very ill clad, seeming to me rather a disparagement than an ornament to the City. *Portugals* there are not many; they us'd to be sufficiently rich, but of late, by reason of many losses by the incursions of the *Dutch* and *English* in these Seas, they have not much wealth, but are rather poor. Nevertheless they live in outward appearance with splendor enough, which they may easily do both in regard of the plentifulness of the Country, and because they make a shew of all they have ; however, in secret they indure many hardships, and some there are who, to avoid submitting to such employments as they judge unbecoming to their gravity,[4] being all desirous to be accounted Gentlemen here, lead very wretched lives, undergoing much distress, and being put to beg every Day in the Evening[5]; a thing which in other Countries would be accounted unhappy and more indecent, not to say shameful, than to undertake any laudable profession of a Mechanick Art. They all profess Arms, and are Souldiers though marry'd, and few, except

---

[1] The population in 1640 A.D. is said to have amounted to 190,000. It now consists of eighty-six persons only.

[2] Domestic slaves were kept by Europeans in India until 1787 at least. In the *Calcutta Gazette* of that year (May 17th) is an advertisement offering a reward of "one gold mohur" for the recapture of a slave, "answering to the name of Christmas", belonging to Mr. R. Hollier. At Goa, the Portuguese nobles (or hidalgos, as they styled themselves) derived the greater part of their income from the manual labour of their slaves. (See Fonseca's *Sketch of Goa*, p. 161.)

[3] The word "lewd" is here used in its original sense of "ignorant" or "unlearned", as in the Short Catechism of 1553 "as necessary for the lewd as the learned". (See Trenck's *Glossary*, p. 121.)

[4] That is, "grandeur" or "greatness".

[5] Tavernier, the French traveller, who visited Goa in 1642 and 1648, also mentions this mark of poverty. It was about this time that the gradual decline of the Portuguese prosperity commenced.

Priests and Doctors of Law and Physick, are seen without
a Sword ; even so the Artificers and meanest Plebeians :
as also silk clothes are the general wear of almost everybody[1]; which I take notice of, because to see a Merchant
and a Mechanick in a dress fit for an Amorato[2] is a very
extravagant thing, yet amongst them, very ordinary,
the sole dignity of being *Portugals* sufficing them (as
they say) to value themselves as much as Kings and
more.[3]

IX.—But returning to my purpose, whilst we were
coming to the City by the River betimes in the Morning, we met the Vice-Roy,[4] who was going to the *Barra*,[5]
to dispatch away *Ruy Freira de Andrada*,[6] whom with
five or six Ships (a small preparation indeed) he sent
to the relief of *Mascàt*,[7] and to make war against the
Persians; having likewise appointed divers other Ships to
be sent after him from *Ciaùl, Dio*, and other Ports[8] of the

---

[1] According to Linschoten (p. 61), suits of silk clothes were owned
in common by several persons. (See also Visscher's *Letters from
Malabar*, p. 32.)

[2] Literally, "a lover", or, as we should say, "a dandy".

[3] An interesting account of the social manners and customs of the
Portuguese at Goa is given in chap. v of Fonseca's *Historical Sketch
of Goa.*

[4] Don Francisco da Gama, Count of Vidigueira, appointed (for
the second time) in 1622.

[5] See *ante*, p. 154. On this bar the *St. John*, man-of-war, under
Admiral Dalboquerque, was wrecked during the siege of Goa in 1510.
(See *Commentaries of Afonso Dalboquerque*, vol. ii, p. 170.) It was,
and is, impassable by ships at certain seasons, viz., during the south-
west monsoon.

[6] One of this family was a learned theologian, who died in 1575,
having taken part in the Council of Trent.

[7] On the east coast of Arabia. Taken by the Portuguese in 1507,
and lost by them in 1648, when it was surrendered to the Arabs. The
"relief" here spoken of was from an attack of the Arabs.

[8] See pp. 17 and 140. In a map of India executed in 1546, in the British
Museum, the ports on the west coast are marked, those connected

Portugals, which, if they go, may be sufficient for some considerable exploit : but as to the Orders of the Vice-Roy in other places, God knows how they will be executed in his absence. The sudden departure of *Ruy Freira* made me sorry that I had not the opportunity to see and speak with him as I extreamly desir'd, and perhaps it would not have been unacceptable to him.

Arriving at the City we cast Anchor under the *Dogana*, or Custom-house,[1] where all Ships commonly ride, to wit, such as are not very great, for these stay either at the bar in the mouth of the River, or in some other place thereof where they have the deepest water.[2] Being come thither, I presently gave notice of my arrival to F. *Fra : Leandro* of the Anuntiation, whom I had known in *Persia*, and who was here Provincial Vicar of the discalceated *Carmelites* of *India* and *Persia*.[3] I also advertis'd the Father Jesuits thereof, for whom I brought sundry of their General's Letters from *Rome*, written affectionately to recommend me to them. F. *Fra : Leandro* came forthwith to visit me in the Ship, where, after some discourse for a while together, he undertook to procure us a House and so departed, having also offer'd me his own Convent with that same courtesie and confidence as was formerly between us.

A little after it was very great contentment to me to see and know F. *Antonio Schipano*, your kinsman, now a

with, or subject to, Portugal being distinguished from others. (See *Commentaries of Afonso Dalboquerque*, vol. ii, pp. 168, 169.)

[1] Called "Alfandega" by the Portuguese, and by the Muhammadans "Mandavi", a name subsequently applied to the river on which it stands. (See Fonseca's *Sketch of Goa*, p. 191.)

[2] The ships were moored at a pier called "Ribeira das Galès", west of the custom-house. (See Fonseca, p. 192.)

[3] The Carmelites established missions in Persia early in the 16th century, and at Goa in 1607. (See C. de Kloguen's *Sketch of Goa*, p. 127, and Fonseca's *Historical Sketch*, p. 68.)

very old man, who was saluted by me upon your account ;
and so for this time I gave him a succinct relation of you,
putting him in mind of your Childhood.   He came to visit
me with F. *Vincenzo Sorrentino* of *Ischia*, whom I had
formerly seen in *Persia*, and who, not living then with the
Jesuits, came with the Spanish Ambassador[1] as his
Chaplain in that voyage.   These two Fathers being
Italians were sent by F. *Andrea Palmeiro*, Visitor of the
Jesuits, and then their Superior in *Goa*, both to compliment me in his Name, and to give him more exact
information of me, whom he had never seen, nor so much
as known by Fame, saving what his General's Letters
signifi'd to him.   Wherefore after they had visited me, and
understood what was my intention to do, they went to give
account thereof to the Father Visitor, saying that they
would return again, as accordingly they did a good while
after, offering me in the Name of the F. Visitor their
Convent of the Profess'd House, where they pray'd me
to go and lodge, at least till I were provided of a House,
adding that they would also provide a convenient
residence for *Mariam Tinatin*[2] who was with me.   I
thank'd them, and accepted the favour as to myself, and
this with the approbation of F. *Fra: Leandro*, whom I
acquainted therewith.   But because it was late that day,
and there was not time to dispatch my Goods at the
Dogana, I did not land, but remain'd in the Ship with
intention to do so the next day.

April the ninth.   Early in the Morning F. *Fra. Leandro*
sent a *Palanchino*,[3] or litter, to fetch *Mariam Tinatin*,
that she might go to Mass at his Church, and afterwards
repair to the House of a *Portugal* Gentlewoman, called
Sig^ra *Lena da Cugna*, living near the discalceated *Carmelites* and much devoted to them, whose House also

---

[1] See p. 188, *note*.   [2] See *ante*, p. 24, *note*.   [3] See *ante*, p. 34, *note*.

stood right over against that which he intended to take
for me. And this was done because the *Portugals*, who in
the matter of Government look with great diligence upon
the least motes, without making much reckoning afterwards of great beams, held it inconvenient for the said
Mariam Tinatin to live with me in the same House,
although she had been brought up always in our House
from a very little Child and as our own Daughter. For
being themselves in these matters very unrestrain'd[1] (not
sparing their nearest kindred, nor, as I have heard, their
own Sisters, much less Foster-children in their Houses)
they conceive that all other Nations are like themselves;
wherefore, in conformity to the use of the Country and
not to give offence, it was necessary for us to be separated;
the rather too because strangers, who amongst the *Portugals* are not very well look'd upon and through their
ignorance held worse than in our Countries Hereticks are,
may easily expect that all evil is thought of them and
that all evil may easily befall them in these parts; so
that 'tis requisite to live with circumspection. And this
may serve for advice to whoever shall travel to these
Regions.[2]

F. *Fra: Leandro* sent also to invite me to Mass at his
Church; and being[3] it was a Holy Day, and the Jesuits
were not yet come to fetch me, as they said they would, I
determin'd to go thither, leaving *Cacciatùr*[4] in the Ship to

---

[1] On this point see De Kloguen's *Sketch of Goa*, p. 171, and
Fonseca (p. 162), who says that "Profligacy had, in fact, become the
reigning vice among the higher classes, and their morals were hope-
lessly corrupt and depraved".

[2] In connection with this piece of advice, two Oriental proverbs
may be quoted, viz.: "Drink not milk under a palm-tree" (lest you
be suspected of indulging in spirituous liquor); and "In a garden of
melons stoop not to tie your shoe" (lest you be suspected of stealing
fruit).

[3] For "since", see *ante*, p. 27, *note*.   [4] See *ante*, p. 126.

M

look to the goods.   I was no sooner landed but I met
F. *Sorrentino*, who in the Name of his Jesuits was coming
to fetch me, and also with a *Palanchino* to carry *Mariam
Tinatin* I know not whither.   She was gone already, and
so I made an excuse for her and likewise for myself to
the Jesuits, onely for that day, being[1] I was on the way
with the *Carmelites;* and although it somewhat troubled
them yet I went to F. *Leandro*, having agreed to return to
the Ship ; and the next day, after my Goods were dispatch'd at the *Dogana*, which could not be done now
because it was *Sunday*, I should then go to receive the
favour of the Jesuits as they commanded me.   Wherefore
proceeding to the Church of the *Carmelites*,[2] which stands
at the edge of the City upon a pleasant Hill, with a very
delightful prospect, I heard Mass there, and stay'd both
to dine, sup and lodge with them.

April the tenth.   Early in the Morning I went to the
Ship, landed my Goods, dispatch'd them at the Custom-
house, and having carry'd them to the House of Sig^{ra}
Lena da Cugna, where *Mariam Tinatin* was, I went to
quarter (till the House taken for me were empti'd,
clean'd and prepar'd) in the Convent of the Profess'd
House[3] of the Jesuits,[4] where I was receiv'd by the Visitor,

---

[1] For " since", see *ante*, p. 27, *note*.

[2] Marked 35 in the annexed plan of Goa.   For a description of it,
see Fonseca's *Sketch of Goa*, p. 256.

[3] The house which still adjoins the church of Bom Jesus.   Founded
in 1585.   For a description of it, see Fonseca, p. 280, and De Kloguen,
p. 115, and *Murray's Magazine* for Nov. 1890.

[4] For an account of the Jesuits in Goa, see Fonseca, p. 64 *et seq*
The Order of the Jesuits, founded by Ignatius Loyola in 1534 A.D.
was established at Goa in 1543, and finally suppressed in the Portuguese dominions in 1759.   Its most famous representative in India
was St. Francis Xavier (from 1541 to 1552), but the members of the
Order did not confine themselves to religious enterprises.   They
engaged in commerce also, and established colleges of secular learning, and entertained travellers with regal hospitality.

the Provincial, the Provost, and the rest with much courtesie, and with their accustom'd Charity and Civility. I found there many Italian Fathers, of which Nation the Society makes frequent use, especially in the Missions of China, Japan, India and many other places of the East; besides the two above-nam'd I found of Italians F. *Christofero Boro*, a *Milanese*, call'd *Brono* in *India* (not to offend the *Portugals'* ears with the word *Boro*,[1] which in their Language does not sound well), a great Mathematician; and another young Father who was afterwards my Confessor, F. *Giuliano Baldinotti* of *Pistoia*, design'd for *Japan*, whither he went afterwards; moreover, in the Colledge, which is another Church and a distinct Convent, F. *Alessandro Leni*, an ancient Roman and Friend of my Uncles, with whom, and especially with Sig: *Alessandro*, he had studied in our *Casa Instituta*, or Academy; and F. *Giacinto Franceschi*, a *Florentine;* all who, with infinite others of several Nations, *Portugals, Castilians* and others, were all my Friends; and particularly F. *Pantaleon Vincislao*, a German, well skill'd in Mathematicks and a great wit, Procurator[2] of *China;* F. *Per: Moryad*, the Vice-Roy's Confessor, and F. *Francesco Vergara*, both *Castilians;* F. *Christoforo di Giovanni*, a *Portugal*, learned in Greek and Arabick; and F. *Flaminio Carlo*, of *Otranto*, Master in Divinity.

Of Fryers I also found many Italians, namely in the Colledge Fryer *Joseph Masagna*, a famous Spicerer[3] and a Man of much business in the Profess'd House, a *Neapolitan*, a *Venetian*, and a *Tuscan*, call'd Fryer *Bartolomeo Pontebuoni*, a good Painter and also a Man of much employment, who were all my great Friends.

---

[1] The word *Borra* in Portuguese means "dregs".

[2] Or "representative". Intimate relations with the King of China were established by Afonso Dalboquerque. (See *Commentaries of Dalboquerque*, vol. iv, p. 206.)   [3] Or "apothecary".

April the eleventh, my Birth-day. The Jesuits shew'd me all their Convent,[1] which is indeed a large and goodly Building, and though not much adorn'd according to our custom, yet, perhaps, is the best thing that is in *Goa;* as also the front of their Church.[2]

April the fourteenth, which was Holy Fryday, I being present at Holy Service in the Quire of the Jesuits because I was still in my Persian Habit, (the *Portugal* clothes which I had bespoken being not yet made) and therefore appear'd not in publick, Sig: *Constantino da Sà*[3] (a *Portugal* Cavalier, or *Hidalgo*, design'd General for the Island of *Zeilan*,[4] whither he was preparing to go speedily with his Fleet) coming also to hear the Office in the Quire, saw me there, and understanding who I was, was pleas'd to take notice of me, and after the Office was ended came, together with the Fathers, very courteously to compliment me, offering himself to serve me (as he said) in the Island of *Zeilan*, if I pleas'd to go thither : whereunto I also answer'd with the best and most courteous words I could. This Sig: *Constantino* had been sent with an Armado of many Ships to relieve *Ormuz* when it was besieg'd[5]; but not arriving there till after the place was taken he return'd back with his Fleet to *Goa*.

X.—*April* the sixteenth, being *Easter-Day*, I first resum'd an Europœan, to wit a *Portugal*, Habit, as 'tis the fashion at *Goa* amongst the graver sort, after I had worn

---

[1] This building is still in existence, though part of it has been destroyed by fire. (See Fonseca's *Sketch of Goa*, p. 282).

[2] The church now called "Bom Jesus"; described by C. de Kloguen in his *Sketch of Goa*, p. 115, and by Fonseca, p. 282 *et seq.*

[3] Don Joãs Dessa (or Da Sa) was captain of Goa in 1515, and may have been an ancestor of this cavalier. (See *Commentaries of A. Dalboquerque*, vol. iv, p. 133.)

[4] Or Ceylon ; see *ante*, p. 109.

[5] By the English fleet in alliance with Sháh Abbas, King of Persia, in 1622. See *ante*, p. 8.

strange garbs for many years together, and ever since the death of my *Sitti Maani*[1] cloath'd myself and my servant in mourning.

April the seventeenth. F. *Pantaleon Vincislao*, my Friend above-named[2] (who was skill'd in the *China* Language, having been many years in these parts, and intended to return thither), shew'd me the Geographical Description of all *China*, written very small, or rather printed in a *China* Character after their way very handsomely. On which occasion I must not omit to note that the *Chinese*, as the said Father shew'd me in their Books, are wont in writing to draw the line, or verse of their writing, not, as we and the *Hebrews* do, across the paper, but (contrary to both) from the top to the bottom, beginning to write at the right side of the paper and ending at the left; which to all other Nations seems a very strange way. Moreover the Letters are not properly Letters, but great Characters, each of which denotes an intire word[3]; whence the Characters are as many as there are words in the Language, and they reckon to the number of eighty thousand[4]; a thing indeed not only strange and superfluous, but also, in my opinion, unprofitable ; yea, disadvantageous, and onely for vain pomp ; for in learning

---

[1] The wife of P. della Valle, who died near Persepolis in the year 1622. (See *ante*, p 122.)   [2] See *ante*, p. 163.

[3] According to the best authorities the Chinese characters were originally purely hieroglyphic, *i.e.*, actual representations of the objects signified, and were gradually applied in a figurative, or metaphorical sense, and finally adopted their present, or idiographic, form by the union of two or more characters to produce an idea resulting from the union of the component parts. A paper, giving information on this subject, was read at the last Oriental Congress. (See *Times* of Sept. 10th, 1891.)

[4] The characters in actual use are, however, said to be only about 40,000 in number—quite enough. According to Dr. Marshman (*Clavis Sinica, or Elements of Chinese Grammar*), in the entire works of Confucius scarcely 3,000 characters are employed.

these Characters they spend many years unprofitably, which might be imploy'd in the acquisition of other better Sciences, without being always Children (as *Hermes Trismegistus*[1] said of the Greeks) ; yea, in their whole life they cannot learn them all ; so that there are none among themselves, or, if any, they are very rare and miraculous, who can write and read all the words and know all the Characters of their own Tongue, which is certainly a great imperfection ; although they say that he who knows four thousand Characters may speak and write well enough ; and he that knows six, or eight, thousand may pass for eloquent.

The *Japanese* seem to me more judicious in this point, having for ordinary and more facile use invented an Alphabet of few Letters, written likewise from the top downwards, wherewith they write all words and all their own Language[2] and also that of *China*. But in the Sciences and more weighty matters the learned amongst them more commonly make use of the *China* Characters, which, as mysterious and sacred, are venerable to all these Nations; and although they have all several Languages, yet they do and can make use of the same writing ; because being[3] the same Characters are not Letters, but significative of words, and the words, although different in sound, yet in all these Languages are of the same signification and number, it comes to pass

---

[1] Hermes Trismegistus, or "Thrice greatest", was so called probably on account of his great learning. He was an Egyptian, or Phœnician, philosopher, who lived, or is supposed to have lived, in the reign of Osiris, and is credited by Sir T. Browne with the striking comparison of God to a sphere—" Cujus centrum ubique, circumferentia nullibi"; though it is by no means certain that he was really the author of it. (See *Notes and Queries* for 1880, pp. 135, 304.)

[2] In the *Times* of August 31st, 1891, will be found an interesting account of the Japanese written language.

[3] For "since", see *ante*, p. 27, *note*.

that divers Nations adjacent to *China*, as these of *Japan*, *Cauchin-China*,[1] and others, although different in Language, yet in writing making use of the *China-Characters*, at least in matters of greatest moment, understand one another when they read these Characters, each in their own Tongue, with the different words of their proper Language, which indeed, in reference to the commerce and communication of Nations, is a great convenience.

April the seven and twentieth   This Morning, being the first *Thursday* after the *Dominica in Albis*,[2] there was a solemn procession at *Goa* of the most Holy Sacrament, for the Annual Feast of *Corpus Christi*,[3] as is the custom.   But in *Goa* it is kept out of the right time upon such a day because the right day of the Feast falls in the Moneths of great Rain ; so that at that time the Procession cannot be perform'd, and therefore they anticipate it in this manner. The Procession was made by the whole Clergy, with a greater shew of green boughs than clothes, and with many representations of mysteries by persons disguis'd, fictitious animals, dances and masquerades ; things which in our Countries would more suit with Villages than great Cities.   Two Ships are now departing by the way of *Persia*, and therefore I have made use of this opportunity ; favour me to kiss the hands of all my Friends in my Name, amongst which I reckon in the first place the *Signori Spina*, Sig^r *Andrea*, Sig: *Dottore*, and Sig: *Coletta ;* upon whom and your self I pray Heaven for all felicity; recommending my self to your prayers also for my safety.—From *Goa, April 27*, 1623.

---

[1] *I.e.*, "Western China", a name given by the Portuguese to the country on the west coast of the Gulf of Tonquin.

[2] Or first Sunday after Easter.

[3] The proper day for the celebration of this feast is the Tuesday after Trinity Sunday, which would, of course, generally be in the month of June.

LETTER III.

From *Goa*, Octob. 10, 1623.

AVING a fit opportunity, according to my desire to make an excursion from *Goa* farther into *India*, more Southwards to *Canarà*,[1] upon occasion of this Vice-Roy's dispatching Sig: *Gio Fernandez Leiton*, Ambassador to *Venktapà Niekà*,[2] a Gentile Prince of that Province, and conceiving that my journey will begin within three or four days, I have therefore determin'd to write this Letter to you, that it may be convey'd by the first occasion of the Ships which are now preparing for a Voyage from *India* into *Europe*[3]; for I know not certainly

---

[1] One of the divisions of the Dakhan, extending from about 13° N. to about 16° N. on the west coast. Also called Carnat, or Carnata, not to be confounded with the "Carnatic territory" on the east coast. It includes the towns of Barcelór, Baticálá, Kárwár, Mangalúr, and Honáwar or Onor. It was ceded to the English by Tipu Sáhib in 1799.

[2] More correctly "Náyak", or "Captain", a title applied to subordinate governors of provinces. Of the "prince" here referred to, history, so far as has been ascertained, says nothing. He was one of the Keladi chiefs, or princes, who began their career as vassals of the King of Vijayanagar (see *ante*, p. 144, *note*), and subsequently moved their capital to Ikkeri, and, in 1639, to Bednur, where they continued to rule until 1763, when their capital was captured by Haidar Áli.

[3] A fleet of merchant vessels was despatched annually from Goa to

how far I shall travel, nor how long I shall stay out before my return to *Goa*, whether moneths or years. As little do I know what other opportunity or convenient place I shall meet withall to write to you ; nevertheless I shall omit none that offers itself, and in the mean time present you with the continuation of my Diary.

Having been here in *Goa* too much shut up in the House of the Jesuits, on the first of *May* I parted from them after many civil treatments and favours receiv'd of them, according to their most affectionate hospitality[1]; and went to the House prepar'd for me, right over against that of Sig^{ra} *Lena da Cugna*, which stands between the Convents of the Bare-footed Carmelites,[2] and the Converted *Nunns* of S. *Mary Magdalene*,[3] in a remote but not inconvenient place,[4] nor far from the commerce of the City, and the more acceptable to me because near the residence of *Mariàm Tinatin*.[5]

May the third. The City of *Goa* lying, as they say, in the latitude of fifteen degrees and forty minutes,[6] then, agreeably to the good rule of Astronomy and the Tables of *Tycho*[7] (according to which, F. *Christoforo Brono* told me, this

---

Lisbon at the close of the south-west monsoon. For an account of the commerce of Goa at this time, see Fonseca's *Sketch of Goa*, p. 23.

[1] Mandelslo, in his *Travels in India*, p. 81, speaks highly of the hospitality of the Jesuits at Goa, and of the delicious canary wine to which he was treated by them in 1639. (See Fonseca's *Sketch of Goa*, p. 281.)

[2] Erected in 1607, or 1612, and in 1707 bestowed on the congregation of St. Philip Neri. (See Fonseca's *Sketch of Goa*, p. 257.)

[3] Founded in 1605 by Archbishop Fr. Aleixo de Menezes. (*Ibid.*, p. 284.)

[4] This place would be somewhere between the points marked 35 and 12 in the annexed plan of Goa.   [5] See *ante*, p. 24, *note*.

[6] The difference of longitude between Frankfort and Goa is 65° 24', equal to about 4 hours, 20 minutes. Making allowance for this difference, our traveller calculates, by means of the Tables of Tycho (in which the time is calculated for the meridian of Frankfort), that the sun reached its zenith at the latitude of Goa at the time indicated here.

[7] Tycho Brahe, the Danish astronomer, born in 1546, died in 1601.

City is in a Meridian different from that of *Francfurth*, about four hours more Eastward), the Sun came to be in the Zenith of *Goa*, that is the declination of the Zenith, at eleven a clock of the night following the said day (speaking suitably to the *Spanish* and *Portugal* clocks). At this time it was the height of Summer, and the greatest heat of the year, as we found by experience. For there may be said to be two Summers and Winters every year in *Goa* and these adjacent Regions ; because the Sun passes over their heads, and departs from them, twice a year,[1] once towards the North, and once towards the South.

May the eleventh. A *Portugal* Gentleman coming from the Court of *Spain* by Land, to wit by the way of Turkie, and, as they said, in a very short time, and with Letters from the Court dated in the end of the last *October*, brought news amongst other things of the Canonization[2] of five Saints, made together in one day, namely, of S. *Ignatio*,[3] the Founder of the Jesuits ; S. *Francesco Xaviero*,[4] a Jesuit,

---

His observatory was in the Island of Huen (long. 12° 41′ E.), whereas Frankfort-on-Oder is in long. 14° 30′ E., and Frankfort-on-Maine in long. 8° 40′ E. It is not clear which of these two places is here referred to, or why the meridian of Frankfort should have been adopted as the basis of calculation.

[1] Owing, of course, to the fact that Goa lies within the Tropics.

[2] The ceremony of canonization succeeds that of beatification in the Church of Rome, and is conducted at St. Peter's with much pomp. In the present day no one can be canonized within fifty years of death, but formerly this rule was not observed.

[3] Ignatius Loyola, born 1491, died at Rome in 1556. He was a native of one of the Basque Provinces, and at one time served in the Spanish army. He founded the Society of Jesus in 1534.

[4] Generally known as St. Xavier. Born at Xavier, in Spain, in 1506, he went to India in 1542, and, after ten years' labour, died on the island of Sanchan, near China, in 1552. His remains were entombed at Goa in a magnificent mausoleum, where they still lie, and have been frequently exhibited to public veneration. An interesting account of this tomb is given in *Murray's Magazine* for November 1890, in C. de Kloguen's *Sketch of Goa*, p. 115, and in Fonseca, p. 286.

and the Apostle of *East-India ;* S. *Philippo Neri,*[1] Founder of the Congregation *della Vallicella,*[2] whom I remember to have seen and spoken to in my Childhood, and whose Image is still so impress'd in my memory that I should know him if I saw him ; Sta *Teresia,* Foundress of the Bare-footed Carmelites ; and S. *Isidoro,* a native of *Madrid.* We had also news of the death of the Duke of Parma, *Ranuccio Farnese,*[3] and how the Cardinal, his Brother, was gone to the Government of that State during the minority of the succeeding Duke. The Currier,[4] who went into Spain with the tidings of the loss of *Ormùz,*[5] this *Portugal* Gentleman said he met at *Marseilles ;* and concerning the Marriage between *Spain* and *England*[6] he brought no intelligence of any conclusion, so that I believe the news of *Ormùz,* lost chiefly by the fault of the *English,* will occasion much difficulty in the Treaty of that Marriage.[7]

---

[1] St. Philippo Neri was born in 1515 at Florence, and died in 1595 at Rome. He was a member of the brotherhood of the Holy Trinity.

[2] A charitable society founded in 1564, otherwise called the "Congregation of the Oratory". The other founders were Cardinal Tarugio, the painter Salviati, and Cæsar Baronius. The object of the society was the relief of poor foreigners, pilgrims, and convalescents. In the year 1707 this Congregation was established at Goa, in the Convent of the Carmelites. The priests are said to be all converted Brahmans. (See De Kloguen's *Sketch of Goa,* p. 131)

[3] In the *Times* of Sept. 12th, 1890, is recorded the death, at Constantinople, of the last representative of the Farnese family, whose history is so intimately connected with that of Italy.

[4] Or "courier".

[5] Ormuz, which had been held by the Portuguese for a century, was in 1622 attacked by an English fleet, fitted out at Surat, in conjunction with Shah Abbas, King of Persia, in pursuance of a design to wrest the mercantile supremacy of the Indian seas from the Portuguese nation. The garrison surrendered after a bombardment and were removed to Goa. (See *ante,* p 8 *et seq.*)

[6] *I.e.,* between Prince Charles, son of James I, and the Infanta of Spain.

[7] Whatever may have been the reason why this marriage did not

May the seventh. Four Italian Bare-footed Carmelites arriv'd in *Goa*, being sent by their Fathers at *Rome* into *Persia;* but having heard at *Aleppo* how the Fathers of *Persia* were troubled by the fate of those new Christians who were discover'd and slain the year before, and especially because they had nothing to live upon, they, not knowing what to do, and being terrifi'd with the Relations of divers Merchants who aggravated things sufficiently, and being so advis'd by some, who, perhaps, like not the coming of such Fathers into Persia, resolv'd to come into *India* and to *Goa*, to the Vicar Provincial, whither they brought no fresh News from *Rome*, having departed from thence eleven moneths before. They came almost all sick, having suffer'd much in the Deserts of *Arabia* and other places of the journey, where they had felt great scarcity; and for all this they would needs observe their Lent and Fasts by the way, sustaining themselves almost solely with Dates, which is a very hot food ; and withall the alteration of the air, both very hot, and unusual to them in the hight of Summer, was the occasion of their being all sick. Two of them arriv'd this day and the two others the day after ; because they came from Muscàt in several Ships. Of these four Bare-footed Carmelites within a few days three dyed, and one alone, after a long and dangerous sickness, escap'd.

May the eighteenth, the Bells of all the Churches of *Goa* rung out with a great noise ; and they said it was for the news of the King's Health then brought from *Spain;* but I said I wish'd they had first recover'd Ormùz, and then rung the Bells with joy for both. A vain people !

May the twentieth. The Bare-footed Carmelites would needs make particular rejoycing for the Canonization of

---

come off, it may be confidently affirmed that Ormuz had nothing to do with it.

their *Sta. Teresia*, and, not confounding the same in one day with that of the Jesuits, they sent two *Portugal* Children on Horse-back, richly clad in riding habit, as Curriers, to declare with certain Verses to the Vice-Roy of *Goa* the Canonization of the She-Saint ; after which the same Boys went up and down the City with a Trumpet before them, scattering other Verses to the people with the same tidings, the Bells of theirs and all other Churches of the City, ringing in the mean-time for joy, being injoyn'd thereunto by the Bishop's[1] Order. At night themselves and divers of their Friends had illuminations throughout the City, and to please them the chief *Portugals* went the same night up and down the street in a great Troop, clad in several disguises, after the manner of a *Mascherade*.[2] I also bore a part in the solemnity, out of my devotion to the new Saint ; and, according to the liberty which every one took of habiting himself as he pleas'd, I put myself into the garb of an Arabian Gentleman of the Desert, which was accounted very brave and gallant. I was accompany'd by Sig: *Antonino*, Son of Sig: *Antonino Paraccio*, my friend a youth of about twelve years old, who was one of those who went in the day time to the Vice-Roy, and I cloth'd him in a Persian Habit of mine, which I had brought from *Persia*, or rather like a noble *Chizilbase*[3] Souldier, very odd and brave ; so that we two were a sufficiently delightful spectacle to the whole City.

May the one and twentieth. In the morning the Barefooted Fathers sang in their Church a solemn Mass *in*

---

[1] Don F. Christoforo Sa de Lisboa, appointed in 1616, who began the rebuilding of the cathedral.

[2] A passage in the original has been omitted here. See p. 192, *note*.

[3] Or Kazilbásh, literally " Red-Head". A warlike tribe of Persia, so called from the colour of their head-dress, adopted by order of the first king of the Sophi (or Safavi) dynasty, as a distinctive mark of the Shi'a sect.

gratiarum actionem for the above said Canonization of
Santa Teresia, upon whose praises an *Augustine* Father
made an eloquent Sermon, the Vice-Roy and a multitude of people being present thereat.

III.—*May* the three and twentieth. The Sun entering
into *Gemini*, I observ'd that the Rain began in *Goa*, and it
happens not alike in all the Coast of *India;* for it begins first
in the more Southerly parts of *Cape Comorin*,[1] and follows
afterwards by degrees, according as places extend more
to the North[2]; so that in *Cambaia*, and other more northern
parts, it begins later than in *Goa;* and the further any
place lyes North, the later it begins there. Whence it
comes to pass that in the *Persian* Ephemerides, or
Almanacks, they use to set down the beginning of
Parsecal,[3] or the time of Rain in *India*, at the fifteenth
of their third Moneth, call'd *Cordad*,[4] which falls upon the
third of our *June;* because they have observ'd it to be so
in the more Northern parts of *India*, as in *Cambaia*, *Sùrat*
and the like, where the *Persians* have more commerce then
in other more Southern places. In *Goa* likewise for the
most part the beginning of the Rain is in the first days
of *June;* yet sometimes it anticipates, and sometimes falls
something later, with little difference. 'Tis observ'd by
long experience that this Rain in *India*, after having lasted
some days at first, ceases, and there return I know not
how many days of fair weather; but, those being pass'd, it

---

[1] From Sanskrit *Kumárin*, the southernmost point of the Indian
peninsula.

[2] This statement refers to what is generally called the south-west
monsoon (from the Arabic *mausim*, "a season"), which term, as is
well known, is applied to the rainy season, as distinguished from the
season when the prevailing wind is from the north-east. These winds
are now ascertained to be intimately connected with the amount of
snow-fall in the Himalaya range of mountains.

[3] See *ante*, p. 32, *note*.

[4] Or Khordàd.

begins again more violent than ever, and continues for a long time together. By this Rain, as I observ'd, the heat diminisheth, and the Earth, which before was very dry and all naked, becomes cloth'd with new verdure and various colours of pleasant flowers, and especially the Air becomes more healthful, sweet and more benigne both to sound and infirm. The arm of the Sea, or River,[1] which encompasses the Island of *Goa*,[2] and is ordinarily salt, notwithstanding the falling of the other little fresh Rivers into it, with the inundation of great streams[3] which through the great Rain flow from the circumjacent Land, is made likewise wholly fresh; whence the Country-people, who wait for this time, derive water out of it for their Fields of Rice[4] in the Island of *Goa* and the neighbouring parts, which, being temper'd with this sweet moisture, on a sudden become all green.[5]

On *June* the fifth I spoke for the first time to the Vice-Roy of *Goa*, *Don Francesco da Gama*, *Count* of *Bidigueira*,[6] Admiral of the Indian Sea and Grand-son of that D. *Vasco de Gama* who discover'd *East-India*,[7] in which this *Don Francesco* had been previously Vice-Roy, and was once taken captive in *Africa* with King *Sebastian*.[8] I delay'd seeing him so long because I was busi'd for a Moneth after my arrival

---

[1] *I.e.*, Mandavi and Zuari rivers, on the north and south sides of the island, called by the natives *Gomati* and *Aganashini* respectively.

[2] The island was formerly known as Kuva, Gova, and Gove.

[3] For a list of these, see Fonseca's *Sketch of Goa*, p. 2.

[4] There are two crops of rice (*Oryza sativa*) in the year. That referred to here is called "Sorodio". The crop grown in the cold weather is called "Vangana". (See Fonseca, p. 27.)

[5] All who have lived in India will recognise the truth of this statement. "A jubilee of nature", as Professor Max Müller well terms it. (*Hibbert Lectures* of 1878, p. 212.)   [6] This should be Vidigueira.

[7] Should be, "made the first voyage to East India by the Cape of Good Hope", in the year 1497.

[8] In 1577, in the war against the King of Fez, which put a disastrous end to the reign of King Sebastian of Portugal.

in changing my Habit and providing a House, so that I went not abroad ; besides that the Vice-Roy was likewise employ'd so many days after in dispatching the Fleets which went to *China* and *Zeilan*[1]; and after they were gone he retir'd to a place[2] out of *Goa*, to recreate himself for many days ; so that I had no opportunity sooner. I presented to him two Letters from Rome which I brought, directed to his Predecessor in my recommendation, one from Sig: Cardinal *Crescentio* and the other from the Duke of *Alboquerque*,[3] then Ambassador at *Rome* for the Catholick King ; and he, without reading them in my presence, said that without that recommendation he should have express'd all fitting Civilities to me, and that he was glad to see and know me, with many other complements and courteous offers. He had no long discourse with me, because many other *Portugal* Gentlemen of the Council and other persons of the Government expected to have Audience; but when I went away he told F. *Moryad*, the Jesuit, his Confessor, who introduc'd me, that at a more convenient opportunity he desir'd to talk with me more at length of the things of *Persia*, and that he would send for me ; and in the mean time desir'd in writing a discourse which I had made a few days before concerning the Warrs of *Persia*, of which his said Confessor who had seen it had given him notice ; wherefore I gave it to him with my own hand, as I had written it in my

---

[1] *I.e.*, Ceylon. See *ante*, p. 109.

[2] Probably in the island of Panelim. (See Fonseca, p. 194, and De Kloguen, p. 88.)

[3] Should be Dalboquerque, a descendant of the great Admiral Dalboquerque, who founded the Portuguese settlement in India in 1509. The family still exists, the present Viceroy of Goa being Senhor Caetano Alexius d'Albuquerque, or Dalboquerque. The name of the family is taken from a castle, Dalboquerque, in Spain.

For further details see *Commentaries of Afonso Dalboquerque* (Hakluyt edition).

Native *Tuscan* Tongue, and F. *Moryad* gave him the Translation of it, made by himself into the *Portugal* Tongue, being[1] the Vice-Roy did not understand *Italian.*

IV.—*June* the ninth. In the Colledge of the Jesuits was pronounc'd, as 'tis the custom every year, a Latin Oration for the Inchoation of the Readings[2]; which, the vacations being ended with the hot weather, begin again with the Rain and cool weather. Letters from some Banians[3] were brought to *Goa*, signifying that the *Moghòl* had encounter'd his Rebel Son *Sultàn Chorròm*, and routed him ; and that *Sultàn Chorròm* after his defeat was retir'd to a strong hold in the top of a Mountain, which they call *Mandù*,[4] and that his Father had besieg'd him there.

June the four and twentieth, being the feast of Saint *John Baptist*, the Vice-Roy with many other *Portugal* persons of quality, as 'tis the yearly custom in *Goa*, rode through the City in Habits of Masquert,[5] but without vizards,[6] two and two alike, or three and three; and having heard mass in the Church of Saint *John*,[7] he came into the street of Saint *Paul*, which they are wont to call *La Carriera dei Cavalli*, and is the best place in *Goa*. Here, after many Companies of *Canarine*[8] Christians of the

---

[1] For "since", see *ante*, p. 27, *note.*

[2] Or, as we should say, "recommencement of the lectures".

[3] See *ante*, p. 78, *note.*

[4] Capital of Malwa, in lat. 22° 30′ N., where the Mogul Emperor held his court at the time of Sir T. Roe's embassy in 1614-18. For a description of the place see Sir J. Malcolm's *Central India*, vol. i pp. 29, 40.

[5] An obsolete word for "masquerade", which nevertheless reproduces the sound of the original Arabic word *Maskharat*, a "buffoon" more correctly than the modern spelling does.

[6] "Vizard" is an obsolete word for "visor", a head-piece or mask.

[7] The only Church of St. John mentioned in the description of Goa s said to have been built in 1685.

[8] *I.e.*, natives of the adjacent district of Kanara (see *ante*, p. 168), generally called "Kanarese".

Country had march'd by with their Ensignes, Drums and Arms, leaping and playing along the streets with their naked Swords in their Hands, for they are all foot, at length all the Cavaliers ran, two Curriers[1] on Horse-back, one downwards from the Church[2] of Saint *Paul* towards the City, and the other upwards, running matches of two to two, or three to three, according as their attire agreed, with their Morisco Cymiters,[3] and at last they came all down marching together in order, and so went to the Piazza of the Vice-Roy's Palace, and so the solemnity ended.

I stood to see this shew in the same Street of Saint *Paul*, in the House of one whom they call King of the Islands of *Maldiva*,[4] or *Maladiva*, which are an innumerable company of small Islands, almost all united together, lying in a long square form towards the West not far from the Coast of *India*, of which Islands one of this Man's Ancestors was really King, but being driven out of his Dominion by his own people, fled to the *Portugals* and turn'd Christian, with hopes of recovering his Kingdom by their help. Yet the *Portugals* never attempted any thing in his behalf, and so he and his descendants remain depriv'd of the Kingdom, enjoying

---

[1] For " couriers".

[2] For a description of this church, see Fonseca, p. 260.

[3] Cimeter is, according to Webster, the more correct form of spelling, though " scimitar" is the spelling now generally adopted.

[4] Lying S.W. of Cape Comorin, or more correctly Kumári, in lat. 7° 30′ N. The word *diva* (Sanskrit *dwipa*) signifies " island", and. *Mala* (Sanskrit) means " chain" or " necklace". They were described by Purchas in 1658, and by Pyrard, a Frenchman, who was wrecked there about the same time, and by Ibn Batuta, who visited them A.D. 1344, and married four wives there. (See Sir H. Yule's *Cathay and the Way Thither*, vol. ii, p. 422.) A translation of Pyrard's voyage has recently (Nov. 1890) been published by the Hakluyt Society. An account of these islands will be found in the *Commentaries of A. Dalboquerque* (Hakluyt edition, vol. iii, p. 201, and vol. iv, p. 251).

onely the naked Title, which the *Portugals*, being now
ally'd to him, still give him ; and because many Merchant
Ships come from those Islands to trade in the Ports of
the Portugals, they force the said Ships to pay a small
matter of Tribute to him as their lawful Sovereign, of
which the Governours of Ports, in whom upon necessity
he must trust, purloin above half from him; nevertheless he gets at this day by it about three thousand
Crowns yearly, and therewith supports himself. The
like Fates have befallen many other Princes in *India*, who,
hoping in the *Portugals*, have found themselves deluded.
Wherein Reason of State is but ill observ'd by the
Portugals, because by this proceeding they have dis-
courag'd all others from having confidence in them ;
whereas had they assisted and protected them, as they
ought and might easily and with small charge have done
upon sundry fair occasions, they would by this time have
got the love of all *India;* and themselves would by the
strength and help of their Friends undoubtedly have
become more potent, as also, without comparison, more
fear'd by their enemies.

June the nine and twentieth. This year the *Moors*
began their Ramadhan,[1] according to the Rules of my
calculation. *July* the five and twentieth, being the Feast
of Saint *James*, the Protector of *Spain*,[2] was solemnis'd
with the same gallantry of Curriers and Dresses as are
above describ'd, saving that the Vice-Roy heard Mass in
the Church of St *James*.[3]

---

[1] Or Ramazan, the ninth Muhammadan month, during which
Muhammadans neither eat nor drink anything between sunrise and
sunset.   The night of the 27th of this month is called *Lailatu 'l
Kadr*, or "night of power", because the Kuran came down from
heaven on that night.

[2] The Spaniards assert that St. James the Greater evangelised their
country.

[3] This church is not mentioned in any of the descriptions of Goa

V.—In the Evening I went with Sig. *Ruy Gomez Baroccio*, a Priest and Brother of Sig. *Antonio Baroccio*, to the Church of Saint *James*, which stands somewhat distant without the City, upon the edge of the Island towards the main Land of *Adil-Sciàh*,[1] which is on the other side of a little River, or Arm of the Sea. For which reason the Island is in this as well as many other dangerous places fortifi'd with strong walls[2]; and here there is a Gate upon the pass, which is almost full of people going and coming from the main Land, and is call'd by the Indians *Benastarim*,[3] by which name some of our Historians mention it in their writings concerning these parts, as *Osorius*[4] *Maffæus*,[5] etc., which Gate, as likewise many others which are upon divers places of passage about the Island, is guarded continually with Souldiers, commanded by a Captain who hath the care thereof, and for whom there is built a fine House upon the walls of the Island, which in this place are very high, forming a kind of Bastion, or rather a Cavaliero, or mount for Ordnance; not

---

which have been consulted. It stands on the eastern coast of the island, near Fort Benastarim.

[1] See *ante*, p. 143, *note*.

[2] Built in the viceroyalty of A. de Noronha about 1564. (See Fonseca's *Sketch of Goa*, p. 153.) The wall extended from Daugim to Panelim, and had three gates (called *passos*), viz., at Daugim, St. Braz, and Benastarim.

[3] The celebrated fort of Benastarim played an important part in the fighting between Afonso Dalboquerque and Adil Shah. (See *Commentaries of A. Dalboquerque*, vol. ii, p. 140 *et seq.*) It was subsequently named the Castle of St. Peter, and became very famous in the annals of Goa, constituting as it did the main defence of the city on its more vulnerable side.

[4] Jerome Osorio, born at Lisbon, A.D. 1500, died 1580 ; author of the *Expedition of Gama*, etc. His works were published at Rome in 1592.

[5] John Peter Maffæus, a learned Jesuit, born at Bergamo in 1536, died 1603 at Tivoli ; author of a *History of the Indies, Life of Ignatius Loyola*, and other works.

very well design'd, but sufficiently strong, wherein are kept
pieces of Artillery for the defence of the place.

We went to visit the said Captain, who was then Sig.
Manoel Pereira de la Gerda, and from the high Balconies
of his House and the Bastion we enjoy'd the goodly
prospect of the Fields round about, both of the Island
and the Continent, it being discernible to a great distance.
The Captain entertain'd us with the Musick of his three
Daughters, who sung and play'd very well after the
Portugal manner upon the Lute, after which we return'd
home. About the Church of Saint *James* are some few
habitations in form of a little Town, which is also call'd
Santiago; and the way from thence to the City is a very
fine walk, the Country being all green, and the way-sides
beset with Indian Nut-trees (which the *Portugals* call
Palms, and their fruit *Cocco*[1]), the Gardens and Houses
of Pleasure on either side contributing to the delight-
fulness thereof, being full of sundry fruit-trees unknown
to us[2]; as also because in Winter-time the very walls of
the Gardens are all green with moss and other herbs
growing there, which indeed is one of the pleasantest
sights that I have seen in my days, and the rather
because 'tis natural and without artifice. The same
happens, I believe, not in this Island only, but in all the
Region round about.

In the field adjoyning to the City, near the ruines of a

---

[1] See *ante*, p. 40, *note*. The word *coco* is a Portuguese word signifying a "burlesque mask", from the resemblance of the three marks
on the shell of the nut to a face. The following description of the
nut is given by Evlia Effendi : "It is a round black nut, on which
all the parts of a man's head may be seen—mouth, nose, eyebrows,
eyes, hair, and whiskers—a wonderful sight !" Called "argell" and
"argellion" by Cosmas (see Yule's *Cathay*, vol. i, p. clxxvi) ; from
Arabic *Nargil*.

[2] For a detailed list of these trees, see Fonseca's *Sketch of Goa*,
p. 29.

deserted building, once intended for a Church, but never finish'd, is a work of the *Gentiles*, sometimes Lords of this Country, namely one of the greatest Wells[1] that ever I beheld, round, and about twenty of my Paces in Diameter, and very deep ; it hath Parapets, or Walls, breast-high, round about, with Gates, at one of which is a double pair of Stairs leading two ways to the bottom, to fetch water when it is very low.

July the six and twentieth. I went out of the City to a place of pleasure in the Island, where was a Church of Saint *Anna*,[2] to which there was a great concourse of people, because it was her Festival. This Church stands very low, built amongst many Country dwellings, partly of the Islanders who live there, and partly of the *Portugals* who have Houses of Pleasure there to spend a moneth for recreation. The place is very delightful amongst Palmetoes[3] and Groves of other Trees, and the way leading to it is extremely pleasant, all cover'd with green. After I heard Mass there Sig. *Giovanni da Costa de Menecas*, a Friend of mine whom I found there, carry'd me to dine there with him at the House of a Vicar, or Parish Priest, of another Church[4] not far distant, and of small structure, which they call *Santa Maria di Loretto*, where we spent the

---

[1] This is probably the well now known as "St. Xavier's Well", in which the Saint is said to have performed his ablutions, and in the water of which a so-called "miraculous" reflection is to be seen. (See Fonseca's *Sketch of Goa*, p. 268.)

[2] Not mentioned in the descriptions of Goa which have been consulted. It was situated in the centre of the island of Goa.

[3] A corruption of the Spanish word *palmito*, a diminutive of *palma*, which is a Latin version of the Greek word δακτυλος, "a finger", originally applied to the date tree, from the shape of its fruit.

[4] Not mentioned in the descriptions of Goa consulted. Loretto is, as is well known, the town in Italy to which the house of the Virgin Mary is said to have been conveyed from Nazareth by angels.

whole day in conversation with the said Vicar and other Friends.

At night, because it rained, I caus'd myself to be carry'd home in one of those Carriages[1] which the *Portugals* call *Rete*, being nothing else but a net of cords ty'd at the head and feet to, and hanging from, a great Indian cane ; in which Net, which is of the length of a man, and so wide that opening in the middle (for the two ends are ty'd fast to the cane) 'tis capable of one person, a man lyes along very conveniently with a cushion under his head, although somewhat curved, to wit with the feet and head raised towards the fastenings, and the middle part of the body more pendulous under the cane, which is carry'd upon the shoulders of two men[2] before and two behind ; if the person be light, or the way short, two Men only bear it, one before, one behind. These Nets are different from the *Palanchini* and the *Andòr*[3] ; for in these from the Cane hang, not nets, but litters like little beds, upon which a man sits with his legs stretch'd forth, or half lying along upon cushions, and so is carry'd very conveniently. Moreover the *Palanchini* and the *Andòr* differ from one another ; for that in the latter the Cane upon which they carry it is straight, as it is likewise in the Nets, but in the *Palanchini*, for greater ease of the person carry'd, that he may have more room to carry his head upright, the said Cane is crooked upward in this form –ᴨ–, and they bend Canes for this purpose when they are small and tender, and these are the most convenient and honourable carriages ; and because

---

[1] Called a "dandy" in the present day in some parts of India, from *danri*, "a pole", to which the net, or "rete", is suspended.

[2] Called "Boyas", belonging to the Mahár, Kúnbi, or Súdra castes. Mahárs carry on the shoulder, others on the head. (Fonseca, p. 34.)

[3] Or "Andola", from which our word "dooly" is derived. Also called "Machilla" or "Manchil", described by Sir R. Burton in *Goa and the Blue Mountains*, as "reminding one of a coffin covered with a green pall". (P. 34.)

there are not found many good Canes and fit to bear
such a weight, therefore they are sold dear, at a hundred
and six score _Pardini_[1] apiece, which amounts to about
Sixty of our Crowns.[2]   Besides, as well the _Palanchinis_ as
the _Andòr_ and the Nets are cover'd for avoiding the Rain
with dry Coverlets made of Palm leaves, to wit those of
the Indian Nut and other such Trees, sufficiently handsome, which being cast over the Cane hang down on each
side, having two windows with little shutters.   They keep
out the water very well, and the Coverlets may be taken
off when one is minded to go uncover'd, and carry'd by
a servant.   Yet I never saw any go uncover'd in _Goa_,
either in _Andòr_ or Nets; but out of the City, in the Country,
many.   I have spoken more at length of these Carriages,
because they are unknown in our Countries, although I
remember to have seen in _Italy_ the Effigies of a Net, or
Rete, engraven in certain Maps of the World, and, if I
mistake not, amongst the ways of travelling in _Brasil_,[3]
where I believe they are us'd, and indeed this mode of
carriage is very usual in _India_, not onely in Cities, but also
in journeys which are of sufficient length ; wherefore to
make experience of it I was minded to have myself carry'd
this day after the manner which I have describ'd : nor

---

[1] Or _párdao_, an Indian coin worth about 1_s._ or 360 _reis_, used at
Goa by the Portuguese. (_Dict._ of P. R. Bluteau, Lisbon, 1720.)
Called _párdan_ by Barbosa.   One hundred and twenty pardini would
be equal to about £6, whereas sixty Roman scudi, or crowns, would
be equal to about £15 10_s._ (old standard).   The old coin called
párdao is described by Varthema as being "smaller than the xerafin
of Cairo, but thicker, with two devils (? Hindu gods) stamped on one
side and an inscription on the other".   (See Fonseca's _Sketch of
Goa_, p. 135.)   For an account of Portuguese coinage at Goa, see
Commentaries of A. Dalboquerque, vol. ii, p. 129, and Fonseca's _Sketch
of Goa_, p. 30.   [2] In the Italian, _scudi_.

[3] Nets of this kind called _hamacas_, whence our word "hammock",
were, and are, used in Brazil, but more usually for sleeping in than
for travel. (See Maw's _Journal_, p. 404.)

must I omit that the men who bear such Carriages are satisfi'd with a very small reward. Going in *Palanchino* in the Territories of the *Portugals* in *India* is prohibited to men, because indeed 'tis a thing too effeminate, nevertheless, as the *Portugals* are very little observers of their own Laws, they began at first to be tolerated upon occasion of the Rain, and for favours, or presents, and afterwards become so common that they are us'd almost by everybody throughout the whole year.

VI.—On the tenth of *August*, I believe, the Sun was in the Zenith of *Goa*, returning from the Northern signes and passing the Southern ; yet for the day and precise hour I refer my self to a better Calculation, according to the good Books which I have not here with me. On the eleventh of the same Moneth I saw at *Goa* a *Carnero*,[1] or Wether without horns, which they told me was of the Race of *Balagat*,[2] not great but of strong limbs, harness'd with a velvet saddle, crupper, head-stall, bridle, stirrups and all the accoutrements of a Horse ; and it was ridden upon by a *Portugal* Youth of about twelve years old, as he went and came from his own House to the School of *Giesù*, which low School of Reading and Writing the said Fathers keep for more convenience of Children, not in the Colledge, which stands in the edge of the City where the higher Schools[3]

---

[1] A Portuguese word for " sheep".

[2] Properly Bálaghat, the eastern part of Maisúr, the name meaning "above the Ghat" (or mountain range), as distinguished from the country below the Ghat, called " Payeenghat". The word *ghat* or *ghatta* (Sanskrit), meaning " step", is here used to denote the mountain-range extending along the western coast of India from Cape Comorin to the Tapti river, whence it bends eastwards, terminating in the vicinity of Barhampúr (lat. 21° 30′ N.). Its greatest elevation is about 8,500 feet above the sea. Its distance from the sea varies from seventy miles to six, but it is generally about forty miles. The range is bare in many parts, but in others is covered with fine forests.

[3] The college here referred to is the new college of St. Paul, generally called the Convent of St. Roch (marked No. 18 in the annexed

are, but at the Church of *Giesù*,[1] which is the Profess'd
House,[2] and stands in the middle of the City, whither
the aforesaid Youth rode daily upon his Martin[3]; and I
observ'd that the beast being us'd to the place knew the
way so well that he went alone at night from the House to
the School to fetch the Youth, without anybody holding or
guiding him, before the servant which drove him, as they
do many Horses. I took the more notice of this trifle
because it seem'd a new thing to ride upon such creatures;
for although in our Countries Dogs[4] and Goats are sometimes seen with saddles and Horse furniture, running,
leaping and capring, yet 'tis onely for sport and with
puppets upon the saddle; but this Martin was ridden upon
by such a boy as I have mention'd, although the beast
was but of a very ordinary bigness.

On the seventeenth of *August* the *Gentile Indians* kept a
kind of Festival, to which a great number of them came to
a place in *Goa*, which they call *Navè*, or, as the vulgar
corruptley speak, *Narvà*,[5] as it were for pardon or absolu-

---

plan of Goa). It took the place in 1610 of the old college of St. Paul,
or Santa Fé, which bore such a conspicuous part in the early history
of the Roman Catholic Church in the East, but which was abandoned
on account of its unhealthy position and is now in ruins. The site
is marked No. 27 in the annexed plan of Goa. For a description and
history of both colleges, see Fonseca's *Sketch of Goa*, pp. 260 and 315.

[1] See *ante*, p. 164, *note*.　　　　[2] See *ante*, p. 162, *note*.

[3] Used for "Freemartin", which name is generally used to denote
an hermaphrodite cow (and perhaps other animals). Such an animal
was called *Taura* by the Romans.

In the *Polychronicon* (written in the 14th century by a monk, Ralph
Higden) is the following passage: "They [*i.e.*, a race of people in
India] gather a grete hoost, and ryden upon wedres, and rammes to
fyght with Cranes."

[4] As is well known, dogs are much used even at the present day in
Holland and Belgium for drawing carts.

[5] Or *Naroa*, on the northern point of the island of Divar (ancient
Divapati). On the bank of a tributary of the river Mandovi are a
Hindu temple and *tirtha* (place of pilgrimage), to which the Hindus

tion, and many came in pilgrimage from far Countries to wash their bodies here, plunging themselves into the Arm of the Sea, Men and Women together all naked,[1] without any respect at all, even persons of quality, and casting Fruits, Perfumes and other things into the water, as it were in Oblation to the Deity of the water in this place, with other Ceremonies, Devotions and the like ; which I relate not more particularly because I was not present at them, because the great Rain kept me from going to see them, as it also was the cause that the concourse of the Gentiles was not very great. Nevertheless I could not but speak thus much in general of it, as being a considerable thing amongst them. This Feast,[2] and their Devotion, last two days, but the first day is the most remarkable.

VII.—*August* the one and thirtieth. A Galeon coming from *Mascàt*,[3] (being the first Ship that came to *Goa* this year since the Rain and the shutting up of the mouth of the Port) brought news how *Ruy Freyra*, having been a few Months before at *Mascàt* with the little Fleet which he had of sixteen Ships, was gone to attempt *Sohàr*,[4] which place being formerly abandoned by the *Portugals* was now fortifi'd by the *Persians* with a strong Garrison ; and that after he had landed he assaulted the Fort but could not take it, though many *Moors* were slain in the encounter,

---

annually flock in great crowds to perform their ablutions. (Fonseca's *Sketch of Goa*, p. 49.)

[1] This is an inexact expression, for men and women always wear *some* clothing on such occasions. (Plato's *Rep.*, Bk. v.) In Bernier's *Travels* is a description of a similar scene at the time of an eclipse.

[2] This may have been the festival of *Pitri Paksh*, held towards the end of the month Bhadra in honour of *Pitras*, or ancestors.

[3] See *ante*, p. 158, *note*. Taken by Dalboquerque in 1507. (See *Commentaries of A. Dalboquerque*, vol. i, p. 77 *et seq.*)

[4] On the south-east coast of Arabia, near Mascat, in lat. 24° 21′ N. It was taken by Afonso Dalboquerque in 1507. For a description of the town, see *Commentaries of Afonso Dalboquerque*, vol. i, p. 91 *et seq.*

and about twenty-five *Portugals;* amongst which were
three or four Captains, men of Valour and Esteem; in
which action some conceiv'd that *Ruy Freyra* had not done
well in hazarding and losing so many people upon a place
of small importance; but he continuing to besiege it, it
was delivered to him upon Articles, the Garrison which
was within marching away with their Arms and Baggage;
after which he raz'd the fortifications, and attempted
another place of that coast of *Arabia*, which they call
Galfarcan,[1] and having taken it, out of indignation, as I
believe, for the many good Souldiers which they had killed
of his at *Sohàr*, and to cast a terror, left no person alive,
sparing neither sex nor age. Which cruel manner of proceeding I cannot approve; because on the one side it will
alienate the minds of the people of that country, and on
the other it will incite Enemies to fight against him more
obstinately and valourously, as knowing they are to expect
no quarter.[2] This is as much as hath been done hitherto
in those parts about *Ormùz*, the doing of greater matters
requiring new and greater Supplies from the Vice-Roy;
but they say likewise that *Ormùz* and *Kesciome*[3] are extremely well fortified by the *Moors*.

September the six and twentieth. Sig. *Don Garcia de
Silva y Figueroa*,[4] Ambassador in *Persia* from the Catholick

---

[1] Korfakan, at the entrance of the Persian Gulf, twelve leagues
distant from Sohar, taken by Dalboquerque in 1507. (See *Commentaries of A. Dalboquerque*, vol. i, p. 94 *et seq.*, where the place is
called "Orfacão". Identical with "Corfacam" of D. B. de Resende.)

[2] For instances of this cruel mode of warfare, in which old men,
women and children were alike ruthlessly slain or mutilated, see the
Commentaries of Afonso Dalboquerque, vol. i, pp. 70, 71, 79, 82, 98,
221, and vol. iii, pp. 15, 127; and also an Arabic work referred to in
vol. i, p. 98.

[3] Kishm, the island near Ormuz, is here meant. See *ante*, p. 2, *note*.

[4] This Spanish statesman and traveller was born in 1574 and died
in 1626. He was page to King Philip II, and distinguished himself
in the war with Flanders. He was sent as ambassador to the King of

King in my time,[1] had (by reason of sundry accidents and the oppositions of the *Portugals* to him as a *Castilian*, as himself saith, or, as others say, because it was his own mind to do so, since the year before, being sent away in a Patache,[2] or Shallop, according to his own desire, he return'd back for fear of a tempest, though without reason) never return'd home into *Spain* to his King ; so that when I arriv'd in *India*, I found him at *Goa*, where we became acquainted with each other ; and coming to visit me one day, amongst other things whereof we discours'd, he told me that he had heard a while since that the Prior of *Savoy*, to wit the Duke of Savoy's son, who was a Prior, was made Vice-Roy of *Sicily* and *Generalissimo*[3] of that Sea[4] for his Catholick Majesty ; which was News to me, and, as a rare and unaccustom'd thing for the Spaniards to place Italians in governments of States in *Italy*, I was not unwilling to take notice of it.

September the thirtieth.   At evening the Dominicians,[5]

Persia in 1614, but, being detained at Goa for two years by the jealousy of the Viceroy, did not reach Ispahan until 1618. He returned to Spain in 1624. An account of his embassy, in French, was published in Paris in 1667.

[1] King Philip III of Spain, who reigned from 1598 to 1631.

[2] See *ante*, p. 61, *note*.

[3] The title of Generalissimo is said by the Seigneur de Balzac to have been first adopted by Cardinal Richelieu about the time here referred to ; but the use of the title in this place seems to throw some doubt on M. de Balzac's statement.

[4] The word "sea" is here used to denote the maritime authority of the Viceroy, and is not a misprint for "see", as might perhaps be suspected.

[5] St. Domingo, who founded the Order of the Dominicans, or Black Friars, in 1215, also instituted the use of the rosary, which he is said to have borrowed from the Muhammadans, who themselves are said to have taken it from the Hindus. It is certain that Hindus use rosaries, but Professor Max Müller (*Hibbert Lectures*, p. 353) doubts whether Roman Catholics adopted them from Hindus. The friars of the Society called " el Rosario" were Dominicans. (See C. de Kloguen's *Goa*, p. 117)

with the Fryers of the Society *del Rosario*, made a goodly procession in *Goa*, with abundance of Coaches and Images cloth'd after their manner, and richly adorn'd with many Jewels ; all the streets where it pass'd being strew'd with green herbs and flowers, and the windows hung with Tapistry and rich Carpets ; to which show, which is yearly made for the Feast of the Rosary, which is upon the first *Sunday of October*, the whole City was gathered together. This great Procession they make the Eve before the Feast, after Vespers, and in the morning of the Feast they make another less one, onely about the Gate of the Church,[1] but with the same pomp, and besides with the most Holy Sacrament.

October the tenth. The Vice-Roy of *Goa* dispatch'd Sig: *Gio: Fernandez Leiton* my Friend, Ambassador to the Gentile Prince,[2] whose Dominion in the Kingdom, or *Province*, of *Canarà*, more Southerly than *Goa*, borders upon *Onor*[3] and the other Territories of the *Portugals* in those maritime parts. This Prince *Venktapà Naicka* was sometime Vassal and one of the Ministers of the great King of *Vidià Nagàr*,[4] which the *Portugals* corruptly call *Bisnagà ;* but after the downfall of the King of *Vidià-Nagàr*, who a few years ago by the Warrs rais'd against him

---

[1] This was the Church of Nossa Senhora do Rozario, or Sta. Maria do Rozario, on the western side of the Holy Hill. (See Fonseca's *Sketch of Goa*, p. 302.)   [2] See *ante*, p. 168, *note*.

[3] Now called Honawar, mentioned by Albulfeda in 1273 and by Ibn Batuta, on the west coast of India, in lat. 14° 18' N., formerly a nest of pirates. There was formerly an English factory here, but in 1670 all the English residents were massacred by the natives, owing to a bulldog belonging to the superintendent having attacked and killed a cow. It was attacked and plundered by the Portuguese in 1569. Taken by the English in 1783.

[4] Generally styled King of Narsinga. See *ante*, p. 144, *note*. The name of the capital is Vijayanagar. (See *ante*, p. 109.) The name Narsinga was given by Europeans to the kingdom founded by Narsing Raja in 1490. (See Wilks' *South of India*, vol. i, p. 15.)

by his Neighbours lost, together with his life, a great part of
his Dominion and became in a manner extinct,[1] *Venk-tapà*
Naieka, as also many other *Naieki*[2] who were formerly his
Vassals and Ministers, remain'd absolute Prince of that
part of the State whereof he was Governour[3]; which also,
being a good Souldier, he hath much enlarged, having
seiz'd by force many Territories of divers other *Naieki*,
and petty Princes his Neighbours ; and, in brief, is grown to
that reputation that, having had Warr with the *Portugals*
too, and given them a notable defeat, he is now held for
their Friend, and for the establishment of this Friendship
they send this Embassage to him in the Name of the
King of *Portugal*, the Ambassador being styl'd Ambassador
of the State of *India ;* and though he is sent by the Vice-
Roy, nevertheless, as their custom is, he carries Letters
written in the name of the King himself, to do the more
honour to *Venk-tapà Nieka* to whom he is sent.

This is the first Ambassador sent to this Prince in the
King of *Portugal's* Name, for before in Occurrences which
fell out an Ambassador was sent only in the name of
some one of those Captains and Governours of the
Portugal Territories which had business with him ; and
this was sent in answer to an Ambassador of his who hath
been long at *Goa*, negotiating with the Vice-Roy the
establishment of the said Friendship. The Ambassador
of *Venk-tapà Naieka* is a Brachman called *Vitulà Sinai*,[4]
and having taken their leave of the Vice-Roy the two
Ambassadors departed together at this time.

I having been some dayes before inform'd of this intended Embassie, and being desirous to see some Country

---

[1] See *ante*, p. 144, note 2.

[2] *I.e.*, Naiks or deputy-governors.

[3] This State comprised the districts of Kelàdi, Barkùr, Mangalùr
and Chandragùtti.

[4] Vitula Sinai should be written Vittala Sinaia.

of the Gentiles, where themselves bore sway, and observed their Rites without any subjection to Christians or Moors, or Princes of different Religion, as in those lands which I had hitherto seen, offer'd myself to accompany my Friend Sig. *Gio. Fernandez Leiton* in this Embassie, and he hath been pleas'd to testifie very great liking of my company. So that I am to take Ship with him within three days, which will be the thirteenth or fourteenth of this present Moneth of *October.* I hope I shall find matter wherewith to feed your Curiosity, and to give you an entertainment. In the mean time I heartily salute all our Friends at *Naples,* and most affectionately kiss your hands. From *Goa,* October 10, 1623.

NOTE.—The passage in the original version, omitted from page 160, is here inserted : " everyone according to his own fancy, some masked and others unmasked, wherein I recognized the tendency which they have towards disorder, and their unwillingness to conform themselves to others in regard to what is fitting.

"The special devotion which I feel towards this great Saint induced me to celebrate the festival like others, so that, besides a device of my own invention affixed to her portrait, which I adorned with twelve figures representing the twelve principal virtues practised by this great Saint during her lifetime, and added to each figure an emblem in accordance with the particular virtue represented by it, to which also I affixed legends in twelve different languages, with certain Italian verses beneath them, in explanation of the emblems, and, since they corresponded with the twelve attributes of the Saint, added at the end three, or four, lines in prose, in the form of a dedication to the bare-footed Carmelite Fathers of Persia, of the College of Oriental languages—besides this device, I say, which I intend some day to have engraved at Rome, because one can have a large number of them printed, I also bore a part," etc.

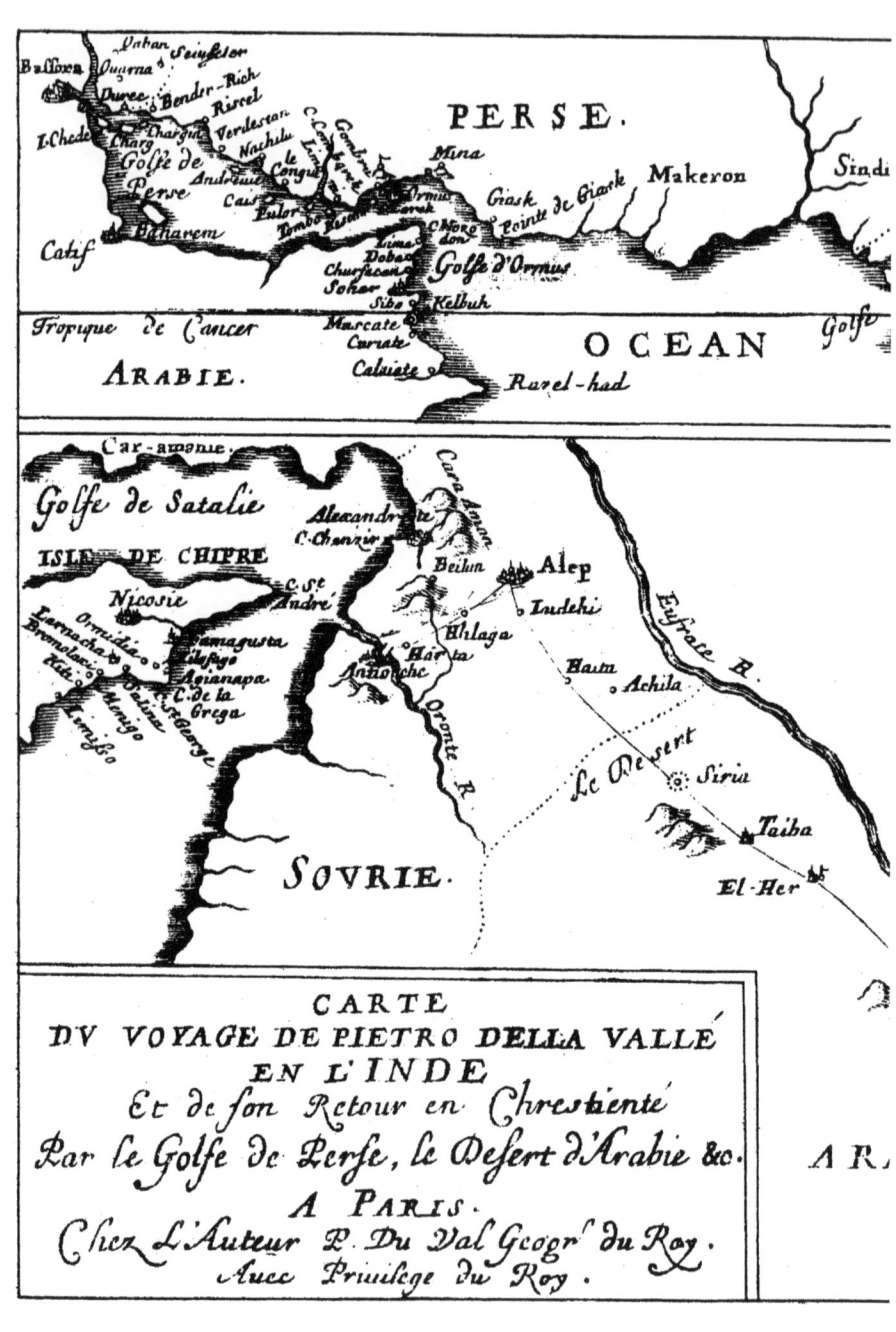

PERSE.

Baſſora
Vahan Seiyßelor
Ouarna
Duree
Bender-Rich
Riſſel
L'Chode
Chary Chargui
Verdeſton
Nachilu
Golfe de
Andreaou
le Congio
Perſe
Caux
Catif
Cauz
Euler
Baſſon
Tombo
Biхарем
Ormus
Carek
C.Moro don
Lima
Doban
Churſacan
Sohar
Sibo
Kelbuh
Golfe d'Ormus

Mina
Giask
Pointe de Giask
Makeron
Sindi

Tropique de Cancer
Marcate
Curate
ARABIE.
Calxiate
Ravel-had
Golfe

OCEAN

Car-amanie.

Golfe de Satalie
Alexandrette
C.Chanzir
Cara Maian
ISLE DE CHIPRE
C.St
Nicoſie
André
Beilun
Alep
Judehi
Ormidia
Famaguſta
Har ta
Hhlaga
Larnacha
Cleſigo
Annonche
Baum
Achila
Bramolaci
Agianapa
Kiti
C.de la
Orontе R.
Mexijo
Grega
Limiſſo
C.de
St George
Le Deſert
Siria

Euphrate R.

Taiba

SOVRIE.
El-Her

CARTE
DV VOYAGE DE PIETRO DELLA VALLÉ
EN L'INDE
Et de ſon Retour en Chreſtienté
Par le Golfe de Perſe, le Deſert d'Arabie &c.
A PARIS.
Chez L'Auteur P. Du Val Geogr. du Roy.
Auec Priuilege du Roy.

A RA

For EU product safety concerns, contact us at Calle de José Abascal, 56–1°,
28003 Madrid, Spain or eugpsr@cambridge.org.

www.ingramcontent.com/pod-product-compliance
Ingram Content Group UK Ltd.
Pitfield, Milton Keynes, MK11 3LW, UK
UKHW040616240426
470322UK00010B/162

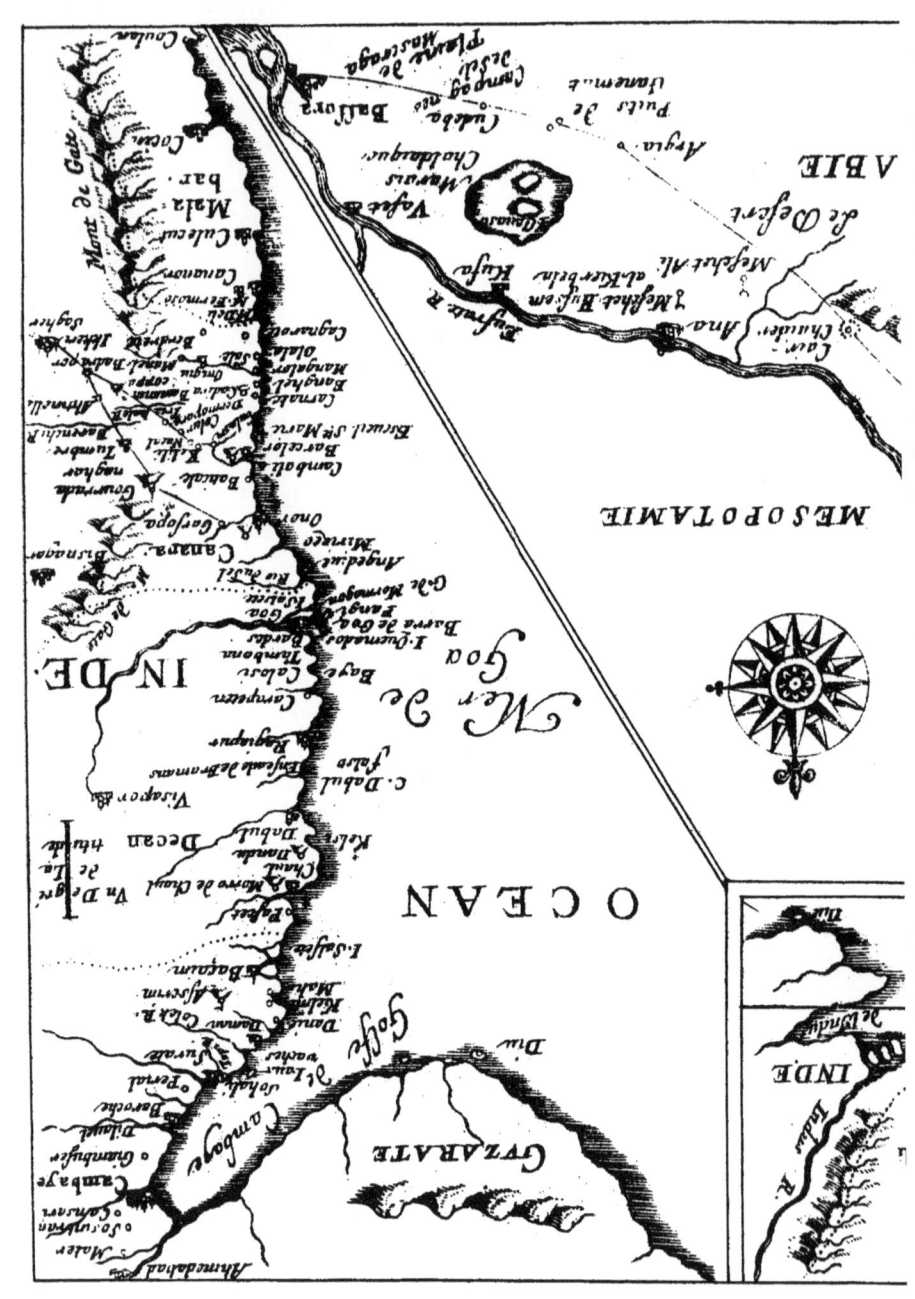